World Development:

An Introductory Reader

WORLD
DEVELOPMENT:
AN INTRODUCTORY READER

Edited by Hélène Castel

The Macmillan Company, New York, New York
Collier-Macmillan Limited, London

The Macmillan Company
866 Third Avenue, New York, N.Y. 10022
Collier-Macmillan Canada Ltd., Toronto, Ontario

Library of Congress Catalog
Card Number: 72-147930

First Printing

Printed in the United States of America

PERMISSION TO REPRINT THE FOLLOWING IS GRATEFULLY ACKNOWLEDGED:

"That Third World," by Denis Goulet, from the September 1968 issue of *The Center Magazine*, Volume 1, Number 6, a publication of the Center for the Study of Democratic Institutions in Santa Barbara, California.

"The Maze of Race and Economics," by Daisuke Kitagawa, from *The Maze of Peace*, edited by Alan Geyer, Friendship Press, New York. Copyright © 1969 by Friendship Press.

"Global Development Strategy: A Moral Responsibility," by Dr. Raúl Prebisch, reprinted with permission of the United Nations Publication Board. All rights reserved. Abridged version TD/B/222, 22 January 1969. United Nations Conference on Trade and Development (UNCTAD), Trade and Development Board, Eighth Session, Geneva, 21 January 1969.

"International Trade and the Developing Countries," by J. F. Rweyemamu, *Journal of Modern African Studies*, Volume 7, Number 2, July 1969, editors, published by Cambridge University Press, London.

"The Revolution of Our Time," by Brady Tyson, reprinted with permission of CICOP, Division for Latin America, Department of International Affairs, United States Catholic Conference.

"Has Latin America a Choice?" by Juan Luis Segundo from *America, The National Catholic Weekly Review*, February 22, 1969. All rights reserved. America Press, Inc., 106 West 56th Street, New York, New York 10019.

To Jacqueline

Contents

ACKNOWLEDGMENTS   xi

INTRODUCTION   xiii

1   THAT THIRD WORLD   1
by Denis Goulet

2   THE MAZE OF RACE AND
ECONOMICS   25
by Daisuke Kitagawa

3   GLOBAL DEVELOPMENT STRATEGY:
A MORAL RESPONSIBILTY   46
by Raúl Prebisch

4   INTERNATIONAL TRADE AND THE
DEVELOPING COUNTRIES   66
by J. F. Rweyemamu

5   THE REVOLUTION OF OUR TIME   92
by Brady Tyson

6   HAS LATIN AMERICA A CHOICE?   113
by Juan Luis Segundo

7   LET'S DARE TO BE AFRICAN   125
by Joseph O. Okpaku

8   *Playboy* INTERVIEW:
    JESSE JACKSON   140

9   TOWARD AN OVERALL ASSESSMENT
    OF OUR ALTERNATIVES   208
    by Robert S. Browne

10 THE CHURCH AND THE
    THIRD WORLD   224
    by João Da Veiga Coutinho

11 THE ADULT LITERACY PROCESS AS
    CULTURAL ACTION FOR
    FREEDOM   248
    by Paulo Freire

12 OUTWITTING THE ''DEVELOPED''
    COUNTRIES   280
    by Ivan Illich

Acknowledgments

THE SELECTION OF ESSAYS in this reader has been in a sense a community endeavor and part of an educational thrust which began two years ago. Numerous people have been directly and indirectly involved in alerting me to significant literature in the field of world development. As many more have given astute criticism and responded to concepts and content of literature shared with them. Among these, I am greatly indebted to friends and colleagues in the Women's Division of the United Methodist Board of Missions and at the Church Center for the United Nations; participants and resource people in World Development seminars and the staff at the Center for Development and Social Change, Cambridge, Massachusetts. My gratitude is of a kind which can hardly be expressed adequately in the form of a simple acknowledgment.

Special thanks are also due Jean Skuse for her invaluable opinions at various stages of the work, as well as to Edna Rouse for her untiring enthusiasm in accomplishing the innumerable tasks that go into preparing and finalizing the manuscript.

Deep appreciation is also extended to the publishers and authors of the selections included in the volume for their reprint permission.

Introduction

IN THE PAST DECADE, even more than ever, a sense of urgency about the world situation has been communicated by research, reports, and statements. Depressing statistics are constantly flashed at us depicting high illiteracy rates, the shortage of schools and teachers, scandalous infant mortality, alarming population increases, food deficiencies, economic gaps. We react with shock that such conditions can exist not only in the developing nations but also in the U.S.A., the wealthiest and most technologically advanced nation in the world.

Yet in a deeper sense, perhaps, we are becoming shock proof to what these statistics say in terms of human indignity. Are we becoming immune to the sense of urgency and resisting coming to grips with reality? One wonders if discussion of the subject is not becoming so prolific that we are in danger of overexposure! This question simply cannot be avoided as we keep hearing of an ever-widening gap between rich and poor, not merely in economic terms but also in terms of genuine communication in a physically shrinking world.

This book contains introductory readings designed to

help people interested and involved in the field of development *to begin* to challenge assumptions, values, and goals about the meaning of development; *to begin* asking critical questions as to the historic, political, economic, social, and cultural reasons for underdevelopment and development before reaching for solutions; *to begin* dealing with underdevelopment not as an isolated problem, but in the broader context of human dignity and justice; *to begin* to distinguish between human development as a goal and the social-economic-cultural-political elements in development as means of achieving a greater humanity; *to begin* to understand that to treat the symptoms of poverty is not enough; *to begin* to create within the individual a humane-developmental attitude rather than going through the motions of study; and finally to get them to pause a while for creative reflection, study, and exploration rather than adapting or adopting partial and ineffective action.

Although each essay offers both conceptual and practical contributions, this book is clearly not a textbook on world development; it does not cover all the issues nor is an integrated theory of development to be found within its mosaic of independent writings. It is hoped, however, that the reader will find ideas which clarify and provoke, ideas which will prick the conscience and lead to concerted effort with others on behalf of authentic development. The assumption is that a new philosophy of development is needed, new policies, new criteria, and new strategies. In fact, for the past two years quite a few of the issues raised in this book, among an array of others, have been part of a difficult, exciting, and only just beginning educational process. The aim of this process has not only been to create an awareness of the urgencies of the world situation but to assess the role of the church, educators, community leaders, and concerned people in development. It is hoped that in future other sectors and disciplines will be included in this educational program. This process of growing awareness has come about through a realization that commitments to world development should not be based on the circumstance that development is an "in" word today, but rather on a kind of knowledge which comes alive beyond policy statements to meaningful programs and individual commitment. Such a process demands genuine self-examination of values and criteria and of our relationship to all peoples. In other words, the goal of this learning experience is that human development become an integral rather than a peripheral part of peoples' lives.

Third World is defined not in terms of geography or government but in terms of people. Furthermore, development is taken here to mean not simply economic growth, or the transference of techniques, modernization, or relief (although these elements are important, particularly when they do not foster dependency or perpetuate themselves). Development is, rather, the process by which powerless people everywhere are freed from all forms of dependency—social-cultural-economic and political—so that they can create a personal sense of history for themselves and thereby express their full potential as human beings. Such a view can be termed utopian; but is there any reason to suppose that people can be stopped from seeking to create a new, just, and more humane world? Can there be true peace and progress without justice?

Due to gains in communications technology, we are now witnessing throughout the world not merely a revolution of rising expectations but a moral revolution of demands for equity and justice. If men are created equal, why and how do such startling gaps in wealth and power arise? This emerging consciousness points, therefore, not only to poverty but to the powerlessness and dependence of people and to the causes of their condition. The questions from the Third World are not only "who am I?" or "who are we?" and "what are we becoming?" or "who defines our destiny?" *but* also "who do I want to be?", "what might be done?", "how can I make a difference?", "what would it require?". We are, therefore, in the midst of a struggle not only for understanding and meaning but for creative humaneness and justice . . . A struggle whereby a people can attain the largest amount of freedom and liberation from dependence to become self-determining and empowered. Only then can people become equal partners. It is perhaps in the visions of the emerging Third World consciousness that we might discover the paths to development with justice . . . if we can listen with humility beyond some of their rhetoric of anger, frustration, despair, and ideology . . . for ultimately, they are motivated by hope, not by defensiveness. In any case, whether they are listened to or not, those on whom they are dependent can no longer avoid being faced with a criticism by another "self." People are no longer judged by their good intentions but by their actions. Social justice is being translated into political-social-economic terms. Social change calls for a removal of all obstacles to development in rich and poor nations alike. World development is a quest for social justice at the personal, institutional, community, national, and international levels, within and between nations. Development is at once a *burden* to those who seek it because the task is formidable, and a *challenge* because it promises a choice—a self-determined choice for a more just and humane life. Finally, development is a *responsibility* in which rich and poor alike must share. Change is inevitable and the development of the broad masses of the people cannot be indefinitely postponed.

HÉLÈNE CASTEL

World Development:

An Introductory Reader

1

THAT THIRD WORLD

Denis Goulet

COUNTLESS ATTEMPTS have been made in the last two decades to find an accurate definition of development. The third world countries seem to like some version of the formula: Development = Bread + Dignity. In some circles Lenin's aphorism of Communism = Soviets + Electrification has been resurrected to express, at least symbolically, the components of socialist "modernization." Still another formulation is that used by U Thant to launch the United Nations' Development Decade: Development = Economic Growth + Social Change. None of these claims mathematical precision, of course, and all leave many questions unanswered:

What if dignity can only be won at the price of going without bread?

What if electrification can be had more cheaply or quickly without soviets?

Is economic progress the objective, or is the object a

Denis Goulet is a staff member of the Center for the Study of Development and Social Change, Cambridge, Massachusetts.

progressive economy? And will any kind of social change do, as long as it is change?

Development is difficult to understand partly because men examine identical realities from many different perspectives. Experts frequently speak as though development were a function of such positive or favorable factors as capital formation, technological skills, managerial ability, efficient bureaucracies, or a combination of these. Others prefer to regard it as a function of eliminating from the underdeveloped countries negative or unfavorable factors like fatalism, low-achievement motivation, weak acquisitional drives, indifference to time, or all of these. Such equations have only dubious value, however. When it is asserted that development results from the sustained activity of the favorable elements we have enumerated, our knowledge has not advanced an iota because there is still ambiguity about development as a *goal*. When development is discussed as a *process,* our vision is blurred by new obscurities.

In broad terms there are four main ways of depicting the development process. Some view it as a historical continuum divisible into stages: lower stages constitute non-development; those immediately above, underdevelopment; those higher still, partial development; and the uppermost, advanced development. This view implies that the passage of time will propel a nation at the lower end of the spectrum through "the stages on life's way." Opponents denounce this imagery as deterministic and a-historical and appeal to a model that stresses historical conditions and the force of human intervention. In these terms, innovations spring from abrupt mutations (in the power structure or in decision-making arrangements) radically different from prior conditions. This revolutionary perspective places its faith in the efficacy of some sort of alchemy that changes social systems through such catalytic agents as the revolutionary conquest of power, ideological enlightenment, or the expropriation of productive instruments.

A third view sees development as an organizational task. Neither history nor ideology but technology systematically conceived and applied is decisive. Societies develop according to their ease in adapting to technology in the realms of production, mobilization, education, and recruitment of an elite. A fourth category of diagnosticians analyzes development mainly in terms of the beliefs and values held by people. To them the supreme factor is the decisive will of a society to assign itself new goals and condition itself to pay the price required to obtain them. In essence, this approach pleads for increasing to the highest degree possible what Daniel Lerner calls "psychic empathy," a man's ability to imagine himself in roles different from those he is actually playing.

My position is that all these four interpretations are essential: disciplined capital formation in order to achieve self-sustained growth, the redistribution of economic and political power, the organization of life in order to increase rationality, and the reconstruction of forces that move men's lives. Anyone who pursues one of these strategies without regard to the others is mistaken. This is so because the idea of development depends on the answer one gives to two questions: What is the good life? What is the good society? These are the oldest of questions, to be sure. But they are also the newest. Raymond Aron, the foremost theorist of industrial society, suggests that the thorniest questions posed by the third world's drive toward development are generated by the possible contradiction that comes from wanting both material development and a good society.

The query into the good life cannot be a ritual unrooted in reality. It needs to be a contemporary question, posed in today's terms. It must be raised against the backdrop of a world in which technology prevails, disparity between the rich and the poor is widely condemned, political domination is a stubborn fact, and challenges to old meanings assume traumatic proportions—a world in which change itself, not permanence, enjoys prima facie legitimacy. The burden of proof now rests on the old ways of doing things. Only in this context do the central questions about development merge into the questions about the "good life."

Much of the confusion surrounding development stems from the failure to grasp the importance of finding the proper definition for it. Development is a total problem, where many disciplines meet: economics, political science, demography, sociology, geography, ecology, among others. My argument is that current thinking about development is characterized by a gross misunderstanding of the real issues at stake. How did we come by this defective understanding? There are at least three major explanations for the failure.

The first is the patchwork historical approach to development aid. The sequence of events after 1945 led developed nations to assume—before they bothered to establish the precise nature of their own objectives—that certain types of assistance were efficacious. Shortly after the Second World War, economists, statesmen, financiers, and industrialists thought that the transition from underdevelopment to development was predominantly a technical problem. The rapid success of the

Marshall Plan in reconstructing Europe bred a euphoria that deluded even cautious bankers into dreaming that the miracle could be duplicated in non-industrialized countries by rapidly industrializing them. The idea caught on that massive injections of capital could do for Africa, Asia, and the poor underbelly of Europe what capital had accomplished in France, Belgium, Italy, and Germany. This optimism coincided with the sanguine first years of the United Nations Organization.

After a while it became evident that the capacity of a nation to make good use of outside capital depended upon the skill of strategically placed people and knowledge of how to make wise investments. As a result, primary emphasis shifted imperceptibly from money to the selective placing of technicians and experts able to administer the outside capital in the most productive way. Engineers would help to build roads because, as everyone knew, roads would shatter the isolation of subsistence communities and precipitate their integration into the market. Agronomists could help boost crop yields and communicate their knowledge of fertilizers, crop rotation, soil preparation, seed selection, the judicious use of insecticides, and crossbreeding of productive strains. Economists could advise governments on how to collect and interpret the statistics needed to prepare over-all plans; they could tell a country what its targets should be, what actual and potential resources it could count on to meet these targets, what monetary mechanisms it might employ to augment purchasing power, and so forth. These technical assistants became legion: educators, administrators, hydrologists, veterinarians, monetary experts, nutritionists, medical personnel, electricians.

After a few years of this, however, a general disaffection set in. Of what use were technical advisers, it was asked, if they had to function within systems or institutions that were not compatible with development? Why request advisers at all if they were not used to train natives to carry on the job after the foreigners departed? Was the work of these expensive experts futile when their recommendations necessarily were based on insufficient statistical data? And what of those experts who did not remain in one country long enough to make recommendations that would be technically, politically, and also psychologically sound? Did the budgetary and foreign-exchange position of the recipient country allow it even to envisage putting into practice the recommended programs and projects? Clearly, the massive economic logjams that resulted from this sort of activity made it necessary to find new and broader elements to be added to the development equation. The new ingredient, the new shibboleth of developers, became institution-building.

This school of thinking declared that trained people with permanent commitments to development are more important than buildings, roads, factories, or dams. What was needed more than programs or projects were human agencies to devise and carry out programs. Therefore the emphasis shifted heavily from bricks and mortar to education and training. Ambitious exchanges of people between the third world and the advanced countries were developed. Students and technicians were sent to the United States, France, Britain, and Israel to learn how to modernize their homelands. At the same time, training programs were instituted in the poorer countries to turn natives into better administrators, educators, plant managers, community developers, researchers, planners, entrepreneurs, soldiers, policemen, communications technicians, journalists, labor-union officials, directors of coöperatives, accountants, statisticians, and foresters. Particular attention was given to three institutions—education, administration (public and business), and politics.

At this point, it became fashionable to say that no underdeveloped country could make significant progress until it achieved a literate mass citizenry, a bureaucracy characterized by the merit system and impersonal loyalty to professional standards, and a firm political commitment to development on the part of leaders who enjoyed popular support. Institution-building came to mean, in practice, that advisers from rich countries came to tell poor countries that they had to abolish ignorance if they hoped to wipe out misery, had to develop honesty and punctuality if they hoped to become efficient, and had to accept political realism before they could build their nations or win economic independence. Obviously, the models for such behavior were the successful countries of the West.

During this period, in the late fifties, developers and developees displayed an almost obsessive sensitivity to "non-economic" or "extra-economic" factors in development. Programs that once had been regarded as mere consumer goods were now defended because, it was alleged, they helped increase production and productivity. This was the case with health care, improved housing, better nutrition, and most education. It was argued that a dollar invested in education generated more development than a dollar spent on fertilizer plants, dams, or steel mills. Development, the argument went, really meant economic growth plus social change. Did educational reform rate a higher priority than new tax legislation? Should land reform be put above controls over foreign exchange or new profit-remittance laws? Or should all take place in concert? If so, how could a policy be devised that would make these changes acceptable enough to entrenched interests for them to be put into practice? Problems of values, motivations, the processes of elite formation, and the like kept cropping up to take the sweetness out of this latest panacea of institution-building. Perhaps the reason for the malaise was that the "non-economic" factors of development continued to be viewed instrumentally; that is, as means for speeding up economic expansion or removing obstacles to economic growth. The assumption prevailed that somehow the "goodies" of development—measured in standard-of-living indices—were beyond criticism. Everyone supposedly wanted them.

An increasing awareness that such thinking was inadequate has paved the way for a new emphasis. It is the opposite of the "instrumental" approach. According to this new view, development is not pre-defined but related to a society's over-all philosophy of what the desirable life and the ideal civilization may be. Economic, institutional, and political modernization is desirable to whatever degree it accords with, or promises to be useful for obtaining, the values held by a given civilization. Whatever the final judgment of this viewpoint may be, one fact is clear: development is no longer primarily thought of as a technical problem. It is now seen increasingly as something less than a fully rational pursuit; the most difficult questions about its goals and costs have never been answered. The complex images that people have of status and comfort appear more decisive than their rates of demographic increase, net caloric intake, or capital-formation ratio. This new perspective on development challenges the conventional wisdom. Its greatest impact is being felt among frontline investigators who are asking the *why* of development, not just the *how*.

The second reason for our failure to understand the real issues of development is that until recently the countries of the third world have not been able—or have not been permitted—to tell others what *they* think development is. By now, however, they seem to have found several ways to get their message across. One of them is the adoption of an ideological stance. When Sukarno preached, as he did for several years, that Indonesia was seeking to establish its political identity in the international arena even if this policy meant disqualifying Indonesia for massive American economic assistance, he was in effect telling the world that industrialization and improved living standards are not as important to Indonesians as some other goals. When Fidel Castro assumes certain postures, he is saying that the construction of a new type of socialism is more important to Cuba than the rapid diversification of agriculture or the quick buildup of heavy industry. Similarly, when Julius Nyerere urges Tanzanians to practice self-reliance in their efforts to modernize the nation, he is implying that for his citizens self-reliance is more important than economic success. And when Eduardo Frei pleads for discipline in walking the tightrope between socialism and capitalism, he is telling the world that Chile sees a "third way" of constructiong a modern society.

A people is describing its ideal of development when it rises in protest against attacks on its own values. If a society suspects that modernization is too destructive of its family structures, social solidarity, rhythms of work and play, it may react negatively to development. Sometimes, it is true, the reaction is romantic and ingenuous, in hoping to keep the old while gaining the new; but there are instances of a fully conscious rejection of the values of modernity. This is true even of as modern a nation as Japan. The phenomenon is strikingly parallel to that of religious syncretism. Christian missionaries to Africa, Asia, or Latin America may have imagined that they had successfully baptized certain pagan rituals, and yet, often enough, they were hoodwinked. Beneath the outward acceptance of Christian practice, old beliefs and rites continued to find a safe haven. This kind of duplicity involves nothing more mysterious than the ancient fight of societies to remain themselves while supposedly being remodeled by others. There is a profound instinct in all human groups to be themselves, and this is asserting itself ever more strongly as societies become increasingly conscious of what development is.

The clearest channel through which the third world has been telling us about its image of development has been, of course, the collective position it has taken in international conferences. At Bandung, Cairo, Belgrade, Havana, at UNCTAD I in Geneva and UNCTAD II in New Delhi, the same message has been delivered. World economic disparities are intolerable, and the third world has lost faith in the will of privileged countries to close the gap; paternalism is unaplatable; vested interests of the first and second worlds, crystallized in the cold war, are not valid excuses for treating underdeveloped nations as pawns; ethnocentrism on the part of Western nations is abominable; all forms of domination are bitter, even if they are sweetened by the promise of higher standards of living (in a word, national birthrights cannot be sold for developmental pottage); native elites will henceforth dictate the terms on which foreign elites may come to the third world, whether to teach, invest, advise, or study.

What all this means, if only negatively, is that the

third world believes development is much more than mere industrialization, modernization, urbanization, rationalization. It is a matter of life-styles.

The third reason that development has been so poorly understood is that we have assumed that underdevelopment existed only in the third world. Such glaring ethnocentrism has reinforced complacency and self-righteousness on the part of "advanced" societies. It has also blinded them to the extent of their own underdevelopment: their domestic misery, structures of privilege, depressed areas, exploited masses, bankrupt political policies. Worse still, the same myopia has beclouded the possibility that the third world may be more developed culturally and humanly than the West. It has led them to assume that they alone had something to teach, while the third world's role was simply to learn. But who will teach the "developed" countries how to run a leisure society, how to humanize personal relations beyond the frontiers of the nuclear family, how to elicit solidarity not by fiat but inner conviction? G. K. Chesterton once described the case of one Mr. Jerome, who was the hardest man to convert because he was so totally convinced that he was a perfect Christian. Perhaps understanding will become possible now that self-satisfaction has begun to ebb because of the growing awareness that our performance has been so poor.

A regulative wisdom is necessary. Benjamin Higgins points out that sophisticated econometrics is fine but adds that his fellow-economists would do well to remember that their discipline began as an offspring of moral philosophy. He cites Keynes in support of his own view that productivity is not development but merely the possibility of development. Development is the ascent of man in all his dimensions, in the quintessence of his humanity. This is why a philosophy of development is needed. Similar arguments have been advanced by regional and urban planners on the ground that their problems require that public choices be made regarding the quality of a society's life. John Howard has called upon planners to transcend pseudointerdisciplinary exchanges and engage in a genuine debate on the basic philosophical issues of how man is to deal with his surroundings. Manfred Stanley and David Apter assert that development is above all a normative concept and therefore a fit subject for ethics and philosophy.

Unfortunately, contemporary philosophers, especially in the United States, have walked away from relevant human problems. When they have not gone into semantic analysis *à outrance*, they have sought refuge in pointless elucubrations that are insulting to man's practical intelligence. Simone Weil and Eric Weil were both right when they held that in a technological age the philosopher must frequent the marketplace, the factory, and the arenas of political debate if he would reflect on liberty, personal identity, the common good, happiness. If we grant that some philosophers and developers acknowledge the need for some kind of framework that transcends descriptions, indices, or typologies—in brief, for a regulative wisdom—it can nevertheless be objected that these are scholars, not men of action. Is the objection valid?

Are engineers, soil experts, organizers of coöperatives, medical educators, and development-bank officials indifferent to the values underlying all development activity? Some are, no doubt; others show greater foresight. An example of the latter was a young doctor who was sent by his government's health service to a small village in the hinterland of Pernambuco, in Northeast Brazil. On his arrival he discovered that the infant mortality rate in the area was two hundred per thousand. Thanks to a strenuous educational and prophylactic campaign, he had reduced this rate by half within two years. However, he finally realized how hopeless the prospects of employment for adolescent males in the region were, and it was then he concluded that his philanthropy had been only a cruel illusion. It was useless to engage in such ad-hoc development unless realistic strategies had been devised to reach the more long-range goals and to master the anticipated consequences of the change on human structures and values.

Similar things have happened to hundreds of developers. Industrial engineers have rushed to build factories because they were deemed essential for development, only to discover afterward that the work force was uninterested in making them run. Experts were unable to carry out resettlement schemes that were technically perfect save in one detail: the settlers' abiding attachment to their former lands, to which they returned as soon as they learned that the drought was over. No practical field developer can be insensitive to the damaging waste that follows upon unreflective activism.

But even if one assumes that a regulative wisdom is necessary, how is it to be obtained? What must one do to avoid dogmatism or hypermoralism in handling the problem? There may be no satisfactory reply at present, but certain ground rules can be proposed.

Development is at one and the same time both art and science. The proof of planning is in performance, not in the elegance of models or the logic of projections. The test of one's understanding of development is success in the course of action one has proposed allied to the endorsement of the action by the population. To paraphrase Marx, development wisdom does not seek to explain the world but to change it. What is needed is not a blueprint of an ideal set of projects but a set of standards for judging how good an idea, an experiment, or a program is. While serving as Brazil's Minister of Planning, Roberto Campos wrote that what was needed was not a plan of factories but a factory of plans; that is, a permanent, human, institutional capacity to devise concrete, well-thought-out innovations. Analogously, the "wise man" of development must not search for some ideal doctrine but for workable ethical tests against which he can measure the degree to which various ventures enhance or dilute human freedom, happiness, man's mastery over his destiny, the quality of his personal and social relations. There is no valid division of labor between thought and action: the thinker is the doer and vice versa.

"Participant observation" does not mean that research observers share the native life but, on the contrary, that they give an active role to the population they are observing in the conduct of their study. Too frequently, these practitioners fall prey to the technocratic elitist bias that makes them discourage participation by the people who are to be developed. To allow this, in their eyes, is to risk inefficiency, a constant shifting of goals, endless debate, and untold other dangers. Certain community developers, it is true, have circumvented summit planners and rejected planning from the top down. On the whole, however, their accomplishments have not generated lasting change beyond the lowest levels. Until a philosophy of planning is devised that links community-development efforts to the highest agencies of decision, most grass-roots efforts will be ineffectual in relation to other such efforts.

It is impossible for men to agree on how they rank identical values. Therefore, there can only be a number of competing (though perhaps complementary) "regulative widsoms." This pluralism is not simply a fact to be tolerated but a value to be fostered. Man has been variously defined as a feeble emergence of spirit, a striving animal, a potential freedom wrestling with absurdity, a network of stimulable ganglia, an illusion summoned to discover true self by liberation from self, and so on. From this diversity of concepts flows a multitude of prescriptions for human happiness. Thus, several development wisdoms may arise out of diverse cultures. This is healthy as long as we do not look for their lowest common denominator but, rather, recognize their complexity and seek the "presumption of concern for truth" on the part of them all. What man must share is full hospitality of the mind whereby the dross of particularism contained in each view is drawn off. Divergent views can have meaning even across the boundaries of ideology.

Biologists and ecologists fear that the human organism will be stunted and some of its potentialities atrophied if its adaptive powers are challenged by overspecialized artificial environments. For example, they think it is dangerous for eighty or ninety per cent of mankind to live in large cities. As it is presently conducted, the drive toward development threatens to impair man's general capabilities because of the excessive demands made on him to adapt to overspecialized environments. For this reason alone it would be folly not to attempt to regulate development in a manner that not only permits but positively fosters diversity. Men ought to be respected for what they are, and their cultures ought to be allowed to develop on their own terms, even if they do not meet the standards of the developers. The most profound wellspring of change, as of stability, is the desire for esteem—self-esteem and the esteem given

by others. It is a tragedy that modernization does not
offer men esteem except in terms of their functions.
This means in practice that development is made possible in many societies only if they accept cultural suicide.

History reveals another important reason for favoring
diversity. Whether it is the American Indian who is
annihilated, or the Montagnard who is humiliated by
the Annamite majority in Vietnam, the quality of
human life is diminished. Irreplaceable positive values
are wiped out. In addition, the man who despises others
dehumanizes himself. Just as the torturer is victim as he
tortures, so the cultural aggressor demeans himself
when he demeans others. To be sure, some diversities
are less important than others and may have to be sacri-
ficed, but it is precisely the exercise of rational discrimination in this area which constitutes a prime task of
regulative wisdom.

Four normative principles should guide the elaboration of any valid ethic of development. The first has to
do with things and may be phrased as a question: What
is the relationship, if any, between the fullness of good
and an abundance of goods? Some people answer the
question in the language of being and having; they have
analogized the contribution made by the goods one pos-
sesses to the enrichment of one's existence. J. Kenneth
Galbraith complains that economists lack a theory of
consumption priorities and a larger view of what production is for. It ought to be evident that no priorities
can be established without passing judgment on the positive or negative influence that different kinds of goods
exercise on human life.

The second normative principle concerns solidarity.
Developers like Perroux, Myrdal, and Lebret have
argued that genuine development can never take place

until men agree to a worldwide plan for the use and allocation of resources. A parallel case can be made for internal and regional solidarities. There is agreement nowadays that the national integration of fragmented ethnic, religious, or tribal groups is imperative for nation-building. It is also generally agreed that the best arrangements of sound geo-economic spaces presuppose regional coöperation far beyond the levels currently practiced. If this is so, a rationale for solidarity must be developed in terms acceptable to men of all cultures, all ideologies, all political and economic philosophies. A reasoned effort must be made as well to determine the limits of that solidarity.

The third pillar of the normative edifice is a position on technology and its relation to freedom and happiness. Jacques Ellul maintains that unlimited technology can provide happiness for all men but only at the price of freedom. Yet, freedom itself is not fully dissociated from images of happiness, whatever we may think of Unamuno's famous dictum about anguished men and contented sows. One of the basic duties of a development wisdom will be to reëxamine the freedom *from* and freedom *for* issues in the larger context of the questions concerning the good life.

Finally, it can be said that neither elitism alone nor populism alone is enough for political or social decision-making. In ideal terms a continuum of alternatives exists—from autocracy, aristocracy, and oligarchy, running through a broad, ill-chartered middle terrain, to the other pole of full communitarian, participatory rule. Preferences obviously reflect diverse social philosophies. More importantly, they reflect the scale and density of the human groups in question, their cultural and psychic antecedents, their varying degrees of well-being in new situations, and the importance they attach to such values as efficiency, productivity, professional mobility. One of the duties of regulative wisdom is to trace the limits of the possible.

Certain proposals can be made to those who are interested in development. The scope of these proposals is intended to be worldwide, not national or regional.

A tiny fraction of the population of the earth uses (when it does not abuse) a disproportionate percentage of the world's resources to keep its wasteful, voracious economy in operation. This inequity is morally repugnant. There is enough wealth in the world to meet the real needs of all men, but there is not enough to satisfy the greed of each one. It is time that the principles of social justice are applied in order to validate the claims on the world's potential resources of those who need them most because they lack them most. This is more important than striving for the redistribution of present wealth. I therefore propose a charter analogous to the United Nations' Charter of Human Rights. Its purpose would be both pedagogical—to educate men to solidarity, and catalytic—to bring real creativity to the quest for new social arrangements governing men's access to goods.

Planners suffer from a twofold occupational hazard: that of acting as though they were omniscient, and that of being obliged to follow the dictates of the quantitative inputs that go into the way in which they formulate their priorities in development. More frequently than not, their targets bear little relation to the aspirations of the people on whose behalf they are presumably planning. Senghor once said, "Africans do not want to become consumers of civilization." But the danger cannot be wished away. Africans, Latin Americans, and Asians may well become consumers of civilization unless some counterweight is found to the technocratic elitism that characterizes current development planning. I therefore propose an Open Letter from the Peoples of the World to the Planners of the World. This letter would be constantly revised in the light of changing popular values. Over time, decision-makers might learn a number of things about people that they now have no other way of finding out.

Development specialists have long worried about the unprofessional manner in which many advisers are recruited for service in third world countries. A few psychologists have even hinted privately at the existence of a special "foreign technician" syndrome. A number of complaints have been voiced about the lack of standards for overseas service in such categories as length of service, chain of command in the country of service, the obligation of the foreign adviser or technician to train native replacements, different pay-scales operating as counter-incentives to qualified native personnel, rules concerning the communication to host countries of information gathered during a mission, and the like. Lebret has urged the international adoption of a code of ethical standards that would assure host countries that they are receiving only qualified, reliable professionals. Yet there is a general reluctance to discuss this publicly. I therefore propose that the idea of such a code be brought into the open and seriously considered.

The legal structure that now governs relationships among countries is irrelevant to the purposes of development. It was originally designed for totally different relationships and a different set of priorities. Fresh thinking, based on premises other than those of a worldwide central legal authority, is urgently needed. New rules of coöperation are called for, a redefinition of national sovereignty, a fresh statement of economic human rights. All this should be explored without assuming that a new world order for law must necessarily be based on world government. I therefore propose an inquiry into a new international legal order suited to development.

A civilization reveals the nature of its goals and values in the environmental conditions it creates. Ecologists warn us that unless rapid action is taken, irreparable imbalances will result from uncontrolled technological disturbance of natural systems. Besides the obvious problems of space and radioactivity, there is urgent need for international control over the oceans. Polar regions likewise need to be placed under international jurisdiction, in part because their protection is essential for ecological health, in part because of their importance in weather control. An equally strong case can be made for new international controls over large river systems—an acute problem now that hundreds of dams for irrigation, industrial uses, and domestic consumption are under construction throughout the world. There exist other problems such as the settlement or resettlement of populations, even within the borders of a country, in terms of political, demographic, and ecological effects. In all these domains, the drift of technology and economics is toward wastefulness, destruction, and irresponsible homogenization of habitats. I therefore propose the creation of an agency for international control of the environment.

Finally, I propose a study of the "pedagogy of the oppressed." The term is borrowed from Paulo Freire, a Brazilian currently working in Chile. His special talent is to help populations heighten their critical, cultural, technical, and political awareness. The study should appraise the main approaches to political education, to community-leadership education, to adult literacy, and to the surveying of those slogans and myths which are now considered relevant to development. All serious writers on development attach great importance to mobilizing popular opinion and eliciting adherence of the masses to the goals and strategies of development. An analysis of the pedagogies of the oppressed employed in Cuba, mainland China, the Malagasy Republic, and elsewhere might reveal the values and leitmotivs that move men most effectively. It might shed light on the true content of ideologies and on the possible discrepancies between the perceptions of elite groups and those of other groups as to which values the people nourish. Also worth investigation would be the adequacies or inadequacies of such programs as U.S. university contracts, UNESCO literacy projects, Peace Corps community-development endeavors, and similar efforts. The aim of the inquiry would be to detect what constitutes good or bad pedagogy and in what ways the "oppressed" man differs, psychically and behaviorally, after undergoing different pedagogies.

Parallel with this should be a study of the content of the pedagogy of the oppressors. In the eyes of the third world, developed countries are not only privileged, they are oppressors. It may be supremely important for Americans, Britons, Russians, or Swedes to learn about the repercussions of their power and their economic forces on the world market or on international conferences. Some years ago, Helder Camara, the Archbishop of Recife, in Northeast Brazil, expressed the hope that if only he and other spokesmen of the third world would present their case to American intellectuals, students, writers, and common citizens, without filtering their information through the distorting lenses of official policy, a revolution in American attitudes toward Latin America would come about. But the effort is gigantic for one man or a few men; it needs to be conducted on a permanent basis by Americans themselves. Questions of foreign investments, profit remittances, insurgency and counter-insurgency, and many others need to be seen in a new light by large numbers of American citizens if their political leaders are to accede to change. The survival of democratic institutions within the United States depends directly on the ability of the country to change its perspectives on the third world.

Although development can legitimately be studied as if it were distinct from other human processes, in the final analysis its goals are the goals of existence itself: to provide an opportunity for men to live fully human lives. In other words, development is good if it helps individuals live the good life. This means that there is no uniform standard for judging the quality of civilizations. It also implies that Toynbee's view may be incomplete. He tests the quality of a civilization by its ability to survive in the face of challenges. I believe it is necessary to go beyond survival and judge societies, as Teilhard de Chardin does, according to how well they meet men's basic aspiration to live more fully. For Teilhard, fullness of life is not found in narrow accomplishments confined to individuals or communities (be they tribal or national or planetary) but in the total ascension of mankind toward solidarity, increasing self-awareness, and expanded creativity. His appeal to cosmic solidarity evokes what may be the supreme arena in which men's will must be tested, the basic ground on which they will choose greatness or mediocrity, perhaps even suicide or survival. This option is implicit in the frame of reference that they choose to define development. The frame dictates strategies of development that are either nationalistic or global, either tied to limited interests or emancipated from them, either favoring privilege or fostering the genuine needs of everyone.

Definitions of development in terms of industrialization, urbanization, modernization, growth, maximization, or even of optimization are bad. It must be defined normatively. Lebret does this when he describes development as a coördinated series of changes, whether abrupt or gradual, from a phase of life perceived by a population and all of its components as being less human to a phase perceived as more human, generating various types of solidarity, both intranational and transnational, based not on homogeneity but on complementarity in the realsm of culture and functions.

Cold- and hot-war divisions have made it impossible for these transnational solidarities to be considered seriously. As the gap between developed and underdeveloped widens, what appears far more likely than worldwide development is generalized alienation—alienation among abundance for wealthy countries; among misery, bitterness, and recrimination for those who have known too much misery. The answer to the question "Development for what?" could well be: the Apocalypse. Or: the division of the globe into a club of rich masternations and groveling slave-nations. Or: a wasteland world of bread and circuses in which universal manipulative technologies deprive men of their capacity to be free or even to have problems. On the other hand, development could create not any utopian paradise but a world in which men will become progressively more free, thanks to social systems that release them from the servitudes of ignorance, disease, egotism, and self-delusion. If they were to achieve such freedom, they might come to dare the exploration of the full dimensions of human potentialities.

Development is a historical task. Marx was convinced that history could begin only after alienation was abolished. If we accept Marx's terms, there can be no doubt that the world is launched on an ambiguous adventure called development that can either make historical beings of men or generate new and more tragic alienations. Development is whatever men will make of it. Human existence is an indefinite process. Even if a man assimilates all the cultural wealth that the past and the present place within his grasp, the possibilities open to him remain enigmatic. Development, like history, never utters its final word.

2

THE MAZE OF RACE
AND ECONOMICS

Daisuke Kitagawa

AT THE TURN of the century, W. E. B. Du Bois boldly
stated that "The problem of the twentieth century is the
problem of the color line—the relation of the darker to
the lighter races of men in Asia and Africa, in America
and the islands of the sea."[1] Events since World War II
have more than borne out the truth of his prediction.
Thoughtful people today are seriously concerned
whether the racial conflict so prevalent throughout the
world may inevitably lead mankind into World War III.
They wonder if all the serious economic, social and
political conflicts may after all be basically racial in
character.[2]

NEW MILITANCY ON THE PART OF
THE COLORED RACES

No one can fail to see how militant the peoples whose
skins have colored pigmentation have become in recent

*Daisuke Kitagawa was Secretary for Urban and Industrial
Mission, Division of World Mission and Evangelism, World
Council of Churches, Geneva, Switzerland, until his death
in March 1970.*

years. They appear to be growing increasingly so. The Black Muslim movement in the United States is a forerunner of this trend.[3] The American public is being confronted by the challenge of Black Power advocates. Many white Americans are saying, "Negroes have never had it so good. Why are they so discontented?" There is obviously something distorted about this point of view.

Until a few years ago, the civil rights movement was the concerted efforts of enlightened black, white and other Americans to achieve racial integration at all levels and in all sectors of American life. This goal has not been completely accomplished. The more articulate black people today sound as if they are striving for an independent development of black people separate from white people.[4]

Some of the radical leaders in the Black Power movement seem to be saying that the old civil rights leaders' approach is no longer tenable. They consider people like Roy Wilkins of the National Association for the Advancement of Colored People (NAACP), Whitney Young of the National Urban League, the late Dr. Martin Luther King, Jr., of the Southern Christian Leadership Conference (SCLC), and a host of other distinguished black Americans to be little less than "white men's Negroes." Moreover, they give the impression that they mean what they seem to be saying by pointing to the recent race riots. They declare that a riot immediately accomplishes more than all the civil rights laws put together, even at great cost in human life and property. One thing is clear: black people are not content to be merely accepted by the white man into the white man's society on the white man's terms. The black American is determined to assert himself as an American in his own right and on his own terms.

The Black Muslim and the Black Power movements in America are both antedated by similar movements in Africa, beginning with the Pan-Africanism championed by George Padmore;[5] the doctrine of Negritude in French-speaking Africa, of which Aimé Césaire and Léopold Sédar Senghor are noted advocates;[6] the emphasis on "African Personality" in English-speaking Africa; and the striving to establish "black governments" in the wake of decolonization all over Africa. Undergirding all these movements are the Western-educated African intellectuals, who for the past few decades have been preoccupied with the effort to restore African identity to their cultural life.[7]

The Communist Revolution in China in 1948, and the subsequent isolation of the People's Republic from the Western world have helped China assert her national identity as distinct from that of the white man. There are other strong racial overtones in that China is eager to establish close relationships with all the developing Afro-Asian nations, offering them all sorts of technical aid while keeping her door adamantly closed to both the USSR and the West.[8]

ONE WORLD INDIVISIBLE: THE CONTEXT
OF INTERRACIAL ENCOUNTER

One of the striking facts of life in the second half of the twentieth century is that the technologically advanced and economically affluent West is being confronted by the increasingly militant Afro-Asian and Latin American nations. This confrontation is taking place as a direct and inevitable consequence of the colonial expansion of the West during the preceding three centuries. It was discussed extensively at the

World Conference on Church and Society in Geneva in 1966.

At that conference, professionally competent participants from many parts of Africa, Asia and Latin America articulated both their aspirations and their frustrations. Christians and non-Christians alike expressed their common desire for their nations to be independent, to assert their respective national identities and to be responsible partners with their former colonial masters in the common task of building the new world community. They expressed their frustration for not being able to achieve this dream because of the growing economic gap between their countries and the North Atlantic countries.

In this encounter three things became clear. (1) The encounter was among other things, between the rich and the poor countries. The vast majority of the rich countries were more or less north of the 38th parallel, and practically all the poor countries south of it. This is the frequently referred to "North and South conflict."[9] (2) The same encounter was almost ipso facto between the white race and the colored races. This implies that the economically affluent, technologically advanced countries are largely inhabited by people of the Caucasian race, while the poor and developing countries are inhabited largely by those of Negro, Mongolian and other so-called colored races.[10] (3) Almost all the countries in the latter category were colonies of those in the former category.

The confrontation between two groups of nations at the present moment of human history cannot be anything but painful. We may even wish that such a confrontation between "have" and "have-not" nations, between established and developing nations, between the white and the colored races could be avoided. But the confrontation between the two sectors of the world is inevitable. Today the only remaining question to be answered is whether the confrontation will lead to the explosion of the whole world, or whether it will result in a mutual reconciliation in a global community.

But why is the confrontation inevitable? The answer is simple: because the two sectors are already integral parts of a world society, interdependent upon each other. This has occurred as a logical consequence of Western colonial imperialism. Through Western colonial imperialism, technological civilization has embraced all of mankind in one economic unit. The world has been compressed into a single entity, and ". . . as a result, what was once a gulf which divided two wholly separate worlds is rapidly becoming a rift which divides one self-conscious human community."[11]

In 1917, President Wilson proclaimed that ". . . there must not be a balance of power, but a community of power, not organized rivalries, but an organized common peace." Commenting on this statement, the British historian, Professor Geoffrey Barraclough, says: ". . . in spite of their rivalry, Wilson and Lenin had one thing in common: their rejection of the existing international system. . . . They were the 'champion revolutionists of the age,' 'the prophets of a new international order.' "[12]

FROM RACIAL STRATIFICATION TO RACIAL POLARIZATION

The rich and poor nations, developing nations and their former colonial masters have been brought to confrontation with each other in a context of a potential world society. It is here that racial tensions between the have and have-not nations come to a head to determine the course of events for the immediate future. As Ronald Segal has said,

> It is the correspondence of rich with white and poor with colored across so much of mankind that promises, by adding to the insurrection of poverty the passion of race, such a future (i.e., race war). The economic may well be the dominant cause; but the racial may become the dominant identification. What has begun as economic discontent has frequently ended in nationalist upheaval. And is the racialist affiliation inherently less powerful than the nationalist one? The Chinese are not alone in increasingly seeing the economic struggle through tinted lenses.[13]

It used to be a common practice among people of goodwill to reduce the race problem to either a matter of education or economics. It was almost as if by becoming more informed or by somehow being assured of economic security, people of all races would automatically get over group prejudice and group antagonism with the result that all forms of racial discrimination would suddenly disappear. Now the problem has begun to seem simpler, and at the same time more complex: no matter what the basic cause or proposed solution may be, the problem seems to be racial.

There is obviously grave danger in this situation. To complicate matters, it seems as if man has regressed rather than progressed in the area of race relations. There are many white people in the United States who are convinced that the 1954 decision to end school segregation and the Civil Rights Act of 1964 have seriously set back racial harmony in this country. However, it is not true that racial awareness is necessarily bad. I for one do not believe it is necessarily bad. In fact, I believe it is—whether good or bad—an absolutely necessary and inescapable stage that mankind must work through before authentic reconciliation can take place between the races. There is a sense in which Black Power is an indispensable element for the "redemption of American life" and for the healing of the nations.[14]

However, this does not in any way imply that there is no danger in the mounting tide of racial consciousness and sensitivity on the part of the oppressed, dispossessed people at home and abroad. I am painfully aware of the time bomb contained in the racism that is prevalent among the rising new generations. At the same time, I am not entirely blind to the tremendously creative possibilities inherent in it. There is a Chinese phrase for crisis that is made up of two characters indicating "danger" and "opportunity" respectively. As in the Chinese, crisis is a dangerous opportunity, and we can see both the danger and the opportunity in the newly aroused racial pride throughout the world.

Three points need to be stressed at this juncture: (1) the sociology of the context in which the recently decolonized peoples confront their former masters; (2) the history of their relationship with each other during the colonial period; (3) the biography of people involved in the encounter.

The context is the emerging one-world society, a society that is a good place to be for the advanced, white nations. But for the developing nations of predominantly colored races, it is a miserable place, in some ways even more miserable than before they gained their independence. In the past, they either were resigned to their state of misery, or else they did not know better. But now they know that it is not necessary for them to stay poor, and they are daily exposed to the luxurious life that is led in the other half of the world that is enjoying an unprecedented state of affluence. This means, among other things, that the colored races are committed to radical change of the status quo, while the white race is more inclined to try to keep the status quo.

The affluent white race is thus basically peace oriented, while the colored races, in the wake of their decolonization, are basically justice oriented. Within this context, the peace that the white man seeks seems to the others to be nothing but the perpetuation of the injustices imposed upon them by the social, economic and political structures of a white dominated world. On the other hand, the desire for justice by the nonwhite world is seen by the white race as nothing short of a socio-economic revolution. The conflict of interest is thus inevitable.

At this point the history of the relationship between the two further complicates the situation. From one point of view it is a history of the conquest and enslavement of the colored races by the white race. From the opposite point of view, it is a history of the gradual emancipation of the colored races from the tyranny of the raw forces of untamed nature, the transition from pre-industrial to industrial economy and the growing dependence of the white race on the colored races to provide raw materials and cheap labor.

The period since Vasco da Gama up to World War II is thus to the white race a period of maritime imperialism and industrial and economic expansion at the expense of the colored races. To the colored races, it is a shameful period of colonization and enslavement, filled with painful memories. But the fact remains that it is this period in which the foundation of the one-world society was laid down, and in which mutual interdependence between white and colored races began to be established. Thus it is not surprising that the white race tends to glory in the past and dread the future, while the colored races are more inclined to forget the past and glory in the future.

This history has been internalized in contemporary man's personal life, his biography. A white man confronting a man of a colored race embodies in himself that history in which his own race dominated the world of the colored races. And quite innocently, without thinking and without meaning to, he faces every man of colored skin with an attitude of superiority, not so much with animosity or despising, let alone hatred, as with a vague sense of being superior. By the same token, a man of the colored races confronting a white man automatically feels the burden of history deep down in himself and finds himself fighting against the inferiority complex that has become a part of his "cultural heritage."

This is why it is almost impossible for even the most liberal of white liberals to be completely free from some vestige of paternalism toward people of the colored races, and even for the most highly cultured man of a colored race not to be somehow belligerent toward people whom he identifies as white. In short, there can hardly be a natural or authentic man-to-man encounter, unhampered by the history of Western colonial imperialism of the last four centuries, between a white man and a man of a colored race—at least for the foreseeable future. Man cannot be raceless, nor can human relationships be without the racial dimension for a long time to come. Man cannot divorce himself from his history. The twentieth-century man will remain a racial man, regardless of which race or races he may belong to, besides being an economic man, organization man and man of culture.

IRREPRESSIBLE CLAIM TO PEOPLEHOOD

The issue at stake is not constituted by physiological and cultural differences, but rather by the distortions of man's outlook and thought patterns. He is a product of the collective experience of his racial group, especially if he comes from a racially stratified or polarized society. One can hardly help "thinking white" or "thinking black" in contemporary United States society, where white and black are sharply polarized one against the other.

If we take colonial Africa as an example, we see that the ruling white always "thought white," never questioning its rightness or soundness, let alone validity. This attitude led him to create a certain set of educational and cultural criteria for black people as a minimum standard for them to become at all acceptable as his social equals. Those black people who made the grade (called *assimilados* in Portuguese territories or *évolués* in French areas) were treated as if they had been transformed into Portuguese or Frenchmen or Belgians, their black skin notwithstanding. In the British territories, neither technical education nor cultural adaptation nor the combination of the two was sufficient to transform a black man into an Englishman. He became at best a black Englishman, that is to say, his black skin stood in the way of complete acceptance into the colonial society. However, it was assumed that he would lead his own people when and if they were believed by the British to be ready for independence.

What is of crucial importance here is that in each case the standards for acceptance were set up unilaterally by white colonials strictly on their own terms. Black people were forced to "think white" in order to be ac-

ceptable to the white man. Those who could not do so
were labeled as uncivilized, and those who refused to do
so were branded as rebels. Exactly the same state of
affairs has prevailed in the United States in the realm of
black-white relationships. White America, always "thinking white," has not fully accepted black people who do
not think as they do, and until recently black Americans
have been forced to accommodate themselves to white
men's criteria. For a Negro physically to pass as white
has been taboo in white society, but for him to insist on
"thinking black" has made him suspect in white America. This double standard has made life in America for
Negro Americans no less a colonial situation than that
of indigenous people of any colony in Africa or Asia.[15]
But there has been a difference in America: in the white
society the black man was neither to assimilate nor to
stand on his own feet, but rather to remain subservient
to the white man. In short, as leaders such as Stokely
Carmichael have put it, the Negro has long been denied
his "peoplehood."[16]

Black Power in America, Negritude in former French
Africa, African Personality in former British Africa are
all expressions of the black man's aspiration to claim his
peoplehood, without which he is destined to remain in-
secure in the white-dominated world. Within America,
Black Power is not alone in what it is trying to achieve.
It identifies itself with Black Nationalism in various
parts of Africa. It is reflected in Red Power, the movement of university educated American Indians to reas-
sert within the constitutional framework of the United
States their lost sense of peoplehood.[17] It is reflected,
too, in the trend among black students at the nation's
major universities to form a variety of Afro-American
student associations.

These movements cannot be dismissed as a stage or a

phase that we must pass through before a fully matured and integrated America emerges, nor can they be dismissed as a current reaction to the civil rights emphasis on integration. They must be accepted as one of the important preconditions for true, authentic reconciliation among racial communities, given the historical context.[18]

IMPLICATIONS FOR CHRISTIAN MISSION
AND MINISTRY

The habitat of man in the second half of the twentieth century is one world indivisible, yet having an economic rift running between the industrialized white north and the pre-industrialized colored south. Less than one-third of the world's population and almost four-fifths of the world's wealth are to be found in the former, and more than two-thirds of the population and barely one-fifth of the wealth in the latter.[19]

Average per capita income is more than ten times as great in the more advanced nations as a whole than in the less advanced nations taken together, and discrepancies run higher than fifty to one between the richest nation, the United States, and the poorest ones. Worst of all, the contrast between rich and poor is growing greater, since the rich nations are moving ahead proportionally more rapidly than the poor countries.[20]

To intensify the tensions between the two inextricably interdependent halves of the world, the rich north (including the Soviet bloc) is Christian in religious heritage as well as Caucasian in race, while the poor south is anything but Christian in religious heritage. This religious-racial-economic gap between the two sectors of "a now unitary world," to borrow Dr. Reischauer's phrase, not only makes these tensions explosive but also makes the Christian's task extremely difficult.

The Christian church at its most ecumenical level is truly worldwide. Beginning with the Reformation and the Counter-Reformation, the church has included all races and nationalities within its community. But it is also true that Christianity is so identified with the Western powers that many non-Christians, especially in Asia and Africa, regard the church as a tool of Western imperialism.

Christians in the West all too often find themselves under the spell of what might be called a majority psychology or a superiority complex in their attitude toward the three-fourths of the world's population that is neither Christian nor caucasian. This attitude has developed because the Christian missionary movement originated for the most part in the older part of Christendom (which coincides with the rich northern half of the world) and moved to the major portion of what now constitutes the poor southern half of the world. The missionaries traveled southward with the attitude of bringing truth to the ignorant heathen. They were superior to the rest of the world in natural science, technology, engineering, industry and economics, and they fell into the trap of thinking that those who were neither Christian nor caucasian were by nature inferior. This way of thinking led the Christian missionary movement to be philanthropically oriented in its foundations.

Many Christians believed that the Caucasian West had attained its highly developed state of civilization because it had been Christian for centuries; thus the evangelistic attitude, though basically philanthropic, was in practice translated into a civilizing mission by exterminating all forms of paganism. The inevitable result was that Christian missions in Asia and Africa were dominated by what can be called the "conquest motif" in regard to all other religions.

The so-called civilizing process meant in effect that Asians and Africans had to be culturally denationalized and religiously Westernized if they were to meet the standards of civilization imposed on them by the Christian missionaries. Their peoplehood was not respected, and converts to Christianity had to be uprooted from the soil of their indigenous culture as a prerequisite or a consequence of conversion. Thus the "new" man that the missionaries produced was something less than man in that he had been completely cut off from his own people. To make matters worse, he was never fully accepted into any Western colonial community, Christian or otherwise, within his own country. He was turned into a stranger in his own land among his own people.

Although this is past history, it is recent enough to be vividly remembered by all the peoples in the poor half of the world. They are preoccupied with the task of restoring their peoplehood and establishing economic, social and political independence. Christians cannot but be suspect in their eyes. How, then, can the church carry out its mission? Or more fundamental yet, what is the mission of the church to the poor half of the world that is non-Christian and noncaucasian? We are not talking here of the mission of the churches in the West to the rest of the world, but rather of the ecumenical church throughout the world that embraces Christians of all nations, regardless of their economic or political status.

The mission of the ecumenical community in the emerging world society is not so much to christianize non-Christians as to humanize all forms of human relationships. In the area of race relations, this means that the church strives not for the assimilation (or integration) of members of minority races into a society ruled by a dominant race, but rather for the establishment of the peoplehood of all racial and ethnic groups in order to bring about a truly pluralistic society.

This means that the mission of the church within the context of a still racially stratified and polarized world is not so much to strive for peace as for justice. A peace that is not built on the foundation of justice cannot be either a just peace or a durable peace. Justice, too, needs to be translated into concrete economic, technological, political and social terms. It needs to be expressed in collective and structural terms, rather than personal and individual terms. For example, in the area of race relations, it is not enough for individual Christians to become personally free from prejudice. The church needs to help to mobilize and consolidate all the forces of justice in order to bring about a structural change in society so that the peoplehood of every racial and ethnic group can be asserted in mutual respect and trust one for another.

For the church to be able to fulfill a mission it needs to impress upon its members, especially those in the richer areas of the world, the need to be emancipated from every shred of the majority psychology (which is the same as Professor Johannes Hoekenidjk's so-called "crusader syndrome"). Christians must outgrow their naïve faith that Christianity has the final answer to every kind of human problem, and that the role of a Christian in any situation is that of the giver, the teacher, the helper—in short, the philanthropist.

This means, among other things, that the philanthropic orientation of Christian mission is totally inadequate in the face of the growing economic gap between the two halves of the world. Millions of CARE packages will not bring about a world in which the living standard of three-fourths of its population is elevated as much as one percent. Even the massive economic and technical foreign aid programs of advanced nations are far from adequate. Dr. Raúl Prebisch, General Secretary of the United Nations Conference on Trade and Development, stated at the World Council of Churches' World Conference on Church and Society, Geneva, 1966:

> In 1961 the proportion of resources transferred to developing countries was approaching the target of one percent envisioned by the Development Decade of the United Nations, that is to say 0.87 percent. . . . But that is not all. World Bank leaders have expressed their great concern about the fact that 50 percent of the new resources transferred from industrial countries to developing countries was absorbed and cancelled out by payments for financial services received from the developed countries. This 50 percent is an average. In some countries and in some groups of countries—for instance in the Latin American region—another study has shown that in recent years the payments for financial and debt services from Latin America to the industrial centers of the world have cancelled out the resources transferred to them. And sometimes payments even exceeded the amount of the new resources. . . .[21]

What does this say to us? For one thing, it says that the developed countries' obligation toward the developing countries cannot begin to be discharged by foreign aid programs, however massive and efficient they may be. I say "obligation" because the West owes its affluence to the Third World. As Franz Fanon has put it:

> This European opulence is literally scandalous, for it has been founded on slavery, it has been nourished with the blood of slaves and it comes directly from the soil and from the subsoil of that underdeveloped world. The well-

being and the progress of Europe have been built up with the sweat and the dead bodies of Negroes, Arabs, Indians and the yellow races.[22]

The basic issue confronting today's world is that ex-colonies have been left virtually without capital and without technical skills necessary to be producers in the world industrial economy. Besides being merely providers of raw material and cheap labor, they are forced to be consumers of goods manufactured overseas. They belong to the same economic orbit as their former colonial masters, but they find the very structure of international trade against them. For being "sellers of raw commodities—too often of only one commodity per country . . . they are dependent for their foreign earnings on goods whose prices are notoriously unstable."[23]

The price of copper, for instance, rose by 42 percent from 1954 to 1955, then plunged by 34 percent in 1957 and by as much again in 1958. Coffee rose by 38 percent from 1953 to 1954, fell by 27 percent the next year and by 33 percent in 1958. Wool fell by over 50 percent from 1952 to 1958; cocoa by as much in the single year 1956. Such fluctuations can deal staggering blows. It has been estimated, for instance, that for every penny by which copper falls on the New York market, the Chilean treasury loses four million dollars, and that each penny drop in the price of green coffee costs Latin America fifty million dollars.[23]

How can the developing countries build up the capital, structures and skilled human resources they so desperately need? Nothing short of a radical reformulation of the basic structure of international trade will be equal to this problem. This is the center of the Christian mission of this generation. It requires that Christians of all walks of life throughout the world become active, intelligent and responsible participants in corporate action in the social, economic and political arenas. For American Christians, this means putting pressure on their government to change its international trade policy. It is only by collective action that an international situation will come into being that will be more conducive to the ministry of reconciliation between the rich and poor nations and between the white and colored races.

Reconciliation cannot take place unless the parties involved are autonomous entities, each standing on its own ready to forgive and be forgiven, to give and receive. Reconciliation of black people with white people and white people with black people is not the same as integration of black people into the white man's society or the white man's concession to the black man's demands. Reconciliation between black and white cannot be realized until the peoplehood of both is asserted with self-respect by one and accepted with respect by the other, from black to white and from white to black.

EPILOGUE

Many white Christians of affluent America may find the significance of this difficult to understand. To them the statement of the late Rabbi Morris Adler may prove helpful:

Being at ease is a luxury reserved for majorities. They are at home in a world which is their world. The society about them reflects their image and its culture is their culture. Their superior numbers provide them with a massive stability and also, paradoxically, permits them to relax in a restful anonymity. Blending with their environment, they are not conspicuous or visible in their racial, religious, or cultural aspect. No outer force, no inner memory impels them to ask: "Who am I?"

But a minority is a breach in the wall of homogeneity, an "outsider," a deviant. The Western World is Christian, the Jew is not. Now he may not be a fervent follower of his tradition; he may even doubt its value or validity. But his birth has stamped him a Jew. Indeed he may become Unitarian or Protestant or Catholic and renounce his faith but, alas, he retains a sense of difference, for he is not native to his new creed. Overt and palpable exclusions strengthen his sense of difference; so do the subtle diminutions of full acceptance he is bound to encounter. Hence he is driven to ask: "What is this thing called Jewishness which makes the difference?"[24]

Replace "Jew" and "Jewishness" with Negro and Negro-ness, Africa and African-ness, Asian and Asian-ness—whatever the race, Rabbi Adler's statement is applicable to all people whose peoplehood has somehow been impaired if not completely destroyed by those whom they believe constitute the dominant group.

✑ NOTES

1. W. E. B. Du Bois, *The Souls of Black Folk*, 1903, Chapter 2, "Of the Dawn of Freedom."
2. Among others, see Ronald Segal, *The Race War* (New York: Viking Press, 1967; also as a paperback, Bantam Books).
3. See C. Eric Lincoln, *The Black Muslims in America*, the first authoritative study of this movement (Boston: Beacon Press, 1961).
4. On this point documentation is hardly necessary, but a few books may be listed:
Charles E. Silberman, *Crisis in Black and White* (New York: Random House, 1964). Lerone Bennett, Jr., *The Negro Mood* (New York: Ballantine Books, 1964). E. U. Essien-Udom, *Black Nationalism: A Search for an Identity in America* (Chicago: University of Chi-

cago Press, 1962; New York: Dell Publishing Co., Laurel Edition, 1964). Stokely Carmichael and Charles V. Hamilton, *Black Power: The Politics of Liberation in America* (New York: Vintage Books, 1967). Charles E. Fager, *White Reflections on Black Power* (Eerdmans, 1967).

5.   George Padmore, *Pan-Africanism or Communism?* (London: Dobson Books, 1955).

6.   George Balandier, "Negritude," in Hughes and Thompson, *Race: Individual and Collective Behavior* (New York: The Free Press, 1958). Franz Fanon, *Black Skin, White Masks*, tr. by Charles L. Markmann (New York: Grove Press, 1967). Originally *Peau Noire, Masques Blancs* (Paris, 1952).

7.   Jan-heinze Jahn, *Muntu: An Outline of Neo-African Culture* (New York: Grove Press, 1961). Victor C. Ferkiss, *Africa's Search for Identity* (New York: George Braziller, 1966).

8.   See among others, Edwin O. Reischauer, *Beyond Vietnam: The United States and Asia* (New York: Vintage Books, 1967), pp. 60–64.

9.   See *World Conference on Church and Society: Official Report* (Geneva: World Council of Churches, 1967). For a popular but authoritative account of this extremely important conference see: J. Brooke Mosley, *Christians in the Technical and Social Revolutions of Our Time* (Cincinnati: Forward Movement Publications, paperback, 1966).

10.   Edwin O. Reischauer, *op. cit.*, pp. 46–52.

11.   Robert Heilbroner, *The Future as History* (New York: Harper & Row, 1960), p. 162.

12.   Geoffrey Barraclough, *An Introduction to Contemporary History* (New York: Hillary, 1965), pp. 104, 119.

13.   Ronald Segal, *op. cit.*, p. viii.

14.   Nathan Wright, *Black Power and Urban Unrest: Creative Possibilities* (New York: Hawthorn Books, 1967), pp. 66 ff.

15.   See "White Power: The Colonial Situation," in Carmichael and Hamilton, *Black Power*; also Fanon, *op cit.* and his *The Wretched of the Earth* (New York: Grove Press, paperback, 1966).

16.   Carmichael and Hamilton, *op. cit.*

17. See Stan Steiner, *The New Indians* (New York: Harper & Row, 1968).
18. Charles Fager, *op. cit.*
19. Edwin O. Reischauer, *op. cit.*, pp. 47–52.
20. *Ibid.*, p. 52.
21. *World Conference on Church and Society: Official Report* (Geneva: World Council of Churches, 1967).
22. Franz Fanon, *The Wretched of the Earth*, p. 76.
23. Robert Heilbroner, *The Great Ascent: The Struggle for Economic Development in Our Time* (New York: Harper & Row, 1963), p. 104.
24. *Who Is a Jew?—a Reader*, compiled and edited by Solomon S. Bernards (New York: Anti-Defamation League of B'nai B'rith), pp. 9–10.

3

GLOBAL DEVELOPMENT STRATEGY: A MORAL RESPONSIBILITY

Raúl Prebisch

IT IS VERY UNDERSTANDABLE, Mr. President, that at a time when I am completing one more stage in my career as an international official I should look back and recall the circumstances in which we began to work for the establishment of this institution. When the Secretary-General of the United Nations appointed me six years ago to take part in the preparatory work for the First Conference and when, in that capacity, I was able to attend the second session of the Preparatory Committee for the Conference, I was struck by the similarity between the concerns expressed by the representatives of Asian and African countries and those which we, who had been responsible for studying the development of the Latin American countries and for helping to devise

Raúl Prebisch is presently Director General of the Latin America Institute for Economic and Social Planning, Santiago, Chile. Until 1969, he was Secretary-General of the United Nations Conference on Trade and Development. This paper is a statement made by Dr. Prebisch in that capacity at the 176th plenary meeting of the Trade and Development Board, January 22, 1969.

ways and means of accelerating their growth rates, have been expressing for the last fifteen years. I also found a similarity in our conceptions of the most appropriate methods of dealing with the serious problems confronting the developing countries at the international level. From that very first moment, Mr. President, I came to the conclusion that that similarity of concerns, of problems, and of ways of tackling them called for a uniting of wills and a search for common methods of action to strengthen certain trends which had for some time been taking shape in the United Nations General Assembly. This gave me enormous encouragement; it opened up new perspectives and, as a result, I was able to submit to the First Conference a report, perhaps the sole virtue of which was that it expressed in systematic form those common concerns of the three regions of the developing world and served as a basis for the organization of action which was both urgent and unavoidable.

Since then there has been considerable progress on the plane of ideas, progress which contrasts with the resistance we encountered at the time when the Economic Commission for Latin America was first set up.

At that time, as now, we came up against resistance in official quarters, resistance, and sometimes contempt, from academic circles confronted with the new ideas which had arisen from the need to explain a new reality —the reality of the developing and emergent countries. Gradually, however, this reality has been perceived. There are a number of fundamental ideas concerning trade and development which, today, are generally accepted; this is a notable advance, although it does not mean that the obstacles preventing the implementation of these ideas are minor ones. We know only too well, Mr. President, that they are not.

What happened in New Delhi [where the Second United Nations Conference on Trade and Development was held in 1968] clearly demonstrates that a considerable and long-term effort will have to be made if we are to reach the solutions we are seeking; the more I think about all this, Mr. President, the more I am persuaded that what we have been concerning ourselves with in UNCTAD is part of a vast worldwide problem resulting largely from the extremely rapid rate of scientific progress and technological innovation. In the brief period of one lifetime we have seen an astounding series of technical advances such as have never occurred since the industrial revolution. This has created a series of major problems, both in the developed and the developing world and we must admit that conventional thinking has not always kept up with the demands of these new facts and phenomena which the scientific and technological revolution has spread throughout the world. I never cease to be amazed that leading industrialized countries are only just beginning fully to realize what the new technologies mean for their own economic and social life. How many people, twenty years ago, were alive to atmospheric pollution, water pollution, contamination of the oceans and the dangerous consequences of a technology which is so rapidly creating so many grave problems? If, twenty years ago, there were a few enlightened persons who foresaw these problems, public opinion and government circles were perhaps apathetic or insensitive to their scope and magnitude.

However, this is not the only field in which we see the need for new ideas and new formulas for positive action. In the United States of America it is now being discovered that there is a problem of poverty, a problem of marginal population—not poverty such as that encountered in the developing countries, but poverty in relation to the enormous rise which technology has made possible in the standard of living of the rest of the population. Today there is an awareness of this problem and of the fact that these effects of modern technology cannot be dealt with merely by the free play of market forces. I am increasingly convinced that market forces play a very important role in a country's economic life, whatever its degree of development and whatever its economic and social system; we have seen the socialist world recognize the necessity for free play of certain market forces in a new concept of competition, of socialist competition, but at the same time it is recognized that the free play of market forces does not provide the solution to a number of basic problems which—as a result of scientific progress and technological innovation —are facing the world as a whole, in both the economic and the social fields, with regard to both production and distribution and to the psychological effects of scientific and technological progress throughout the world and particularly in the developed countries. The unrest manifesting itself among young people in the larger countries, which is also beginning to make itself felt elsewhere, is in large part a result of the very rapid development of science and technology and the delay with which thinking is adapted to the needs created by these new economic and social phenomena. There is a growing recognition of the fact that this new situation calls for new attitudes and a new type of action—action consciously designed to take advantage of all the fruits, all the enormous benefits offered by modern technology, and, at the same time, to combat its negative effects on the economy, on society, on the very concepts of life and human values.

If this is the case in the great industrial countries, how can we not note what this modern technology has in store for the developing countries? There are enormous possibilities; I believe that within fifty years those who look back to the past will be amazed to see how slow we were in adopting new ideas and new approaches to this phenomenon and in harnessing the full potential of modern technology for the definitive solution of the problem of the developing countries. This problem of the use of technology and overcoming its adverse effects is much more acute, I believe, and occurs on a much larger and more complex scale in the developing world than in the industrialized world, because in the industrial countries the problem consists essentially in a series of adaptations and adjustments to the requirements of technology and in the need to eliminate and correct its adverse effects. In the developing countries, on the other hand, along with this problem, which is also present, there is another problem of basic importance, namely, that of transforming the economic and social structure, changing attitudes, and achieving a true development discipline in order to make full use of the new technology. This calls for new ways of thinking and I believe that in UNCTAD, as in other United Nations organs, a real contribution is being made to the understanding of these problems and to the search for new solutions.

I should like to refer to what I believe is one of the most fundamental and important—I would even say disturbing—aspects of the impact of technology on the developing countries, especially those which have made the most progress in industrialization. In these countries, economic and social contrasts are being created to which we must pay the most serious attention. If we examine the course of industrial evolution we find that, historically, the modern sector of the economy was initially very small but gradually expanded until it embraced a large part of the economically active population. This phenomenon is still in progress in the industrial countries which still have problems of technical backwardness to solve in agriculture and other fields. But that problem is relatively small compared with the formidable one now facing the developing countries. In many of these countries, including those which have made the greatest progress in industrialization, the proportion of the economically active population which has been absorbed in the modern sector of the economy is still very small. In a considerable number of developing countries, nearly 50 per cent of the ecnomically active population is still employed precariously in agriculture, where productivity and incomes are low. Furthermore, a growing proportion of the population consists of persons who have left farming for the towns but have not yet been absorbed by the modern sectors of the economy and thus constitute a marginal population. It may be argued that, historically this also took place in what are now the industrial centres of the world. Why then should we worry? Why not be patient and allow the long-drawn-out process whereby the industrial countries were able gradually to absorb their less productive and low-income population into the modern sectors of their economy to take place also in the developing countries? To adopt such an approach would be to disregard other aspects and effects of present-day technology. In the nineteenth century, for example, the spectacular development of mass communication media for the transmission of information, ideas and aspirations with which we are familiar today had not yet taken place. The backward population which constitutes the bulk of the economically active population of the developing countries is today subjected daily to continuous stimulation, as it were, by all these communication media, which make known and attempt to inculcate not only the ways of life and consumption habits of the industrial countries, but also new ideas and new political concepts which engender fresh aspirations as yet unknown in the nineteenth century. This, then, is another effect of modern technological progress which, although presenting an enormous potential for the improvement of communications, is nevertheless disquieting from the standpoint of the ease with which these communications grow, unaccompanied by measures for rapidly giving real satisfaction to the new aspirations thus created.

There is also another factor which was not present during the economic development of the major industrial countries in the same degree as it is today in the developing countries. This is the familiar problem of the high rates of population growth experienced in the developing countries today—rates which were hitherto unknown in the history of mankind or in the brief period which has elapsed since the industrial revolution. In some developing countries the annual rate of population increase has reached 3.5 per cent. As we know, this is due, not to an increase in the birth-rate, but to the fact that, thanks to science and technology, the mortality rate has been considerably reduced. A development which thus brings enormous benefit to mankind, by alleviating suffering and extending life expectancy, has, at the same time, a dark side, since the high rate of population increase is an extremely inhibiting factor in the task of speeding up the rate of economic and social development. Do not think that I am viewing this demographic problem from a narrow economic viewpoint. It has social, psychological and other aspects which the economist must also respect. Nevertheless I believe it to be our duty to draw attention to the importance of this high rate of population increase. That im-

portance is clear to us today. Twenty years ago it was
not clear because, although the population growth rate
was already rising, the consequences of this growth had
not yet had any impact on the economic sector. Only
today are we realizing fully the effect of the rapid increase of population on the manpower problem, i.e., the
growing number of economically active persons whom
the modern sectors of the economy are unable to absorb
satisfactorily in the developing countries. This is a factor of crucial importance, not only because it is creating
this conflict between the growth of the economically
active population and the inability of the economic
system properly to absorb it, but also because it helps to
reduce the capacity of the developing countries to mobilize their own internal investment resources. Thus we
have the further problem that population growth is generating or to some degree accentuating in all the developing countries a continuous social pressure for the satisfaction of the people's entirely legitimate social demands for education, housing and health and other services. The drawback of these quite legitimate and understandable requirements, however, is that they reduce
the amount of the investment resources which the developing countries might otherwise obtain to accelerate
their rate of development.

However, this is not the only problem. There is another tremendous contrast with the nineteenth century.
In addition to the very rapid population growth and the
consumption and social investment demands, there is
the fact that the modern technology which the developing countries must now try to assimilate requires a very
large and ever increasing amount of capital per capita, a
requirement contrasting with the persistence of a low
level of income in those countries.

Wherever we look we can see that despite the vast

capacity of modern technology to solve the problems of the developing countries, the application of this technology brings with it a range of adverse effects, of vast contradictions, between the requirements of the technology and the existing economic and social structure. A further drawback is the adverse effect on the periphery of the economy of technological and economic development in the industrial centres. We are all well aware that the demand for primary commodities in the large industrialized countries is, with a few exceptions, expanding relatively slowly, precisely because of the impact of economic growth and technological discoveries, which are increasingly providing substitutes for raw materials from the developing countries; and this compounds the very great existing difficulties due to the development of technology within the developing countries themselves.

For all these reasons and considering what has to be done in order to derive benefit from this technology and to remedy these drawbacks, we are driven to the conclusion that much of what we have been seeking in UNCTAD and in other United Nations organs is, in the last analysis, a response to the problems created by technology. Why, for instance, do we place so much emphasis on better access to the major markets for primary commodities? Why are we seeking to establish a system of preferences for the manufacturers and semimanufactures from the developing countries? In order to try to remedy the adverse effects of the economic and technological development of the industrialized countries on the exports from the peripheral countries. Why do we stress the need to increase the transfer of financial resources from the developed to the developing countries? In order to try at least to alleviate the problems of the contradiction between the scanty financial resources available and the vast need for capital owing to modern technology and, in addition, the problems of population growth and the constant incentives to new kinds of consumption. Everything that is being done here springs from the gradual realization of the need for major transformations caused by the absorption of modern technology and the far-ranging economic and social changes caused by the adoption of technology by society, which in turn demand from us a completely new outlook and a thorough reappraisal of our modes of thinking. It is not simply a matter of repeating the processes of the past. We can certainly learn from the past. However, while a study of the past can give us some sort of a basis for facing the future, that will not suffice. We are forced to revise our ideas and seek new forms of action within a new strategy of economic and social development. In my view, it is here that UNCTAD has a basic contribution to make, as, indeed, it has been doing. A process has begun and, if we carry it further, I believe we must eschew oversimple or partial solutions. What is a matter of great concern to me—because I see this kind of solution cropping up every day—is that despite the considerable amount of knowledge already gained—imperfect though it may still be—concerning the manner in which these phenomena of economic and social development occur in the peripheral countries and their relation with the phenomena of the industrial centres, and although there is an increasing awareness of the complexity of the problem as a whole and of the interdependence of its many factors, there is a tendency towards overly simple and partial solutions of the problem in preference to over-all solutions or the combining of convergent measures which is essential for solution of the problem. Thus we see that in some circles there is insistence that the solution to the problem of the developing countries lies in birth control and comparisons are made between what an outlay of $100 on birth control could achieve as compared with the investment of a far greater sum in other fields. This is a false presentation of the problem; I believe that a well-thought-out demographic policy is necessary, but let us not carry our appreciation of this factor to the point of believing that it is *the* solution, independent of a whole series of other measures which require to be taken.

Emphasis is also rightly being placed on the need to increase agricultural productivity in the developing countries. I am in agreement with this too, but we must not declare this to be *the* solution to the problem, for there are other things which require to be done besides increasing agricultural production, and they must be done precisely in order that agricultural productivity may increase. Some go a little further and do not limit themselves to one simple solution but combine two: in their view the solution to the problem of the developing countries lies in increasing the fertility of the land and decreasing the fertility of its inhabitants. It is true that measures will have to be taken regarding these problems, but there are many other things which must be done as well. What would be the consequences for the developing countries of an increase in agricultural productivity? One of the results will be that the proportion of the active population employed in agriculture will have to be smaller. This has been the experience everywhere, irrespective of the economic or social system in force, and therefore, while an effort must clearly be made in regard to agriculture, both in order to increase the production of foodstuffs and to meet the urgent need to raise the incomes of the enormous rural population of the developing world, this very sensible policy requires a simultaneous acceleration of the pace of industrialization and of the rhythm of development in the modern sectors of the economy. If this is not done, the already very serious problem of the inadequate absorption of the expanding economically active population into the modern sectors of the economy will become even more acute. On the other hand, in accelerating the pace of industrialization in order to absorb this increased population which agriculture will no longer require, other internal and external obstacles to faster growth will also have to be attacked more vigorously. The more a developing country speeds up its industrialization and thus increases its need for imports, the more serious becomes its tendency towards an imbalance in its foreign trade and the more important and urgent therefore become the measures to be taken in the industrialized countries to facilitate exports from the developing countries. In these circumstances there is also a greater requirement to expand trade among the developing countries themselves. In this connexion, I must again voice my concern at the fact that while the developing countries are knocking on the doors of the industrialized countries and bidding them open their markets, they nevertheless remain unaware, for the most part, of the need to open their own doors to exports from other developing countries. The policy of expanding trade among the developing countries is moving very slowly and very considerable psychological obstacles must be overcome if the necessary progress is to be made in this area of trade policy.

Thus, whatever aspects of the problem of development may be considered in isolation, it will be seen that by taking action solely on one or other aspect we shall succeed only in creating new problems or aggravating existing ones unless we proceed from an overall viewpoint and with a clear understanding of the interdependence of the different aspects and the need to develop a set of concerted measures in order to deal with them. This, in short, Mr. President, is the justification for a global strategy of development. Why global? For two main reasons; first, because each country, in its own strategy, must take into account all its own economic and social phenomena and, secondly, because the overall strategy must be global in a geographical sense since purely internal measures taken by any one country will not be very effective without full international cooperation and because, furthermore, international cooperation can be largely wasted and come to naught if there is no serious policy of internal development. Hence the global character which we are attempting to give to the development strategy for the second United Nations Development Decade and to the subsequent stages and efforts which will be required in the case of a large number of countries, however optimistic we may be regarding the prospects.

We must not, however, fall into the trap of believing that the whole problem is essentially an economic one. There is a growing concern in the developing world. I have perceived it during my travels and especially in my conversations with young people, with whom I am, happily, still capable of communicating. In them I perceive not only a generous desire to assist in raising the standard of living of the masses who have been left behind by the economic process but also a persistent questioning. "Where are we going?"—they ask—"What kind of man is to be created in this process? What will be his concept of life? Are we going to absorb everything being done in the industrial centres as if they have achieved, or are achieving, perfection in these social and psychological aspects of development, something we would be most reluctant to believe?" Thus, in addition to the economic problem, social, intellectual, moral and psychological problems of the highest importance are being raised. It is becoming increasingly evident that there is a certain concept of human values which must be preserved or attained despite the penetration of technology which threatens to develop certain concepts of life incompatible with man's basic aspirations. Of course, this concern of the developing countries also exists and manifests itself in the industrial countries since it is a general problem. But, in the developing countries, this problem can become and is becoming much greater and has a much more serious effect because it is combined with other problems arising from inadequate economic growth and from the adverse effects of unequal technological penetration. I am becoming increasingly convinced that the potential of modern technology and the growing awareness, particularly among the younger generation, of the problems it engenders creates for us an inescapable moral obligation. I was profoundly impressed, a few days ago, when, having been invited by the students of Louvain University, I found in many of them not only a knowledge of the problems of the developing world, a familiarity with the literature produced on the subject—especially by the United Nations—and a very deep awareness of these problems, but also a generous and enthusiastic resolve to contribute to their solution. I had an opportunity, a few months ago, to observe the same reaction, among the students of the Universities of Lund and Stockholm, in Sweden, and among other groups. I had not realized to what an extent this interest in and sense of moral responsibility for helping the third world to obtain all the advantages of modern technology had developed among the younger generation in the industrial countries. As is commonly the case with the younger generation, all this is inspired by the moral imperative which I mentioned, by generous feelings free from any immediate economic self-interest. I consider this to be of great importance since—and I say it quite frankly—I do not think that any vigorous movement will develop spontaneously from the routine activities of many administrations in either the industrial or the developing countries. Such administrations are preoccupied with the day-to-day problems of economic and social life and are frequently restricted by various political alignments already approved by parliaments and congresses. The movement, therefore, will have to come from outside; the drive will have come from the new generations, from the ecumenical movement, from greater understanding of these problems in various intellectual, trade-union and other circles. This seems to me to be of the greatest importance at the present juncture.

The movement must also come from enlightened economic self-interest. To some extent, the problem of development has been presented in a distorted manner. It is sometimes presented as a philanthropic problem and sometimes as a policy according to which ample resources must be donated to suppress an existing or imminent problem in this place or that and, inevitably, a considerable proportion of the resources mobilized internationally are going to be wasted. I believe that this is a very serious error. If mankind is ever to acquire foresight, if it is to try and peer into the future and see what lies ahead, as it must do in the light of technological progress—and this applies both in the large industrial countries and the developing ones—we must see clearly the great economic importance for the industrial countries of ensuring satisfactory development and an adequate growth rate in the developing countries, for an enormous new commercial frontier will be opened in the world if, in the next ten or twenty years, a vigorous international trade and financial aid policy is put into effect. The trade which could develop in this way offers, in my view, great possibilities for development of the legitimate interests of both the developed and the developing countries. It also holds out enormous possibilities for technological expansion. Consequently, it is not a phenomenon or problem which should be approached from a philanthropic standpoint, however important such a philanthropic approach to the problem may be. It should not be forgotten that economic self-interest is of vital and basic importance and that it offers us the opportunity of creating a new field of international economic expansion which will be of benefit to all, irrespective of economic and social systems, although considerations of a political and social nature cannot, of course, be avoided and are not, in fact, avoided when these problems are being examined.

I do not wish, Mr. President, to make predictions about the future or to create apocalyptic images with respect to the developing world, but I wish to be frank about what I see in the part of the developing world that I know best—or, if you prefer, about which I am least ignorant—that is to say, Latin America. In that region —and I mention it because I believe that there is a parallel which sooner or later will arise in other regions —the modern sectors of the economy are failing to absorb the increase in the economically active population, and this is not only generating increasing social tensions through the inequalities it creates in the distribution of income and in the levels of living, but it is also giving rise to a sense of frustration among the more dynamic elements of the younger generation. By dynamic elements I mean not only those which may decisively affect the course of economic and social development but all men of initiative and ability, who are forceful and forthright and who come from different social groups and various occupations and professions. If Latin America continues to develop at the same rate as it did during the last Development Decade, there will be an increase in the number of these dynamic elements who are not absorbed by the economic system and remain on its fringe, and thus will become frustrated and disillusioned men, men who conspire against social stability. I do not say that to conspire against social stability is an evil in itself because it is frequently necessary, in order to create a new order, to undergo a period of instability—and there is sufficient historical experience to warrant such a conclusion—but the fact is that any *ad hoc* solution will not get to the root of the problem, namely the inability of the economy to grow.

I believe, Mr. President, that this poses a problem which responsible persons whether in the centre of the economy or at its periphery cannot continue to ignore, for it is going to be a source of major movements of which I believe there are already clear signs. A few months ago, in Catholic circles of Latin America, there was a very interesting discussion on the acceptability of the transformations of economic and social structures by violent means. I followed that discussion with a philosophical interest because, in my opinion, it is not ideology but events which are going to decide whether the transformations in Latin America and in the developing world will be violent or not. If the developing world continues to drift, if there is not a strong policy of international co-operation, if there is not an equally strong internal resolve to cope with these transformations in a rational manner—whether or not the philosophy of violence is considered—the probability is that the transformations will be violent. These, then, are the two alternatives currently facing the developing world and I believe that we all have a great duty to speak clearly. Violence may have a historical role—it has had such a role in the past; but given the nature of the phenomena confronting the developing world and which the industrialized world, too, must face, even supposing that a violent transformation of society in a developing country is successful, the problems, the international obstacles will remain the same, and there will be no escaping the need to promote and increase industrial exports, to stabilize prices by commodity agreements, and the need for international financing to ensure that domestic sacrifices are not excessive or lead to extremes which are politically and socially inconceivable and indefensible. Seen from this angle, the planning of a policy of international co-operation, therefore, is independent of social and economic systems, although this does not apply to domestic planning.

Sometimes, when I discuss these problems with friends in the industrialized countries, I come across the following attitude: the developed countries need the products of the developing world less and less, since synthetic products offer great possibilities. If this is so, if the new nuclear technology enables us to disregard the developing countries from a military standpoint, there is no need for concern; the developing world will have to evolve slowly—with or without violence—since the industrialized world is strong enough to assume an attitude of indifference towards what is happening in the third world. I am of course presenting the problem in what are perhaps somewhat exaggerated terms in order to bring out its nature more clearly. But I ask myself whether the situation is really so. Europe and the United States are trying to fight the "Hong Kong flu" which is approaching from the periphery to the centre and the centre has to recognize this reality. It may be that medical technology will within a few years make the centres immune from such epidemics on the periphery, but because of the remarkable progress in communications, of satellites which enable the centre to know what is happening on the periphery—above all to know about major events on the periphery—and the periphery about major events in the centre, a phenomenon entirely new and unique in history is emerging: a certain emotional unity in the entire world which leads men of every country to feel the tragedies of others, to become infected, as it were, with their problems. When we see these new generations in Europe and the United States which are following the problems of the developing world, which are not insensitive to what is happening, I ask myself whether the centre can be immunized against what is happening on the periphery. I ask myself the same question when I talk to the young people of the industrialized countries and when I note that the men of the periphery, self-denying, courageous, of great vision and making great personal sacrifices, have—whether they are mistaken or not—already become symbols in the countries of the centre, symbols of the need for transformation, the need to create, new attitudes at the cost of sacrifices and to react against certain prevailing habits, symbols which show that the tendency to emotional unity, unity of action and sentiment in the world is very strong and, in my judgment, irreversible. I do not know what is going to happen, but I ask myself and I ask the men of the centre whether they believe that there is no need for a strategy to attack the problems of development, whether they think that they can immunize themselves by means of new scientific and technological discoveries against the troubles and convulsions of the world on the periphery. I do not think so, but perhaps I am mistaken. But whatever attitude may be taken, I believe in the vital work of the United Nations and of UNCTAD in throwing light on these phenomena and in the need to carry out the task of convincing those who do not think as we do. Persuasion is the only instrument we have: we must inform people, find new approaches and call for that action which, after all, is a relatively small effort to ask of the developed countries.

4

INTERNATIONAL TRADE AND THE DEVELOPING COUNTRIES

J. F. Rweyemamu

THE SETTING: THE WIDENING GAP

THIS ARTICLE IS CONCERNED with an analysis of the causes of the poverty of the developing countries. The decade of the 1960s opened with a new wave of optimistic expectations for the periphery.[1] There were, first of all, the massive decolonisation efforts, which to many implied the eclipse of imperialism and the possibility of meaningful economic reconstruction by the former colonial people, now that political power was in our own hands. 'Seek ye first the political kingdom and all things shall be added unto you,' succinctly if unaptly captured the prevailing mood of the time.

Secondly, even the United Nations General Assembly enthusiastically designated the 1960s as the Development Decade, expressing the 'desire of the world com-

J. F. Rweyemamu is Senior Lecturer in Economics and Dean of the Faculty of Arts and Social Sciences at The University College, Dar es Salaam, Tanzania. An earlier version of this article was read to the Tanzania Economic Society in July 1968.

munity to accelerate the development process in the less fortunate areas of the world.' In fact, the General Assembly also expressed its conviction that the expansion of trade and the resulting increase in foreign exchange earnings offered the most rapid method of aiding the development of new nations.[2]

But, as the so-called development decade gradually wore on, it became increasingly evident that these political 'winds of change' and the promised international efforts were not being accompanied by commensurate economic prosperity and well-being in the developing countries. On the contrary, as the 'Group of 77' representatives meeting in Algeria observed, 'the lot of more than a billion people of the developing world continues to deteriorate as a result of the trends in international economic relations.'[3] This tendency is borne out by a good deal of statistical data. Accurate figures are difficult to ascertain and their absolute values may be debatable. But both their relative magnitude and their significance point in the same direction, and reveal several clear trends.

First, the share of the developing countries in total world exports declined from 30.4 per cent in 1938 to only 19.1 per cent in 1966, as shown in Table 1. In the first half of the 1960s, total world exports grew at an average annual rate of 7.8 per cent and exports of developing countries, excluding oil exports, grew at an average rate of only 4 per cent. Furthermore, whereas the average prices for primary products exported from developing countries have decreased by 7 per cent since 1958, those for primary products exported from developed countries have increased by 10 per cent in the same period.[4] Indeed, the purchasing power of exports from developing countries has been steadily declining. In the mid-1960s the developing countries were able to buy, for a given value of their *traditional* exports, one-tenth less imports than at the beginning of the period. The loss in purchasing power amounted to approximately U.S. $2,500 million annually, which represents nearly half the flow of external public financial resources to the periphery.

TABLE I

Percentage Share in World Exports of Major Economic Areas[5]

Area	1938	1955	1960	1966
Developed market economies	62.3	64.6	66.8	69.6
Under-developed countries	30.4	25.3	21.4	19.1
Centrally planned economies	7.3	8.5	10.2	10.3

Secondly, during the same period, the developed countries have, through rapid technological progress and continued exploitation of the periphery, increased their capacity for economic development. At the same time the developing countries have become—politically, economically, and technologically—more dependent on the centres.[6] This is indicated not only by the fantastic rise in the developed countries' incomes, but also by the rise in the value of their trade among themselves. Indeed, the fact that the economically developed countries are each other's best customers is now more than ever a central feature of world trade. It is chiefly within a small circle of countries that international trade is now expanding. Thus, in 1966, these countries exported to each other as much as U.S. $105,600 million, or approximately 75 per cent of their total exports, valued at U.S. $141,400 million. In 1960 the proportion was only

70 per cent. The developing countries, on the other hand, increased their trade among themselves by only 0.3 per cent in the same period, and it made up only 16 per cent of their total exports.

Thirdly, while less than one-fifth of the world's people, who live in industrialised lands, enjoy three-fifths of the world's wealth, three-fifths of the world's people, in China, Africa, and India, share little more than one-tenth of its wealth.[7] And the most alarming phenomenon is the fact that the differences are becoming sharper, as the wealth and incomes of the rich countries increase very rapidly while those of the poor countries stagnate.

The most obvious question that comes to mind is, Why is it that, despite the vigilant efforts of the countries of the periphery to step up their levels of living after attaining political independence, they have not been able to better the lot of their peoples? What can and should be done, nationally, regionally, and internationally, to put this right? These are some of the issues I shall try to explore in this article. I shall argue that the observed symptoms of under-development—namely, the increasing degree of structural dependence of the developing economies on those that are developed, and their consequent poor performance in international trade, widening the gap of power, wealth, and income between the industrial centres and the periphery—are to be largely traced to the historical relationships between the metropolitan powers and the former colonial countries. I shall also argue that the prevailing international division of labour not only tends to accentuate the misallocation of resources and the inequality of income—a natural tendency for an economic structure dominated by mature capitalism—but also creates economic classes on an international scale, as the contradictions between the relations of production and property become manifest. Finally, I shall attempt to outline some policies which might rectify these trends.

THE "CLASSICAL" EXPLANATION

The classical explanation of the above pattern of international trade is, of course, the international division of labour. On this hypothesis, it is argued that basically countries trade with each other because they possess different comparative advantages in the cost of production of goods and services. These cost differences are largely attributable to differences in relative resource endowments, as reflected in their price structures. In other words, the *raison d'être* for the international division of labour is greater specialisation of production, which—under conditions of free trade, perfect competition, zero transport costs, and so on—can be shown to be distributed in the most advantageous fashion in the given circumstances. It also follows that international trade—given the above special conditions—tends to equalise the prices of commodities in different countries, permits countries to specialise in the production of those goods for which they have comparative advantages, and tends to equalise the prices of factors of production as between countries.[8]

But the record of the widening gap set out earlier certainly does not conform to the above picture. In the first place, it has been observed by Professor Chenery that, while the share of certain industries in the domestic product of the industrial countries declines, there is never any actual contraction in absolute terms;[9] this means that, as less capital-intensive industries are gradually set up in the capital-scarce countries, there is no likelihood that such industries will disappear from the capital-abundant countries. Secondly, as Prebisch has argued, the faster technological progress in the industrial countries has not resulted in the falling of industrial prices relative to those of primary products;[10] yet one would expect this to happen, given the above assumptions. Thirdly, the enormous differentials between the developed and the developing countries, noted above, indicate that the price of labour (and other factors of production) is far from tending towards equality among the various regions of the world.

What then is wrong with the international division of labour? Or, at any rate, what is wrong with the classical explanation given above?

I think it is worth exploring the underlying obstacles to the theory of comparative advantage if we are to understand the reasons why some economists, as well as the U.N. General Assembly resolution quoted earlier, are mistaken in their belief in foreign trade as an 'engine of growth.'[11] For, in the first place, it is wrong to regard so-called 'natural endowments' as an absolute and unchangeable criterion on which to base the international division of labour, especially under conditions of changing demand patterns and technology, since what is a comparative advantage today may cease to be so tomorrow.[12] Secondly, comparative advantages cannot be realistically calculated on the basis of market prices, for, as is now well known, capitalist prices are influenced by a number of non-competitive forces such as monopolistic profits, bargaining power, and so on. Thirdly, and most important, the theory of comparative advantage assumes unlimited and responsive demand; that is to say, elastic markets and prices. If both the prices and the markets for certain commodities which are the speciality of a given region are inelastic, then the very notion of comparative advantage becomes not only suspect but meaningless. I will show presently that in fact the demand for the traditional exports of the periphery is today typically inelastic.

Finally, the continued emphasis on the assumption of 'perfect competition' in international trade theory would seem to be grossly misplaced. In fact, the growth and development of what Professor M. Bye calls the 'multi-territorial unit' has rendered the assumption of vertical capital immobility untenable.[13] The growth of oli-gopoly in the advanced countries seems to be related to the problem of under-development.[14] Let me examine some of these points in greater detail.

In the first place, it should be recognised that the pattern of demand in the industrialised countries has changed in such a way as to result in a smaller growth in demand for primary than for manufactured products. This arises from a conglomeration of various factors, enumerated below.

1. *Engel's Law*. Ever since the days of Adam Smith, economists have confirmed his observation that 'the de-sire of food is limited by the narrow capacity of the human stomach; but the desire of the conveniences and ornaments of building, dress, equipage and household furniture, seems to have no limit or certain bound-ary';[15] and therefore the demand for food tends to be-come a smaller proportion of spending as income rises, while spending on industrial goods takes up a higher proportion of the budget. The effect of this so-called 'law' is that there have been relatively small increases in the consumption by industrial countries of the tropical beverages and food exported by the developing coun-tries. For example, coffee consumption in the U.S., the major coffee importer, has remained static at 2.97 cups per person per winter day in the 1960s.[16] In general,

one can say that the relative shift in the demand for beverages, food, and tobacco accounts for a significant proportion of the fall in developing countries' total exports. This problem has been compounded by the increasing inequalities of income in the developed market-economy countries, in so far as the high-income group in the population has shifted its tastes to the more expensive qualities and varieties which are often produced within the devloped countries themselves, such as butter instead of margarine.[17]

2. *Changes in the structure of production and the use of synthetics.* There has been, *pari passu* with the above developments, a tendency towards autarchic production in the industrial countries, through the substitution of home production for imports. For example, the fall in demand for vegetable oils in the industrial countries can be attributed partly to a shift in consumer demand from soap to synthetic detergents and partly to the substitution of animal for vegetable oil in soap-making. The expansion of soya beans in the U.S. and of beet sugar in Western Europe has led to a decline in oil-seed and cane-sugar exports respectively from the developing countries.[18] In industrial production the developed countries have increasingly substituted raw materials which they themselves have processed for those formerly imported. The main substitutes have been aluminium for copper, and to a lesser extent for steel and other materials; man-made fibres for cotton, silk, and wool; synthetic for natural rubber, sisal, jute, and hemp, and plastic materials for a wide range of traditional textiles, paper, wood, and other materials.[19]

At the same time there have been significant structural shifts in production in the industrial centres. The most important changes have been sharp increases in production in engineering and chemicals and small increases in textiles. It is obvious that such an irreversible shift in the industrial countries' structure of production has had a substantial adverse effect on the exports of the primary-producing countries, because the import content of engineering and chemical production is small, while that of textiles is large.[20]

3. *Commerical policies of the industrial countires*. Despite their 'excessively rigorous verbal devotion to lopsided liberal trade principles'[21]—as exemplified in the rules of G.A.T.T.,*for instance—the developed countries have intensified their protectionist attitudes, to the detriment of developing countries' trade. As Dr Onitiri has pointed out, this is the more unfortunate since the developing countries as a whole are the least able to carry out structural adjustments in their economies.[22] The escalation of tariffs with higher degrees of processing of tropical products by the developed countries is to be greatly deplored. It is of course no accident that at the Second U.N. Conference on Trade and Development the O.E.C.D.** members were willing to grant preferences to manufactured products *other than* the processed and semi-processed agricultural products. Furthermore, the industrial countries have placed quantitative restrictions on the import of cereals, dairy produce, textiles, toys, sports goods, and leather products and have supported, through subsidies or minimum price guarantees, the production of beet sugar, oils, soya beans, and oilseeds. Moreover, as if the above restrictions were not enough, it has become part of the fiscal system of most industrial countries to subject certain tropical commodities, such as coffee, tea, tobacco, tropical fruits, and cane sugar, to heavy taxation.

* General Agreement on Tariffs and Trade.
** Organization of Economic Cooperation and Development.

In sum, one can say that the necessary conditions assumed by the theory of comparative advantage, which alone make it possible to advocate international trade as an engine of growth for the developing countries, are largely absent. Numerous factors—the technological revolution in the industrial countries which has altered their pattern of demand and structure of production, their enviable sustained rate of economic growth, the diversity of demand that accompanies high income, the reduction of trade barriers within Europe and America, and the intensification of communications—have all contributed to the spectacular rise in trade between the developed countries, especially in manufactured products. Developing countries, on the other hand, have, by the unhappy concatenation of a series of more or less special circumstances, which I will describe very shortly, been unable to restructure their economies so as to reap similar benefits of development.

From what has been said so far, I think it is clear that the under-developed countries cannot rely on economic growth being induced from outside through an expansion of world demand for their traditional exports of primary commodities. Nor can the necessary foreign exchange gap be narrowed considerably by the inflow of foreign capital from developed countries, both private and public. On the one hand, the amount of development assistance has levelled off in absolute terms and has declined as a proportion of the gross national product of developed countries. This has been explained as due to the current balance-of-payments problems of the major donors. However, these problems are a result partly of the monetary crisis (which reflects the impending overproduction crisis), partly of their failure to restructure their economies away from processing towards industries at higher levels of technical advancement, and partly of imperially initiated wars. In such circumstances, the prospects of increasing the level of aid to developing countries are very bleak indeed.[23]

But aid, quite apart from its meagre scale, has a detrimental effect on the developing economies in so far as it reinforces the centre-peripheral relationship. The *quid pro quo* for the aid given by the developed countries is the safeguarding of the principal economic positions which they either occupied before decolonisation or have established after independence. Thus it is no accident that over 90 per cent of French aid goes to francophone countries. In other words, the industrial countries want to keep control (either directly or through the subterfuge of joint-owned companies) of all the principal sources of raw materials, including minerals and oil, as well as the major industrial constellations.

The methods of ownership and control have obviously changed since (or even before) the period of decolonisation, but the effects are basically the same. Thus one may quote the former chairman of the World Bank; although he was addressing U.S. businessmen so as to induce them to understand and accept foreign aid on their terms, he underscored the major economic motives of the aid programme by stating the benefits of foreign aid programmes from the point of view of the U.S., as follows: (i) to provide a substantial and immediate market for U.S. goods and services; (ii) to stimulate the development of new overseas markets for U.S. companies; and (iii) to orientate national economies towards a free enterprise system, in which the U.S. could prosper.[24]

Two significant conclusions follow from the above discussion. First, I think that the U.N. General Assembly emphasis on trade *under the existing international division of labour* is not only misplaced but may be regarded as a calculated strategy by the capitalist countries to mislead the developing countries. For it must be quite evident that the new nations of the twentieth century cannot follow the nineteenth-century pattern of development of the so-called regions of recent settlement, such as Canada, Australia, and New Zealand, where the export sector was the leading sector, or of those areas that received large doses of investment from their mother countries designed to produce raw materials and food for the latter in return.[25] This is because, as shown above, economic development is diffused through trade only when the pattern of advance in the industrial countries happens to be such as to cause a rapidly rising demand for imported foodstuffs and raw materials.

Furthermore, the continuation of the imperially initiated specialisation in traditional exports is detrimental to both our long-term economic growth and our autonomy as independent countries, since the traditional export sector—lacking sufficient backward and forward linkages[26]—fails to provide a focus around which an integrated economy can develop; and the export-led economies which were originally imperially dominated have tended to develop patterns of income distribution and economic/political power bases which thwart modern industrial and agricultural growth.[27] For both these reasons it is meaningful to reaffirm the late Professor Nurkse's words that the emphasis on trade under existing patterns of international division of labour is indeed 'out of place and could be interpreted as a hangover from by-gone days.'[28]

If it is in the case, as I have argued above, that the emphasis on trade is misplaced, because it is unlikely to be the engine of growth, a second conclusion follows: that one must examine the fundamental cause for this state of affairs, in order to discover the growth options now available to the periphery. My view is that the misery of the developing countries is to be traced to their *historical* relationship with the metropolitan powers, which has led to their being firmly integrated with the world capitalist system as 'satellites.'[29] It is the speed with which and the process by which this situation is overcome that will determine their economic prosperity and their social and political well-being. These assertions are supported in the section that follows.

THE FUNDAMENTAL CAUSE OF UNDER-DEVELOPMENT

It is generally recognised that the developing countries have been, for the most part, the former colonial or semi-colonial regions—in other words, the agricultural plantations and raw-material hinterlands of the big capitalist powers, which have exploited these areas as sources of cheap raw materials, labour, and foodstuffs. But the implications of all this for the potential growth of the periphery have largely gone unnoticed. Yet it should be obvious that a historical relationship of the metropolitan-colonial type tended to breed at least two major obstacles to the development of the dependent countries: (a) their integration in the world capitalist market as satellites, involving foreign ownership and control of the periphery's resources and commercial institutions; and (b) their domestic structure, with an export enclave intimately interlinked with the network of world capitalism, which allied the most powerful interest groups of the periphery with those of imperialism. It is perhaps because these historical and institutional conditions have been ignored that the Japanese model of development is often recommended for adoption by the periphery.

To the extent that these relationships did not change at the dawn of independence—indeed, they may have deepened or new ones may have been established—it is likely that the nature and direction of existing trade flows reflect both this pattern and also the persistence of certain precolonial divisions of labour and patterns of trade. In other words, international trade perpetuates the *artificial* international division of labour between the developing countries and the metropolitan centres, a division established by imperial power and maintained by lop-sided trade. For the kind of trade relations imposed by the colonial powers did not usually displace the existing social and economic structure of the colonies. While those relations, in the earlier stages, were confined to plundering and establishing a network of trading posts without affecting production itself, the next stage of colonial expansion included the introduction of primary production for the market, both agricultural and extractive. The specialisation of a colony was determined by the colonial power—either according to its own needs or because of its likely profits as an intermediary between the colony and other countries—and had little to do with the optimal allocation of world resources. In this way different modes of production were set up.[30]

This integration of the less-developed capitalist countries into the world capitalist market, as reliable and continuous suppliers of natural resources, results in a continuous dependence on the centres of monopoly capital, further cemented by the market institutions (export-import houses, banking, insurance facilities, commercial and government purchasing facilities, shipping, and so on) which evolve from this dependency.

This tendency is reinforced quite naturally by the pattern of colonial and neo-colonial investment (in the choice of both sectors and techniques). Such investment was concentrated in the primary-export industries together with their associated infrastructure. Consequently, not only is the industrial output of the periphery meagre, as shown in Table 2: but, even where it is substantial, it does not reflect a significant and consistent integration with the rest of the economy.

TABLE 2[31]

Product of Manufacturing Industries of Non-Socialist Countries (as a % of total value added, 1958)

Region	All industry	Light industry	Heavy industry
Africa and Middle East	1.5	1.7	1.2
Latin America	3.7	5.3	2.7
Asia (excluding Japan and socialist countries	2.1	3.5	1.1
Sub-total (periphery)	7.3	10.5	5.0
U.S. and Canada	49.9	47.5	51.5
Europe (excluding socialist countries)	37.6	36.6	38.2
Japan	3.5	3.5	3.7
Australasia	1.7	1.9	1.6
Sub-total (industrial centres)	92.7	89.5	95.0
Total	100.0	100.0	100.0

The concentration of finance capital has deepened with the greater economic integration of the periphery with the metropolitan centres, whose international oligopolies have tended to establish their subsidaries in the periphery.[32] Furthermore, realising the deteriorating terms of trade for unprocessed primary products, the plantation interests have now established processing plants, leaving production to the smallholders. There is thus a beginning of consumer-goods industries and export-oriented processing industries. But the result remains the same as in the colonial period, in so far as most of the subsidiaries use the same techniques of production as in the centres, import most of their machinery, enjoy a monopoly position (sometimes protected!), and repatriate most of their profits.

Not only is the value added very small, and the drain of foreign exchange large: they also have the disadvantages of perpetuating the periphery-metropolitan dependence. The result of such a pattern of development, so well described by Baran a dozen years ago, has hardly changed:

> Their exploitation was multiplied; yet its fruits were not to increase their productive wealth; these went abroad or served to support a parasitic bourgeoisie at home. They lived in abysmal misery, yet they had no prospect of a better tomorrow. They existed under capitalism, yet there was no accumulation of capital. They lost their time-honoured means of livelihood, their arts and crafts, yet there was no modern industry to provide new ones in their place.[33]

SOME POLICY IMPLICATIONS

The most important aspect of all these problems confronting the developing countries is the fact that their economies are intertwined with the international capitalist system, their resources, economies, and societies being geared to the needs of the imperialist powers. Among the many implications of this fact, particularly for our purposes, are the following:

1. their extreme reliance on exports of primary produce, especially agricultural and mineral output for a significant proportion of national income, although export prospects for these commodities are not very promising;

2. the existence of lop-sided investment, favouring a sector that is scarcely related to the economic structure of the country concerned, at the expense of the diversification of the internal market;

3. the orientation of transport networks, commercial and government purchasing policies, banking, insurance, shipping, and other commercial institutions to the metropolitan power rather than domestic (including regional) needs;

4. the continued lip-service paid by political leaders and economic bureaucrats to regional (horizontal) integration among developing countries, while they encourage vertical integration with the centres, thus perpetuating the dependence of the developing countries on them;

5. excessive faith in the likelihood of economic advancement through a gradual, reformist strategy, including the quinquennial exercise of drawing up caricatures of 'development plans'—mostly by expatriates—plans which do not take into consideration the historical relationships of the periphery and the industrial centres; and

6. the political effects of economic weakness in tying them to the chariot-wheels of the very imperialism from which they strove for political independence.[34]

In so far as the fundamental cause of the underdevelopment of the periphery has been traced to its structural dependence on the metropolitan centres—a relationship forged during the colonial era and continued in the post-independence era—it would seem that the periphery has at least three significant options: (a) to eliminate its status of 'satellite' *vis-à-vis* the centre; (b) to transform itself into a metropolitan member of the system; and (c) to opt out of the system.[35] These alternatives are not mutually exclusive, nor do they lead to the same development process. They all involve, however, a much more *radical* transformation of the periphery-metropolitan relationship than has often been recognised by the architects of the so-called 'development plans'.

Furthermore, regardless of the choice they make, the countries concerned will have to determine a number of distinct though connected issues, such as the relative importance to be assigned to foreign trade and to mobilising internal resources, the order of priority to be assigned to different industries or sectors, and the choice of techniques in the economy at large and in particular industries. Such decisions must take account of the structural changes required in the economies of the developing countries, if they are to achieve meaningful economic growth. Two important requisites for change may be emphasised here: the need for industrialisation, and for internal reorganisation (economic and political).

A well-defined industrialisation strategy

This in effect implies making industry a leading sector in the development plans. The primary and essential role of industry in the development process is now fully demonstrated from the lessons of history. Maizels, in his definitive statistical study, summarises the evidence conclusively and exhaustively. In particular, he shows that industrialisation has been the key to economic progress in most countries and that the main reasons are that it

(i) tends to *raise physical output per head*, and (ii) *changes the pattern of output* in response to changes in the structure of demand. But, having arrived at such useful results, Maizels goes on to say, unperturbed, that 'this well-established picture implies *no* precise rules about the stages of development of at present under-developed countries,' and that the availability of aid and technical know-how, as well as other special features, 'makes possible changes in the pattern and thus acceleration of industrial growth and economic development!'[36]

However, there are at least two major economic justifications for industrialisation on the periphery. The first is the balance-of-payments situation, the elements of which have already been described in Part I, above. For the inherited export enclaves of the developing countries make them dependent on the export earnings of their primary products, the prospects for which are very bleak indeed. Imports, on the other hand, have been growing faster than exports, while the terms of trade have deteriorated considerably. This has considerably curtailed their ability to sustain high rates of capital investment, in spite of the capital available from the developed countries. In the absence of integrated basic industries at home, they have to keep on importing capital goods; and yet their ability to do so is determined by the level of exports and the prevailing terms of trade.

Secondly, there is the justification for expanding the capital-goods sector. In so far as investment should be concentrated upon methods and lines of production which will increase the investment potential still further, and to the extent that one of the most important limiting factors is the output capacity of the industries which produce capital goods, the growth rate in the future will be higher, the larger the proportion of current investment that is directed towards expanding this sector. Such a view runs contrary to the conventional wisdom which advocates gradualism and 'consumer goods first.' But it is based on the belief that a bigger share of a total which is growing more slowly will be greater in the long run than a smaller share of a total that is growing faster.[37]

However, I must point out that carrying out an industrialisation strategy is not easy in the face of strong imperialist pressure to reduce its importance in development, aided by planners with old habits of thought. It is often argued that the industrialisation of the capitalist countries in the nineteenth century was made possible by a particularly propitious constellation of events which no longer exist in the twentieth century (except of course, for the successfully industrialised socialist countries!). Thence it is concluded that to follow the example of the present-day industrialised countries will be to miss the target, and that the production of raw materials corresponds much more to the conditions of under-developed countries! At the same time, certain relative, practical difficulties of industrialisation have been given an *absolute* character: for example, the lack of capital and of a skilled labour force, the uneven distribution of raw materials, or the danger of dislocating the balance of payments. These difficulties are, however, used to substantiate not only the necessity for an inflow of capital from the developed capitalist countries but also for giving preference to the development of agriculture.[38]

Yet similar justifications of a very narrow specialisation on agricultural raw materials once led Marx to declare: 'You believe perhaps, gentlemen, that the production of coffee and sugar is the natural destiny of the West Indies. Two centuries ago, nature, which does not trouble herself about commerce, had planted neither sugar-cane nor coffee trees there.'[39] It is therefore necessary to lay stress on the following policies:

1. The available capital resources must be invested, not in the conglomeration of industries recommended after a static consideration of 'import-substitution' and 'export-promotion' needs, but rather in basic industries that will meaningfully integrate the economy, create internal demand, and reduce the periphery—centre dependence. For the past pattern of demand for imported consumer goods is only a very limited guide for altering the consumption-investment mix for the future, and it is least useful when considering the future demand for capital and intermediate goods. So it can hardly be over-emphasised that import substitution and export promotion are not relevant as basic selection techniques.[40] Instead, greater weight should be placed on forward and backward linkages with the rest of the economy, and on the amount of value added.

2. To give priority to industry, as I have advocated, does not imply neglecting agriculture. Indeed, agricultural production has to increase, to meet not only the growing needs of the agricultural sector itself but also the increased demand in the industrial sector for food and raw materials, as industrial output and income rise. Indeed, it is the very development of an integrated industrial sector that will speed up agricultural development, by the production of more efficient agricultural implements and intermediate goods such as fertilisers and pesticides.[41]

3. Regional integration among the developing countries must also be pursued, vigorously and untiringly, especially by harmonising their industrial programmes. The intermediate- and capital-goods industries I have advocated are those in which the economies of scale and

external economies are the greatest, requiring, in the non-industrialised countries, regionally-integrated markets.[42] However, the periphery must be careful lest their integrated regions become the sphere of influence of the imperialists.

Internal reorganisation of the economic base and the political superstructure

It must be pointed out that the international capitalist system is not the only constraint on the productive potential of the periphery, although it has been given prominence in this article. Equally important, but derived from the periphery-centre relationship, is the reactionary power base of the periphery. Tanzania is one of the few countries that have tried to tackle the institution of a progressive power base, and some of the problems arising, by launching the Arusha Declaration; but even here much remains to be done. It is true that the social ownership of the means of production implies new *opportunities* for economic development, such as proper planning, using the means of production in the interest of society as a whole, and so on; but it should be realised that these are *only* opportunities, which do not automatically guarantee the attainment of these objectives. But beyond the problem of control, which is partially solved by nationalisation, is that of the very nature of socialist planning. How can a plan drawn up by 'experts' who consider mainly the internal consistency of the programmes, far removed from the needs and conditions of the people, be said to be directed by the will of organised society? It would seem that, if economic development is to be directed by organised society, then planning must be what the late Professor Lange called 'active economic planning'.[43]

The analysis of this article has shown that the sun of imperialism, far from being eclipsed at the dawn of independence, still glares down on the most impoverished half of the planet, rather more fiercely than before. This is revealed by the growing inequality of development, the constantly widening gap between the level of development of the advanced capitalist countries and that of the economically and politically dependent—the so-called 'developing'—countries. The recognition of this fact is the first necessary step towards our economic reconstruction. For only then can we examine meaningfully our development options and the corresponding strategies required to attain them.

NOTES

1. In this article the term 'periphery' will be used to refer to the 'under-developed' or 'developing' capitalist countries in the world. It originates from R. Prebisch, 'The Role of Commercial Policies in Underdeveloped Countries,' in *American Economic Review Papers and Proceedings* (Menasha, Wisconsin), May 1959.
2. U.N. General Assembly Resolutions 1710 and 1707 (xvi), passed on 19 December 1961.
3. Group of 77, 'Charter of Algiers' (Algiers, 1967, mimeo).
4. U.N.C.T.A.D., 'Review of International Trade and Development, 1967' (Geneva, 1967, mimeo.), TD/15, part 1.
5. Sources: ibid. and G.A.T.T., *Trends in International Trade* (Geneva, 1958).
6. The word 'centres' will be used to denote developed market economy countries. Cf. A. G. Frank, *Capitalism and Underdevelopment in Latin America* (New York, 1967).

7. M. B. Brown, *After Imperialism* (London, 1963), p. 4.

8. H. G. Johnson, *Money, Trade and Economic Growth* (London, 1964), p. 29.

9. H. Chenery, 'Patterns of Industrial Growth,' in *American Economic Review* (Menasha, Wisconsin), September 1958.

10. R. Prebisch, 'Commercial Policy in Underdeveloped Countries,' ibid. September 1960.

11. This term, now accepted in economic literature, was introduced by D. H. Robertson in 'The Future of International Trade,' in H. S. Ellis and L. S. Metzler (eds.), *Readings in the Theory of International Trade* (London, 1957), pp. 497–513.

12. Cf. I. Sachs, *Foreign Trade and Economic Development of Underdeveloped Countries* (Bombay, 1965), pp. 25–6; and H. Myint, 'The Classical Theory of International Trade and the Underdeveloped Countries,' in *The Economic Journal* (London), June 1958, pp. 317–37.

13. M. Bye, 'Self-financed Multi-territorial Units and Their Time Horizon,' in *International Economic Papers* (London), viii, 1957, pp. 147–78.

14. See G. Arrighi, 'International Corporations, Labour Aristocracies and Economic Development in Tropical Africa,' in D. Horowitz (ed.), *The Corporations and the Cold War* (London, 1968). For a contrary view see H. Myint, 'International Trade and the Developing Countries,' a paper read at the International Congress on the Future of International Economic Relations, Montreal, Canada, 2–7 September 1968.

15. Adam Smith, *The Wealth of Nations* (New York, 1937 edition), p. 164; see also H. Houthakker, 'An International Comparison of Household Expenditure Patterns: commemorating the centenary of Engel's Law,' in *Econometrica* (Amsterdam), xxv, 1957.

16. Pan-American Coffee Bureau, *Annual Coffee Statistics, 1964* (New York, 1964).

17. However, even in these cases, developing countries' exports are limited greatly by the developed countries' import restrictions. For example, Kenya's butter and Ghee is of good quality but is not exported to any developed country.

18. U.N.C.T.A.D., 'Commodity Survey, 1967' (Geneva, 1967, mimeo.), TD/C.1/46/add.f; F.A.O., *Commodity Review, 1967* (Rome, 1967).

19. The extent of substitution may be grasped from one example: whereas in 1950 synthetic rubber was only 24 per cent of total world rubber consumption, by 1968 it had risen to 65 per cent. F.A.O., *Commodity Review, 1967*; and *Rubber Statistical Bulletins* (London), 1960–8.

20. A. Maizels, 'Recent Trends in World Trade,' in R. Harrod (ed.), *International Trade Theory in a Developing World* (London, 1963).

21. Statement by A. M. Maalim, Minister of Commerce and Industry, leader of the Tanzania delegation to U.N.C.T.A.D. II, New Delhi, 13 February 1968.

22. H. M. A. Onitiri, 'Capital Movements, the Volume of Trade and the Terms of Trade,' in J. H. Adler and P. W. Kuznets (eds.), *Capital Movements and Economic Development* (London, 1967).

23. At U.N.C.T.A.D. II, only the small donor countries expressed their desire to reach the aid target of 1 per cent of national income.

24. Reported by Harry Magdoff, *Economic Aspects of U.S. Imperialism*, Monthly Review Pamphlet no. 24 (New York, 1966), p. 5.

25. Cf. R. Nurkse, 'International Trade Theory and Development Policy,' in H. S. Ellis (ed.), *Economic Development of Latin America* (London, 1962), especially p. 23G.

26. This latter-day newcomer to the dismal scientists' lexicon has been generously given to us by Professor A. O. Hirschman, *The Strategy of Economic Development* (New Haven, 1958), especially ch. 6.

27. Arrighi, loc. cit., and Frank, op. cit. See also R. H. Green and A. W. Seidman, *Unity or Poverty? the economics of pan-Africanism* (London, 1968); I. Sachs, *Patterns of Public Sector in Underdeveloped Economies* (Bombay, 1964).

28. R. Nurske, *Patterns of Trade and Development* (London, 1961), p. 50.

29. The metropolitan-satellite relationship is explored fully by A. G. Frank, op. cit.

30. Sachs, *Foreign Trade and Economic Development*, pp. 28–9.
31. P. Jalee, *The Pillage of the Third World* (New York, 1968), table v.
32. Ibid. p. 78.
33. Paul Baran, *Political Economy of Growth* (New York, 1957), p. 144.
34. Cf. M. Dobb, *Economic Growth and Underdeveloped Countries* (London, 1963).
35. A fourth option—to follow the traditional capitalist road as a satellite, which normally implies relying on foreign capital and subordinating development to the sectoral interests of monopoly capital—is excluded here because it conflicts with the aims of the periphery.
36. A. Maizels, *Industrial Growth and World Trade* (Cambridge, 1963), p. 10, my italics. See also Chenery, loc. cit.
37. For a clear elaboration of this point, see Dobb, op. cit. ch. 5.
38. Cf. Jerzy Rutkowski, 'Some Problems of Socialist Industrialisation,' in O. Lange (ed.), *Problems of Political Economy of Socialism* (Warsaw, 1962), p. 58.
39. Karl Marx, *The Poverty of Philosophy* (New York, 1955 edn.), p. 207.
40. Contrary to the views of E. J. Stoutjesdijk, *Uganda's Manufacturing Sector* (Nairobi, 1967), p. 6, among others.
41. See A. F. Ewing, *Industry in Africa* (Oxford, 1968), and René Dumont, *False Start in Africa* (London, 1966), esp. p. 104, for further elucidation of this point.
42. In this connection, the implications of the balkanisation of Africa, so well described by Kwame Nkrumah in his *Neo-colonialism: the Last Stage of Imperialism* (London, 1965), should be taken very seriously.
43. O. Lange (ed.), *Problems of Political Economy of Socialism*. See also E. Boorstein, *Economic Transformation of Cuba* (New York, 1968).

5

THE REVOLUTION OF OUR TIME

Brady Tyson

REVOLUTION IS THE NAME GIVEN to those traumatic epi-
sodes in human history when the structures of society
are radically changed to permit a different distribution
of the effective exercise of power, and the dominant
mentality of a society is radically altered to include new
aspirations and a new vision of human society. Revolution in itself in nothing new, though it often comes in
different forms, seeking different goals. Revolution has
generally meant a breakthrough against opposition in
the continuing search of men and society for wider and
more meaningful participation of more people in the
goods and decision-making process of a society.

In our time, characterized as it apparently is by an
apparent "speeding up" of the historical process, several
emphases seem to be compressed in the current "time of
troubles" that is by some of us hopefully called "The
First World Revolution." All of these apparently sepa-

*Brady Tyson is Professor of Latin American Affairs, School
of International Studies, American University, Washington,
D.C. This paper was prepared for the 1970 Catholic Inter-
American Cooperation Program* (CICOP) *Conference.*

rate movements are also known, increasingly, as "The Movement." By this is meant the anti-imperialist, anti-colonial, anti-neo-colonial, the civil rights movement, the student power, the university reform, the church renewal, the anti-paternalism, the anti-racist, the Black Power movements, and the movements of solidarity of the so-called "underdeveloped" or poor nations and peoples of the world. There perhaps is a great common denominator in the anger of Fanon, the sorrow of Mannoni, the nationalism of Tito, the prophetic and suffering love of Martin Luther King, Jr., the plaintiveness of the flower children, the new freedom of the Hippies, the determination and earnestness of the intellectuals of the "New Left," the Quixotic romanticism of Ché Guevara, the desire to be themselves of Fidel and Stokely, the courage of desperation of the anti-war and anti-draft demonstrators, the frustration of many American university students with their academic life, the small but growing revolt against computers and careerism of many white, middle-class American graduate students, professors and professionals, the bitterness of the Black Power movement, the earnestness of the young Roman Catholic priests and nuns and laymen who love their church though it sometime persecutes them, and the pastoral rage tempered by compassion of Father Helder Camara of Recife. All of these, and many more, are seeking, against one form or another of imposition, freedom, dignity, equality and their own identity.

Perhaps the beginning of this Great World Revolution can be dated from the "Civil Libertarian" phase as manifested in the English, French and American Revolutions. These were revolutions made (particulariy of each case noted) by the "Magistrates" against the absolute and personal power of the monarchs, and they produced those dreams that are now common to almost all of mankind (though nowhere fully realized, and in the majority of places still largely dreams) of freedom of speech, regular democratic processes of popular participation in the setting of the major goals and priorities of a society, freedom of religion, freedom of the press, a secular and limited state, etc. But as the revolutions established themselves and time wore on it became apparent that not only could the revolutionaries become corrupt but that the revolution was itself nurtured on only a partial vision of the task of human emancipation. There were other forms of power and imposition, other forms of injustice and humiliation that were not touched by liberal, democratic political institutions and mores. The Civil Libertarian Revolutions became the victims of the victors: The Magistrates themselves became the new establishment, the new nobility, and created a society dominated by middle-class, commercial, industrial and capitalist interests and values. The new, industrial middle class began early to accommodate the rhetoric of the French, American and English Revolutions to their own interests, and finally lost their drive to "share the blessings of liberty" with those less fortunate, and began to think of themselves not as magistrates-with-responsibility and servants of mankind, nor even as the more fortunate, but as the virtuous who had been recognized and who deserved what they had, even as those who were not free and prosperous obviously did not deserve these things until they had "earned" them.

The subsequent phases of the Great World Revolution can be seen as successive, widening circles of participation by people in society as subjects rather than objects of history. As the first phase emphasized the political, the second great phase turned to economic injustices and inequalities. The Socialist Revolution against entrenched economic power, as typified in the Mexican Revolution, the Russian Revolution, the two Chinese Revolutions, and the Cuban Revolution, is striving to overcome the inequalities of dignity and opportunities in life caused by the distribution of wealth or property on bases other than need: the equal dignity of all men, and the welfare of the whole society. Like the Libertarian Revolution, it is nowhere complete, but has everywhere become part of the common expectations and dreams of the vast majority of men. Thus, the first phase of the Great World Revolution sought and still seeks "liberty," the second sought and still seeks "equality," and the third phase—not widely perceived as yet although already a tremendous force—seeks "fraternity," or acceptance and love-in-human-community. As the first phase was largely political, the second mainly preoccupied with economic injustices, so the third phase is taking an anti-racist and/or racist form. As the tyranny of the absolute monarchs precipitated the first phase, the cruelties of capitalism the second, so the racism of the imperialist powers has precipitated the third phase.

Of course, liberty means equality, and equality means fraternity, and fraternity means liberty, and this all together means a human community of love and mutual respect, of "non-coercive concern, for all, by all." For such a society, with its full participation, full responsibility, and full realization for all, man gropes not knowing exactly what forms such a society-of-communities will take, but still knowing he was meant to be free, equal, and accepted.

The world today must needs make all three struggles at once—now that history has caught up (or better, men have seen a bit more of the pattern of history), and the interrelatedness of the three phases is clearly seen.

The struggle for human community and liberation has, however, become significantly more difficult given the emergency of the "systems managers" of the great middle-class capitalist bureaucracies, and the great middle-class socialist bureaucracies, who prize predictability and stability above any mere dreams or human aspirations. And this dominant middle-class mentality— the mentality of the "organization man"—is not just the pattern of the United States; it is the pattern of the world-society in which we live today. That is, the rich or "developed" nations are those who consider themselves the "magistrates" of the world system, advocating their own virtues before the world majority of proletariats. It is the rich nations who are convinced of their own right and competence to continue the tutelage of the "underdeveloped" or poor nations of the world.

As the First World Revolution was made against the absolute monarchs by the emerging middle class, so the present phase of this continuing World Revolution is the stirring of the world proletariat against the modern magistrates—the good, gray decent middle class of the world. Against the managers, the social engineers, the technocrats, the moralists and the bureaucrats. Against a style of life that stifles community and smothers creativity and spontaneity. Against ascriptive authority, against the imposition of mass-produced identities of people-made-passive to let the rulers continue to rule. Against the continued massification and homogenization of mankind by the mass-culture machine. Against the designation of men as only producers and consumers. And as uncomfortable as it may be for those who are still prisoners of the old, liberal vision, middle-class democracy is no longer a vital, dynamic force, and anyway it is not enough. It is not enough because there is not enough real participation, not enough real tolerance or acceptance of diversity, creativity, spontaneity and ambiguity. Not enough stimulation of real individuality, not enough real community and love. Not enough individuality, not enough freedom, not enough compassion, not even enough real conflict to be creative. Middle-class democracy let its soul perish as it satiated itself at the table of plenty, and as it began to identify affluence with authenticity. Middle-class democracy, and the world-style of the affluent nations, means too much competition (as differentiated from conflict), too much "putting-down to stay-up," too much up-tightness, too satiated and thing-oriented, too un-loving and closed.

Strange to say, the great world movement of our time for revolution was precipitated by the same middle class that now seeks to stifle it, because the dreams that were forged in the struggle against the absolute monarchs were couched in universal terms, and they have seeped out of the narrow bounds of the white, European and middle-class societies, and become the dream of great numbers of brown, black and yellow peoples, who are poor and non-European or North American. Perhaps the most radical statement in all history—at least for our time—is that "all men are created equal." This proposition, when held up against the great and obvious inequalities of wealth, opportunities, prestige, acceptance, power and education of the world of today— inequalities that are increasing rather than diminishing —is enough to make a sensitive humanist long for radical change, and to frustrate him and drive him to despair when he considers the lack of evident progress. Gone or going is the once-full confidence in "electoral politics," in appeals to the reason and humanity of the powerful, in appeals to morality and compassion, in mass-education of the poor as a means of their libera-

tion when that education is in the hands of the powerful.

In our time the old, liberal structures of the west,
including the Marxist structures (of thought, institutions and power), have tended to harden, and to justify
themselves with pretentious myths that conceal the satisfied magistrates who profit from these social orders. The
inherent paternalism of the middle class and of the west,
with its basic fear of real popular, spontaneous democracy that can well up from the soul of a people, has
deformed the true mission of the magistrate, which is to
liberate and not to perpetuate domination. The paternalistic magistrate of the west distrusts individual and
group spontaneity, distrusts the poor, distrusts the colored, distrusts the non-westerner, and seeks to make
them all over in the image of the satisfied white middle-
class technocrat. In short, the west no longer believes in
democracy because it no longer believes in people, and
because its power has made it arrogant and insensitive
and isolated it from the needs of the people over whom
it has so much—too much—power and influence. Even
as once the monarchs become insensitive, isolated and
indifferent to the societies over which they ruled and
used ancient myths to defend privilege, so today the
middle-class and affluent and powerful nations and
classes of the world have done the same thing.

The insistence that "stability" is the prerequisite for
"progress" (understood as imitating the west), that
"order" is the beginning of "civilization," shows how
easily the west has forgotten the conflicts and dreams
that characterized its own period of dynamic creativity,
and belies its professions of belief in the ability of
common and poor people to participate meaningfully in
the formation of their own destinies. Even the acid of
cultural relativism (a comfortable ideology for middle-

class social scientists) has failed to corrode the spiritual arrogance that characterized so much of both the Communist and non-Communist west. Small wonder that there builds slowly a gigantic reservoir of resentment in the proletariat of the world, who see in the insensitive middle-class nations their oppressors and condescending would-be tutors.

But even as at home, as the vast numbers of university students (soon to be joined by high school students) and minority groups join the "Third World" in their rage against a system interested only in its self-aggrandizement and perpetuation, the techniques and power of skillful repression, "cooption" and social engineering increase at perhaps a more rapid rate. Thus seen, the World Revolution is not just a phase, but the continuing nature of the human condition. Its exact forms and issues are given to us by the historical moment, but the very nature of society and history is perhaps to demand a continuous struggle. "Life is struggle."

WHY LATIN AMERICA NEEDS A RADICAL, SOCIAL REVOLUTION

Radical social revolutions become the only possible avenue of the expansion of humanism when existing structures in a society are constructed to perpetuate the domination of a minority and there is little hope of erosion of this position. Even though the dominant classes of Latin Americans have professed for over a century the old, liberal ideals of the civil libertarian first phase of the Great World Revolution, progress towards the creation of an egalitarian community of mutual confidence and common mission has been, to say the least, negligible. It is in part the failure of the elites to lead and to share. There is little "egalitarian thrust" that has been the chief drive in the moderately successful North American progressive and evolutionary process in the Latin American culture. But the egalitarian dreams are beginning to penetrate the hitherto docile and submissive masses, even though the techniques of manipulation and repression are also improving.

But the stagnation of Latin America is also in large part due to the nature of the economic, cultural, military and political tutelage imposed by the rich Western powers (in our time, the United States) on Latin America. Even if we could imagine a paternalism that could remain enlightened and devoted to the eventual liberation of the dependent, the United States has not been interested in even an evolutionary process that would liberate Latin America. The United States has also contributed massively to the inability of the Latin American republics to move towards a more just and egalitarian society. At any rate, the results are obvious: between the elites and North American imperialism, the evolutionary approach in Latin America is barren of significant results.

Three hundred years of domination by elites who profess liberal doctrines, but who in practice do not even believe in "dribble-down" theories of economic and cultural development, and who are only capable of twin policies of repression and condescending paternalism, has left a massive sea of potential popular wrath. And though there are several dramatic centers of development in Latin America today, these centers are still surrounded by great and still silent masses who are not participating in the modernization process. It is nowhere more true in the world than in Latin America today that the rich are getting richer, and the poor are not only getting poorer, but becoming more numerous. It is difficult to affirm whether Latin America today is in the grip of a stagnant process propped up by the United States, or whether there is real social, economic, cultural and political regression in the area. The dominant classes of most of the Latin American republics are more closely allied with and identify more with the developed nations than with their own fellow citizens who are poor.

It has been argued that in such a situation North American technocracy and capital—assuming that enough of both are forthcoming and Latin American nationalist pressures do not become too "obstructionist" —can effectively "develop" Latin America. But such a style of development—assuming its possibility—would not only be from the top down, but from the outside, and therefore not only doomed to perpetuate paternalism but to inflict alienation on Latin American society. The best that could be hoped for would be for United States capital and skills to be made available to non-governmental and popular forces in Latin America to give them the capacities to make their own revolution, from the bottom up, and from inside. Development or modernization, "U.S. style," is only introducing a new class of managers, as has begun to emerge in the United States, which imposes on Latin America the technocratic managerial paternalism that is one of the enemies of an indigenous and liberating process of development. Assuming the best of intentions, there are still great limits on what one nation can do for another to help it develop—aside from get out of its way. The true meaning of development perhaps is the conquest of self-determination and the affirmation of one's own true identity—and these are things that people, and nations, must do for themselves.

Latin Americans share in common with mankind the

great aspirations and dreams, and also the growing, gnawing realization that the technical skills and the resources are available to realize many of these dreams for all men—if society were but organized more rationally and justly. It is the rage of knowing that men can now "invent their own future" that couples with the rage of centuries of mass misery that produces the double rage of some contemporary Latin Americans. The long list of failures—from the Liberators to the nineteenth century liberals, through the Good Neighbor period, the collapse of populism, the failure of the Alliance for Progress—further causes despair over patience as an answer and remedy.

Perhaps the Mexican Revolution better than any of the other revolutions of the twentieth century combined in its aspirations the longing for liberty, equality and fraternity. It was a struggle against tyranny, for social justice, and for a new sense of national community and purpose. Like all revolutions it shows today a tendency to worship its past victories more than to realize the great ennobling dreams of its heroes. But here at least we saw the power of a people with a dream. And in the Mexican revolution there were efforts—long since abandoned—to find meaningful participation in the political societies and structures of the nation for all the people. Like the United States, Mexican society is now pretty well "safely" in the hands of the managers. But the dreams remain.

But it is not just the power of the idea of a just society, but also the traditional structures' inadequacy and refusal to adapt that make revolution in Latin America a necessity. The gap between man's dreams and his potential to realize those dreams on the one hand, and the performance of the Latin American power elites on the other, demonstrates the isolation from reality of the traditional elites in Latin America. Indeed, the ineptness and unwillingness to even give an inch has already led to their replacement by modernizing military elites, largely trained by the United States army, who are interested in managing their societies but not in justice, freedom and equality. The old system is breaking down, and being replaced by one of military technocrats.

In addition to the intransigence of the traditional power elites, the imposition of an exploitive system by the United States, the denial of popular aspirations by the new modernizing military technocrats, one must also add the inevitable "population explosion" and "rising expectations." Both of these are results of the first penetrations of the technology and dreams of the modern western nations, but both work against the continued dominance by the west.

A revolution in Latin America is not inevitable—as necessary as it may be. As an ancient Chinese proverb has it, "Nothing is so bad that it couldn't be worse." Latin American traditional elites could be replaced by more competent, North American trained and dependent technocratic elites, who could manage misery so expertly that there was no release. Indeed, the trends are in this direction—aided and abetted by "U.S. Aid."

WHO ARE THE ENEMIES OF THE REVOLUTION IN LATIN AMERICA?

If a revolution in Latin America is so necessary, and yet seemingly so far away and difficult, it must be because of the tremendous obstacles to its realization.

Therefore it would be perhaps useful to describe in a little more detail the enemies of the revolution.

The people of Latin America are not held back from taking control of their own destinies by pure inertia, docility and lack of the necessary skills and education. Strong forces are allied in defense of the *status quo,* and as it is always well to know the strength of those opposed to the revolution, it is well to know who, and why.

First, there is the traditional oligarchy. Often melancholy over the increasing inroads of modernization, literacy, urbanization, and industrialization, they are nonetheless committed to defending as long as possible their vested interests, and utilize their strong hold on the ancient cultural symbols to continue the vassalage and immobility of millions of their fellow Latin Americans. They are prepared, like the useless kings of Balkan republics, to go into permanent but affluent exile when they can no longer hold the dike against inevitable change. They believe that they have been born not only to rule, but they have been born superior to the great majority of the human race—especially of their own nation. At best, they believe that it takes some five or six generations to "civilize" a peasant—and by civilization they mean being like they are. Their favorite verb is to "orient," that is, to mold someone in a predetermined fashion to fit into the wisdom of the ages (middle ages, that is). They commonly believe that the peasants are "little better than savages," and that they are the essence and flower of western civilization. They look with secret (convenience dictates secrecy) horror upon popular democracy, with its exaltation of the wisdom and power of the common man, and consider democracy a form of government that cheapens culture. They believe idleness is the mother to true culture, but that the majority of men cannot use leisure correctly, and thus should have to work to insure idleness and culture for the few.

Second, there is the new oligarchy, new creation of the modernizing and industrializing dynamics. They are interested in change, but have shown a marked inability to involve their wealth and energy in any significant programs for social improvement and justice. They have such a limited confidence in the future of their own nations, and so little interest in promoting the concept of the common welfare, that they usually are not even interested in the development of a mass, internal market. They want stability in order to get richer, and believe they are the rightful heirs of the traditional oligarchs' mantle of power, which must soon drop. They are "nationalist" because they would like to hamstring competition by North American private enterprise, and not because they really believe in true national development. They crave and demand protection and support from their governments, but argue against any suggestion that they have public responsibilities in return. They are open advocates of an unchecked capitalism that has not existed for some decades in the United States—and they are unblessed by the guilty Puritan conscience that has provided some of the great monuments of "benevolence" in the way of libraries, universities, and foundations in the United States. They take their tax deductions in deposits in Swiss banks and the purchase of U.S. stocks, and the purchase of gold squirreled away somewhere against the rainy day of the revolution. They are not interested in humanist values for the whole society—their energies are devoted to their own pursuits.

Third, the emerging "modernizing military elites," the

Ibero-American Nasserites. These military technocrats and bureaucrats are interested in social change, and in modernization and industrialization, and probably understand much better than the new oligarchy built by industrialism itself the dynamics and requirements of a modernizing national system. But they see development only as "systematic development," and are unaware or unconcerned with its human significance, and very little interested in human development except as it affects the national system. The "military managers" offer little hope of meeting the needs of the revolution because their view of national development affords no room for innovation-from-below, for democratic feedback, and for significant citizen participation in planning the national destiny. The military mentality is not likely to encourage significant dissent, or to really believe in a pluralist society, and is likely to prize national power as the ultimate goal rather than the liberation of men to be themselves, and likely to emphasize competition rather than work for the world community that is the necessary precondition of a truly just society.

Fourth, the Modernizers of the United States, in their assorted varieties. There are U.S. Aid officials, military technocrats ("advisors"), businessmen, bankers, missionaries, social scientists, educators, etc. Interestingly enough, they all share some of the same defects: they all usually fail to see the development process as a whole, they all usually fail to understand their own built-in cultural values and biases, and they all are likely to feel (consciously or unconsciously—it doesn't make any difference) at least a little bit superior, if for no other reason than that they are "helping." Furthermore, as a result of the spontaneous way in which American political processes grew, they all fail to understand how to stimulate meaningful participation in the political, social and economic life of the society. Strange that North Americans in Latin America demonstrate so clearly the deterioration of the democratic idea of confidence in the common man as a political actor, even while this same idea is so much still a part of the North American political mythology. But this, too, is a result of the rise of the social managers and technocrats. Coupled with the traditional and deep messianism of the American people, this set of techniques of social, political and economic manipulation has created a new kind of manager. But there he is, the North American in Latin America working to achieve "stability" because he is afraid of the dynamics engendered by dispossessed and repressed groups trying to organize themselves, and join the nation. Therefore, though he is often genuinely interested in modernization, and sometimes even motivated by a desire to help-from-above, still the dominant strains of cultural imperialism and messianic national mission to civilize and modernize remain constant. And then, too, the later evolution of American society has tended to make irrelevant the traditional articulations of the humanist dream of freedom and justice for all, and Americans have not continued to develop their humanist sensitivity and aspirations as fast as they have developed their technology and manipulative skills.

Fifth, the "vanguard elites" of those "revolutionary" political groups who believe that in the name of the people they should seize power from the traditional and/or dominant groups in order to guide the people in the "correct" path of national liberation and development. These elements, many believing themselves to be truly revolutionary or, indeed, the "only" revolutionaries, must be judged counter-revolutionaries even though they are against the system. Counter-revolutionary because they only want to substitute the rule of a new elite or class for the rule of the old elite and the old class. Counter-revolutionary because they, too, are paternalistic, arrogant, and do not really believe that the people are capable of taking control of their own destiny. "Democratic centralism" and "guided democracy" are counter-productive ways of bringing about the liberation of the individual from social and political pressures, because they build in new ones, implemented by the latest techniques of pressure and manipulation. Rather than *deliver* liberation, they *promise* liberation, and deliver a new messianic slavery. Vanguard elitism works against true communities by building small communities of "true believers" who cannot embrace the dissenter, and who are threatened by pluralism in their own numbers, and in society around them. Vanguard elitism is revolutionary ideological triumphalism, as bad as the old religious and political triumphalism it seeks to replace. It has to be admitted that our imagination has lagged behind our needs, and the demands of rapidly changing and industrializing societies are especially difficult. It is true that we do not have too many clear ideas as to what type of democratic institutions would be adequate to insure significant participation by the citizen in the making of the political, social, economic and cultural decsions that directly affect him. But there is little hope of even the experimentation necessary to develop such new modes of political association and participation as long as the magistrates continue their domination, buttressed in their own minds by a newer but not much subtler version of the "white man's burden," which is the paternalism of the bureaucrat-technocrat. And, unfortunately, recent history has shown how difficult it is for a vanguard elite not to become like the traditional elite that it replaces. How much more diffi-

cult—and rewarding for freedom—it is to have a serv-
ant elite than a vanguard elite.

Sixth, the guerilla warriors and their apologists must
also be seen as impediments to the process of national
liberation, because they vainly imagine that they can
conquer violence by violence, and then rule without
violence. They imagine that the answer to arrogant
paternalism is organized mass hatred. They vainly imagine that they will purge themselves of their lust for
power and violence by purging those who lust for power
and violence. They vainly imagine that an elite can for
long stay disinterested and in touch with the majority of
the people, and at the same time enjoy a majority of
power over the people. Power not only corrupts, it iso-
lates, and de-sensitizes. They vainly imagine that guerilla warfare is a catharsis, and see it as the portal to
purity of motive, vainly forgetting the lessons of all of
history. They are inverse copies of the military, modernizing technocrat, or the U.S. aid technocrat, differing
only in that they do not have power. If warfare could
liberate men from slavery to other men, from hate and
fear, from insecurity and tribalisms, it would be worth
the effort. History to date shows that violence only produces the seeds of more violence, hate of more hate,
and that the great promises necessary to move men to
great violence are like heroin, not only capable of creating sustained illusions, but habit-forming as well. The
death of Ché Guevara is an extended parable that serves
only to make the bitter, more bitter, and to drive some
few desperate ones into more desperation. But it is also
a typical incident whose meaning is not only mythologi-
cal. It shows us that the United States has succeeded in
dominating the Latin American military establishments,
and in turning them into domestic peace forces—against

"subversion." The anti-subversion techniques that began to be developed soon after the Nixon riots have become increasingly more widely disseminated and understood (through U.S. training programs), but increasingly more sophisticated and effective. Perhaps the folk wisdom of the peasant is here more trustworthy than the despair-fed romanticism of the intellectual revolutionary, who forgets to note and count where the guns are. Suppressed peasants have learned in the hard school of centuries of hopelessness that adventurism is hard on the defeated, and that hope and dreams alone do not a revolution make. Since there is today no real chance for the supplying or training of any significant guerrilla band in Latin America, calls for such are counsels of despair of those who imagine that radical thought can substitute for hard thinking and imagination when confronted with apparently insurmountable problems. Because the call to violence can only serve to perpetuate a society (whatever new form the victors—whoever they may be—impose) based on hate and violence, and because the objective conditions in Latin America do not exist today, calls for guerilla warfare are today counter-revolutionary, and anti-human.

All of these enemies of the revolution have one thing in common—and this is what makes them enemies of the revolution: they all want to rule society from the top, either in their own interest, or in the interest of their ideals, or of "the people." All have an exaggerated estimate of their own virtue and disinterestedness. All presume too quickly to know what other people want and what is good for other people. All are incurably paternalistic and arrogant. All secretly disdain the capacity of the peasants and workers to be responsible for anything. All have difficulty in understanding and listening to the peasant, the poor urban worker, the slum dweller. They are all enemies of the true revolution because they all rely on violence to dominate, all rely on purely structural changes and manipulation of others, and because they all are potential "new classes," either occupying the positions of power or impatiently waiting in the wings to seize these positions. All of them are corrupted by the almost inherent paternalism, arrogance and triumphalism of the west. All of them are more interested in the form of society than they are in the building of community. To hold power by violence, to rule by violence, or to take power by violence, is to be by violence corrupted—made insensitive, to be isolated, and finally indifferent.

They are the true radicals in Latin America—and in any society—who desire to destroy the old chains of bondage, but who do not aspire to forge new ones for the people. They are the New Breed of Revolutionaries who envision and seek to realize in their own lives and relations with other people a style of life that is radically egalitarian, and that seeks to replace coercion with bonds of love and mutual respect. They are the true radicals who deem community more important than politics and government, and who are determined that the state should serve men and not men the state. Who are determined that freedom from anxiety and the possibilities to be a part of an "affinity-community" without taking from others, or putting others down, is the function of politics. They are the true radicals who have discovered behind the ancient symbols a new and an old and a timeless truth—that men were meant to be free, and that men can live by faith, and love and hope. They are the New Breed of Revolutionaries who have already become free men in the midst of all the social, cultural, economic and political structures of our time, men who are free in the midst of the national systems of bondage, imperialism and colonialism. Men who are free, yet who long for that day when all men will be free at last.

6

HAS LATIN AMERICA A CHOICE?

Juan Luis Segundo

NOT LONG AGO, I read in *Criterio*, a Catholic monthly from Buenos Aires, the following figures on the Third World's progress toward development:

In the developed countries, per capita income is increasing by about $60 each year; in the developing countries, it is increasing by less than $2.

Exports of the developing countries have dropped from 27 per cent of the world total in 1935 to 18 per cent in 1967.

The average unit price of raw products exported by the poor countries has dropped 7 per cent since 1958; in the same period, the unit price of the products they have purchased from the developed countries has risen 10 per cent.

In 1962, the development loans granted to poor coun-

Juan Luis Segundo, S.J., is Director of the Peter Faber Center for Research, Montevideo, Uruguay. This article is a condensation of a talk he gave on January 29, 1969, at the Inter-American Forum.

tries represented 0.87 per cent of the loaning countries' gross national product; in 1966, the figure had fallen to 0.62 per cent.

The external debt of the developing countries has grown from $10 billion in 1955 to $40 billion in 1966.

In 1964, in Geneva, at the first UN Conference on Trade and Development, the developed countries promised to devote a minimum of one per cent of their national income each year as assistance to developing countries. But at the second UNCTAD Conference, in New Delhi, February, 1968, representatives of 132 countries withdrew this pledge.

I read in *U.S. News and World Report,* a brief paragraph commenting on the facts given in the *Criterio* article: "Does there still exist a minimum hope for Latin America? The reply of the most experienced observers is a weak yes. The hope can be reduced to a small light on the horizon. But the immediate outlook is that of a Latin America ruled by poverty, instability and tyranny."

Reading articles like these during the past three or four years, a rapidly growing number of representative Latin Americans are coming to see the future of their continent in a new light. They have been struck by the failure of the Alliance for Progress, the death of Che Guevara and the extinguishing of hope for a successful guerrilla warfare. All these, together with the open or veiled militarization of many Latin American regimes, have forced them to re-examine their position on the possibilities of peaceful evolution and of violent revolution.

The new reaction can be summed up thus: "There is going to be neither evolution nor revolution. All we can do is—hang on." Perhaps if I can describe their way of thinking, it will help North Americans understand them.

WHAT THE PROSPECTS ARE FOR EVOLUTION

The ideas of this growing minority of informed Latin Americans on the possibilities of evolution can be boiled down to two.

1. A radical evolution (i.e., one that aims at giving solutions and not merely palliatives for existing problems) may or may not lead to increased production, but it will certainly—and immediately—trigger an increase in people's needs. In other words, it will step up their consumption, imports, indebtedness, inflation, and their feeling of privation, whether real or imagined.

A subject that has been much discussed, for example, is the increase of literacy. It would undoubtedly be a fine thing to teach the 50 per cent of Latin Americans who still cannot read to do so. But such a development would lead to a dramatic rise in demands for all sorts of things: for better hygiene, for social reforms, for more and better tools. It would accelerate the migration to the cities. It would, in fact, lead in a very short time to violent revolutionary explosion. For a continent that hungers in as many different ways as Latin America does would come to realize in short order how acutely hungry it is.

A great deal of assistance has already been given, of course, to stimulate an evolution. But most of this has been diverted—away from a genuine, radical solution that might have set society on the road toward development—to the satisfaction of more imperative but short-range needs: housing, food programs, etc. And this means that we are not grappling with the core of the problem.

2. It may be asked if industrialization cannot satisfy (instead of stimulating and then denying) the expectations of a wretched people to whom we have allowed a glimpse of a better life.

As the UNCTAD conferences at Geneva and New Delhi showed, the monopolies of the international market are never going to give, out of their strength, the slightest break to the infant industries of the developing countries, which obviously are too weak to compete with them. These conferences, in fact, now have a familiar, bitter connotation for the average intelligent Latin American.

Gradual industrialization through our own resources might seem a further possibility. But the poor countries are also, separately or even collectively, very poor markets. And they have to import the new techniques, the machinery, even the research, to make such industrialization possible—and all this is extremely costly. It is almost cheaper, if we want to provide income for our workers, to pay them *not* to work and buy the products manufactured in industrialized countries.

If there are, none the less, some industries today in the Latin American countries, it is because foreign capital finds in them certain governments so accommodating that it is worth their while to open factories and to manufacture there. But because profits so often leave the country—and personnel, too, as soon as it reaches a certain level of skill—these industries are most unlikely to be the beginning of a true national development. Anyway the giant international combines are careful not to let any of them grow big enough to become competitors.

Not long ago I read with astonishment that a Mexican bus manufacturer had won a bid to supply buses for Dallas, Texas, in competition with no less a rival than General Motors. A photo of the Mexican bus caught my attention, as it was obviously a General Motors product. Reading on, I learned that General Motors of Mexico had won the bid over General Motors of the United States because—quite apart from whatever unspecified privileges the Mexican government may have granted—wages in Mexico are so low and because part, if not all, of the profits can be siphoned back to the United States.

According to a recent issue of the German review *Deutsche Aussenpolitik,* General Motors made a profit in 1968 of 25 per cent in the United States and about 80 per cent in their Latin American branches. No one will be surprised at these figures. I offer them only as an example of the innumerable bits of information that help to mold the Latin American's thinking about the United States.

"The financial assistance of Washington to Latin America is relatively modest when compared with the profit the United States derives from it." This admission by Covey Oliver, Under Secretary of State for Latin American Affairs, which I read in *Le Monde* on October 24, will surprise no one who is acquainted with Latin America's problems.

One may ask, then, what interest the Latin American countries have in U. S. investments, what they expect from this kind of industrialization. The answer is that they expect practically nothing. Even those countries which, like Brazil, have adopted a policy of welcoming U. S. branch industries, do not expect thereby to move toward a profitable, Brazil-owned industrialization. All they look forward to is somehow to hang on—which is another way of saying that all they look forward to is despair.

WILL OTHER COUNTRIES FOLLOW THE EXAMPLE OF CUBA?

If evolution seems to be out of the question, what about revolution?

If a revolution takes place in Latin America, or to be more exact, in any country of Latin America, it will certainly not be for the distribution of wealth. It will be for the purpose of placing at the service of the whole country's development the wealth that today is banked abroad or wasted on luxuries, or even is used for repression.

Who will be surprised, therefore, if many Latin Americans want their countries to follow the example of Cuba? Not that Latin Americans think that everything in Cuba is ideal. The great majority of them would have preferred in Cuba a purely and exclusively Latin American revolution. But they know there was simply no other choice. As a matter of fact, many of us suspect that Cuba, obliged to choose between a less than total revolution, one that wasn't really radical enough to deserve the name "revolution" (the tragic dilemma of the Chilean Christian Democrats) and one that involved Soviet backing, may have chosen the lesser evil.

It happens, however, that the image of Cuba-as-model, of Cuba-as-vanguard-of-revolution in Latin America, is similarly being questioned. Quite apart from all the slogans and even the slogan-makers, it must be asked, and actually is being asked, whether Cuba in fact opened or closed to the Latin American countries the possibility of realizing their revolutions (and even the very possibility of realizing any Marxist-Leninist revolution).

Let us look at the principal arguments behind this second hypothesis. Again, the reason is not that I am persuaded by them, but rather that they help to understand the mentality that I see rapidly gaining ground on the Latin American continent.

1. The possibility of slipping from a national revolution, i.e., the insurrection of a whole people, to an ideological one, whether Marxist-Leninist or not, seems to have ended with Cuba.

In the first place, North American policy makers and even conservative groups in Latin America, after observing the case of Cuba, know that for tactical reasons the repetition of a Batista cannot be permitted—the rule, that is to say, of a dictator that elicits a desperate and practically unanimous reaction from the people, a reaction capable of being channeled, not toward new elections, but toward the radical transformation of the economic, social and political structures. As a matter of fact, none of the many subsequent Latin American dictatorships offer at this time, nor would they be permitted to offer, an opportunity for a unanimous national uprising or, for that matter, any widespread uprising. (Haiti, of course, is an exception, but its dictatorship predates the Cuban change.)

Consequently, violent revolution is bound to seem—and does seem—ideologically tainted. In other words, it appears as a force that would upset much of the good that has been accomplished and alienate all the existing interests. Guerrilla warfare deceives no one: either one is an extreme leftist, or else one is against it ideologically or by inertia. How are we to interpret the Cuban case against this background?

2. Repression is no longer carried out by the classical political and military methods used in Batista's Cuba. If the guerrillas are organized, so is the control, and much more powerfully. Moreover, it is organized now on a continent-wide basis, so that national conflicts will not be tolerated. Thus, support by a very small percentage of the population is enough to make the machinery of repression highly effective. It may not be effective enough to end the armed struggle, but it can keep the guerrillas indefinitely off balance and prevent them from taking over the government.

3. Even granting a successful seizure of power under such circumstances, the economic pressure of a blockade by the United States would be so far-reaching at present, in agricultural and even more in mining countries, that no Latin American country could hold out even for a few months in a revolution that would forcibly estrange the strong interests of international industries and set off corresponding reprisals. At least it could not do so without the support of some other equally strong economic system.

4. The Cuban blockade made it crystal clear that unless a blockade or imbalance of world dimensions occurs, the two main powers will not challenge each other in their respective spheres of domination: consider the cases of Czechoslovakia and Santo Domingo. After Cuba, Che Guevara's call for a series of Vietnams to be created in Latin America seems a political pipe dream. Even where the people of a given country are brave and united in their ideals, no one is going to be able to ignite Vietnams in Latin America. For that to occur, the great powers would have to get involved, either openly or behind the scenes. But Latin America cannot count on that to happen—and knows it.

Once again, cynical though it may sound to idealists,

the proper tactic to the strongest and best-structured revolutionary groups in the continent is just to hang on.

NORTH AMERICANS MUST UNDERSTAND THE SITUATION

What conclusions may be drawn from what I have said? I do not say there is no solution. But North Americans, if they really want to understand our plight, must recognize how increasingly desperate it is. Two important sociological facts can illustrate this.

The first of these is external to Latin America, though it affects that continent most vitally. The President of the United States has stated—and the directors of the World Bank for Development have said the same thing —that we must reduce our population or at least not let it increase. It may be true, as President Johnson affirmed, that the sum of $5 spent on birth control is more effective than $100 spent on development, but one is tempted to ask: "Effective for what?" Certainly not for development, if that word means what it says. He must have meant that the $5 would enable us at least to hang on a while longer.

In a world that is tightly structured and determined not to change its structures, the only way to keep rising pressures from causing an explosion is to lower the pressure—and that means, in our case, to have fewer Latin Americans. Then we survivors can hold out a while longer, we who still can find enough to eat and something to peddle on the world market to those who thrive—and mean to keep on thriving—from the sale of our raw materials.

The second fact is an internal one: the passivity, the

indifference even, that people now show to the increasingly frequent seizures of power by the military.

As I see it, for more and more Latin Americans the military are no longer a hated symbol of conservative ideology; they are seen, rather, as the guarantee of a world in which we can at least plod on from day to day. In other words, as men come to realize that there are no political solutions, they stop looking for political figures.

In recent decades, the military men—that faceless, anonymous group (not to be confused with identifiable figures like Peron, Rojas Pinilla, Perez Jimenez, Odria, etc.) with no particular political convictions any longer —have come to symbolize that primitive desire of all men: to hang on till tomorrow.

They are no longer either resisted or applauded. They are merely the caretakers to whom one turns over a hopeless country. Who, aside from military men, can be expected to efficaciously maintain a minimum of order and continuity, no matter how unjust and inhuman, when nothing can be done to seriously transform the situation?

It is they, the military, who will make it possible for the millions who are dying off in the present world structure, as a direct result of poverty and malnutrition, to die in silence. They can now at least die quietly, without asking what sense it makes, without raising insoluble problems, without suicidal violence.

THE AMERICAN EMPIRE'S EXTERNAL
PROLETARIAT

As Toynbee and others have shown, all great empires were built by the sweat of a vast proletariat. But today, unlike what happened in earlier centuries, the proletariat that makes possible the life and prosperity of the great empires is principally external to them; that is, it lives far outside the frontiers of the metropolis. Russia itself, in order to survive as a world power, has had to adopt this approach. And certainly so has the United States, the largest, strongest and most prosperous empire of all time.

The proletariat of Europe, in the first stages of that continent's industrial capitalism, managed to hold on, despite glaring inhumanities, until today its rights have been more or less acknowledged and implemented. What of present-day Latin America, the principal external proletariat of the American Empire? It too wants to hang on a while more. But how long can it?

The fact that the proletariat that produces the great prosperity of the United States is external, living on another continent far to the south, is most important. Because it is external, that proletariat can do nothing to remedy its plight. I am not denying that waves and waves of desperate Latin Americans might not someday take to violence. My point is rather that, whether they like it or not, the ultimate decisions about their fate are going to be made in the United States, the metropolis of the empire.

We in Latin America are naturally apprehensive about these decisions, and for two reasons:

1. The U. S. democracy is based on the principle that legislation—like taxation—without representation is unjust. But when an empire is built on an external proletariat, millions and millions of men are excluded from political representation, from making the decisions that concern them most. Their life or death, their human dignity or indignity, will be determined by what is called, with deadly precision, foreign policy.

Would the American minorities fight to change this situation, which leaves those directly interested in the matter, those who stand to benefit from it, as the only representatives to decide the life and death of millions of human beings?

2. And now we come to the second, more serious, reason for our apprehension. It is not really correct to say that, because U. S. policy toward Latin America is directed toward an external proletariat, that policy is therefore not decided by interested parties. For all U. S. citizens, rich and poor, are interested in perpetuating what is the real source of their well-being and progress. That source is the international economic structure, with its growing imbalance between prices offered for raw materials and prices demanded for manufactured goods.

Is it possible that the beneficiaries of this policy would decide to change it? Is it possible that while engaged in an economic-political struggle with a rival power, the United States would assume the dangerous task of opening an internal front: the restructuring of its economic-political empire?

The very fact that I, a Latin American, have raised this possibility shows that I believe in it. I realize very well that this is one of the most arduous challenges ever presented to any people. In any case, the reply to the question "How long will we have to hang on?" can be only this: "Until this hope becomes a reality."

7

LET'S DARE TO BE AFRICAN

Joseph O. Okpaku

AN EXAMINATION OF the speeches, writings, goals and actions of most of us who pride ourselves on being African intellectuals reveals a painful fact—our alienation. It is not the culture-conflict nonsense of the "Heinemann writers' club" nor the once-useful anachronism of their French-speaking counterparts. Our alienation has so changed our thinking and values that often common sense has yielded to an undesirable "Western sophistication." Perhaps it is time to suggest that we bring the machinery of African development to a grinding halt and ask ourselves a question: Where are we going?

That the West has always had a pejorative attitude toward Africa is self evident. That some have modified this to an often condescending, always reprehensible patronage exhibited in "defenses" of Africa is perhaps not quite so apparent. What does seem clear is that most of us so-called African intellectuals have consciously or

Joseph O. Okpaku is an author and publisher of Third Press, New York.

unconsciously swallowed hook, line and sinker the same pejorative attitude toward our own continent. Our literature, our politics, our scholarship, our language—what does not show it? At the Dakar Festival in 1966, Wole Soyinka said he prefers to be called a writer, not an African writer. When an Englishman speaks of an "African writer" he implies inferiority, and when Soyinka says "don't call me an African writer" he accepts this implicit judgment. What Soyinka forgets is that when a Westerner speaks of a writer as such, he means a Western writer, yet I am sure Soyinka would deny that he wants to be called a Western writer. (My criticism of Soyinka has no bearing on my opinion of his arrest and imprisonment, which I deplore and have publicly protested.)

How does an African writer become great? London "discovers" him, proclaims him great, publishes him, and adds his name to the list of those whom the West has chosen for Africa, which then sings a chorus of praise that London has written. Not only does London or its extensions in Africa decide what our written literature should be, it also decides what our taste must be. It chooses our heroes for us.

What then is the yardstick for African writers? Simple: That writer is best who achieves the nearest approximation to Western literature. With no regard for African literary taste and indifferent to the far-reaching consequences, our African writers and those who call themselves critics have taken the position that the best in the arts is Western art and that therefore, to achieve the best, we must aim at the highest in the Western tradition. How does this differ from what the missionaries have always done?

Soyinka is Africa's Number One playwright because he has the best mastery of the English language and, allowing for a little welcome exoticism, he writes most nearly like a "Western" playwright. Chinua Achebe is the Number One novelist because he is the nearest thing in Africa to a Western novelist. As for criticism, Lewis Nkosi has asked with all good intentions that the critical standards applied to Western writers be applied to African literature. What they all forget is that critical standards derive from aesthetics, which in turn are primarily culture dependent. Thus Western love, with kissing in the streets and other overt displays of affection, strikes all but the most alienated African as public show or pretension. On the other hand, it is common knowledge among Africans who have had love affairs with Westerners that the African concept of implicit love—"I don't have to hold you and kiss you to reassure you that I love you, you should know it"—is often regarded as cold, if not inhuman. It seems clear then that an ideal Western love scene would strike an African reader as melodramatic, while the ideal African love scene would appear crude and grotesque to a Western reader. Yet both are valid. How can we use the critical standards of one in judging the other?

The non-African will derive meaning from African art by "studying" the African audience in order to understand the African writer. With this understanding, he can then recast the meaning within his own Western cultural context in order to make it relevant to his culture. This, precisely and no more, is the job of the Western critic: to interpret African arts to Western audiences. In like manner, the role of the African critic is to interpret African arts to Africans using the means common to both critic and audience—namely African culture, hence African critical approaches and standards —and to interpret non-African arts to Africans using once again the means common to him and his audience:

African culture. But like the Western critic of African literature, for the African critic to interpret Western literature to an African audience, he must first understand Western literature within its own Western cultural context.

So far as Africans are concerned, literature and the other arts—in fact even politics—can only be judged by African standards. If by such standards they fail, then they have failed. Anyone who wishes to enjoy art outside his own culture should develop a taste for differences and a knowledge of what the other cultures consider beautiful or meaningful. The Western world has learned to appreciate Noh drama (or at least pretend to) or leave it alone, yet by Western standards it could not be called drama at all. Does this mean that it isn't? To the Japanese, Noh drama is one of the highest forms of art. If the Western world is interested in Japanese drama it must accept the Japanese thesis. The same is true of African art. Africans must decide what they consider good art and then set up their gradations. The non-African who wishes to enjoy African art should accept this thesis, or in ignoring it should not attempt to tell the African what is good art.

The validity of art is cultural: If a work is valid as African art, then it is valid in itself. Thus, as a prescription for Soyinka's problem, the important thing is to be a good *African* playwright. When he achieves this and is acclaimed by African critics using African critical standards, then the world, if it has any respect for African culture and aesthetics, should accept him as a playwright per se. There is no universal aesthetic, and if there were it would be undesirable. It is possible to be universally meaningful, but this is achieved only by being meaningful to the culture within which the art is expressed. The problem is that there hasn't been a good African writer by African standards in recent times.

Though African writers have sought to deny it, art is communication. Since communication implies the awareness of a listener, the "means" of communication are determined by the particular audience. Consciously or subconsciously, a good writer shapes his language, imagery, and figures of speech to the cultural makeup of his readers—yet it seems much easier for an African writer to write for Europeans than for Africans. Why praise them in the name of "internationalism" or "universality" when their readers are already sated with the work of Europeans? In much of our scholarly writing, literature, and drama we are not addressing Africans, but are speaking discreetly to the ears and microphones of the Western world. We only use Africa as a platform, as an excuse for big, impressive spiels to the West. As if to add insult, some of us excuse ourselves by arguing that Africans are not sophisticated enough or educated enough to understand us. Our scholars regret that their subject matter is too abstruse. Our writers say there isn't a reading audience in Africa! What nobody asks is, What use is our academic sophistication, our literary genius, if we cannot answer our first call—to communicate with our own people? And so I ask: Africa, who will write for you?

Let us recall the day when, on returning home from the first term at boarding school, Grandma addressed us in our native tongue and we replied in English or French. Or when it was time to eat, we decided that eba or fufu was no longer good food, that all we now wanted was bread, butter, and a cup of tea. If you had a grandmother with a sense of humor, she probably laughed in your face or lamented your newly acquired "corruption." Unfortunately, many years after boarding school, we still possess that corruption, except that it is now deeply entrenched—in other words, it is more "sophisticated."

Before, it was the Western man who told us we were inferior. Now it is the "progressive, sophisticated" Africans who say that Africa is inferior. Ironically, they are the first to emphasize, "of course, *we* are not inferior." The difference in who purveys this preachment of inferiority is central to our present dilemma in Africa and will be even more important in the period of change to come. Against the Western man, the reaction has been nationalism, anti-imperialism, and anticolonialism. Against the "sophisticated African elite" it will be an uprising of those we often call "the masses," and in that sweep everything must go—our intellectualism, our academicism, our sophistication, and any other absurdity in which we dress ourselves today. Perhaps we condemned too quickly the alleged slaughter of the educated elite in the Congo. Perhaps we didn't learn a lesson from it. In fact the only lessons we learn from events in Africa are those which Western analysts tell us. We, as Africans, are too close to events to be "objective."

An examination of Négritude (despite the political role it played, largely through the enthusiasm of those who misunderstood its implications) and of practically all of our cultural, social, and political behavior today reveals the crucial fact that we intellectuals carry on our existence in purely Western terms. Négritude was never addressed to the black "masses" of Africa. Its language, its implications were all aimed at a dialogue with the white; it was and is a statement made to the Western world about Africa. So far, no philosophical statement has been made by Africans *to Africans.* Essentially, Senghor says to the white world, You say we are inferior? False. We are at least your equal. Meanwhile, what have we to say to the millions of people who have never heard of Négritude or "whitetude"? Our philosophy exists only because the Western world has an attitude toward us. Without "whitetude" there would be no Négritude. Our consciousness of Westernism resembles the American preoccupation with communism. In both cases our action is determined by the thing we claim to be fighting against. In hate as in love, we are subservient to the object of our passion; we are only free when we are disinterested.

But Africa cannot yet boast of independent thought, much less action. Our energies are continually being wasted in trying to relate to the Western world—to convince, to explain, to reassure. Of what? That we are not primitive (African), that we are or can be civilized (Western). It would take a volume to state the degree to which this unconscious habit of placing the West and not Africa at the center of our thought has brainwashed most of us educated Africans. A few examples must suffice. Novel after novel reveals a great effort devoted to "describing" African culture—"explaining," "apologizing," and "defending." Obviously we are not describing African culture to Africans (unless for a special purpose), and it would be absurd for us to apologize for or defend Africa to Africans. It is clear then that we are conscious of someone else—the Western reader. We cannot blame the Westerner for this, except as he may demand such explanations as a condition for publication. It is quite legitimate for him to want to add to his knowledge. But perhaps our writers should answer this: did Shakespeare try to explain the English culture he wrote about to us Africans? Does any Western writer today bear us in mind when writing? Most of our writers are students of literature. In order to understand Western writers, they have had to study Western history and civilization. By the same token, Westerners who want to understand us fully should study our civilization. If they are interested enough, they will. If not, too bad. It is their headache, not ours.

In politics the results of our "brainwashing" have sometimes been disastrous. To Nigerians, for instance, it seemed for a long time that their main goal was to be called "democratic" by the Western world. It mattered little what democracy meant or whether Nigerians really cared for democracy as such. While the West viewed Nigeria with a kind of reverence and proclaimed it the yardstick of progress in West Africa, an inordinate passion to meet Western expectations became a driving force in Nigerian political life. For a time it went smoothly, and praise flowed in from London and Washington, DC. With the beginning of the crisis in the Western Region in 1962, much public time and money was spent to reassure the Western world that despite its troubles Nigeria was still essentially democratic. Thus began the glossing over of hard realities within Nigerian society and politics. With the military coups, West Africa's leading democracy came tumbling down—to the astonishment and dismay of all but Nigerians who had long expected it. Throughout the subsequent troubles, no one has seriously asked whether democracy (or socialism or communism) is really relevant to Nigeria's problems.

In our intellectual life, many of us seem to have been led to believe that the highest level of scholarship is the most "objective"—meaning, in practice, without regard to its applicability to situations of vital concern to Africa. We seem to think there is value in a Hamlet type of intellectualism—the kind that cripples us from acting. But the sad fact is that any intellectualism or academicism which does not have a utilitarian value, immediately or in the foreseeable future, is of small value in Africa. Thus, though it may be an interesting academic exercise to speculate on who in Western political history Kwame Nkrumah most resembles, such a study is useless to us unless it is used, for example, to help us Africans understand what Nkrumah and his actions meant to us and how his thoughts might influence our future political behavior. For our scholars to dismiss the relevance of Nkrumah to African political thought by putting a Western label on him to enable a librarian or scholar to know how to classify him in Washington or London is a gross disservice, not only to Nkrumah himself but to all Africans who are seriously concerned with the future of the continent.

By virtue of himself, Nkrumah in particular demands a detailed interpretation by African political scientists because he is the one person the West is obviously not anxious for us to understand—unless to reject or discard him. He is the one person who has made the greatest effort to put down his thoughts in writing so that the people can read and debate them. Despite his political shortcomings, we owe him high regard as a valid and authentic leader of African thought—and this despite *Time* magazine, the *Washington Post,* or *West Africa,* and, with due respect, despite the present Ghanaian Government, which unfortunately feels compelled to try to erase Nkrumah from the minds of the people. If even the Western world cannot forget him, how much less could the African people who love him and most of the time agree with him, in spite of his obvious faults.

What all this boils down to is that our thoughts and actions are, at this point, determined by a non-African system. When we think for ourselves, we do so in Western terms; and if we are not thinking, we pay Westerners to lead our thought for us.

The provision of Western experts to Africa has become a flourishing business. Let us consider their role as advisers to African countries in fields other than technical or scientific, for example in education, art, music, drama, and architecture, where culture plays a major part in determining standards and objectives and where thought and taste can be greatly influenced. Let us assume that the "expert" really is one, and that he is honestly concerned with serving the best interests of the employing country. The crucial question immediately arises: What does he consider to be in the best interest of the African country? If he is like most of his fellow countrymen and like his compatriot missionaries before him, he believes there is only one evolutionary process and that along this path the West is ahead of Africa. Consequently, progress for Africa means becoming more Western, and since there are radical cultural, aesthetic, and philosophical differences, this means becoming less African. Result? Alienation. If, on the other hand, he is one of the few who have become aware of this absurdity, he might decide to base his judgments on African cultural preferences. Now, how does a Western man go about trying to understand African taste and then "expertly" advise Africans on how to apply their taste? Not only could he not stay long enough in Africa to really understand it, but the cost of bringing him over would be unjustifiable. Obviously this is a role that only an African can play meaningfully.

The same can be said of several of the foreign manpower advisory boards that African governments have acquired a fascination for. Development is broadly culture dependent. Progress is based on what is considered important, and this depends on culture. An error of the manpower experts has been their insistent advice that what Africa needs today is technology. They say Africa most needs technicians and engineers, not social scientists and certainly not humanists—a familiar song to any African who has sought a scholarship at home or abroad. The Lord knows how many Africans better disposed toward the humanities have been pressured to enter the sciences through false appeals to their national responsibility or by financial need. Yet one need only examine African societies to note the overwhelming emphasis on humanism rather than materialism, scientific or otherwise. In Africa, man comes first; the family system, the communal life all show this. Then why, in the name of some half-understood theory of development, is scientific materialism imposed as the top priority? We are told that it is because we have a long way to go. Where? If the Western world in which man stands dazed and confused on the brink of self-destruction is the goal we are rushing to, it seems hardly worth it. To say "technology now, culture later" would presuppose that cultural development can be manipulated as technology can, and that all we need do is build machines and skyscrapers and then reach down and pick up culture.

I do not for a moment mean to imply that Africa does not need technological development. That would be unrealistic. But I do say that Africa must continue to be culturally aware, and that cultural growth in itself, not vis-à-vis Western culture, is more vital to a people than technological development. Technology is a useful tool to help man live more gratifyingly, but culture is life itself. Technology must therefore be subordinate to humanism, which it should serve. Is it right that part of our progress should repeat an error the Western world has made?

Indeed, the best hope for Western man may lie in a humanism which perhaps only the non-Western world can provide. One need only compare the young Western adult, who feels that he has been reduced to a punch hole in a computer card, with his African counterpart, who has a sense of identity and a confidence in his place in society despite the alarmed cries that Africa is "falling apart"—a thought that seems to disturb non-Africans much more than Africans. While the technical advantages are desirable, the dehumanization that has accompanied Western development is certainly not. If Africa can acquire technical knowledge while preserving its humanism—and I am convinced that it can, if we start relating to and valuing our humanism—then well and good. If the two were incompatible, we should forget about technological development. Fortunately, these aspects of development are not mutually exclusive.

With all of this emphasis on technology, what has happened to African humanities? We have left the field to Western scholars who write books and critiques not only for Western students, but also for African students to use in studying their own cultures. Not only are some of these works nonsensical, they also adopt a viewpoint which at best could be called "interesting" to an African. Their very approach, and their use of terminologies and concepts ("Conradian," "Kafkaesque") presupposing a background in the Western tradition, mean that they can relate primarily to a Western reader.

Though the Western critic who compares Chinua Achebe to Joseph Conrad cannot expect to convey much to the African reader, he is by no means useless. His proper role is to interpret African culture to Western audiences, leaving to the African humanist and critic the primary task of interpreting African culture and thought to Africans. Thus far, however, the African —perhaps from an awareness of which side his bread is buttered on, or more often without conscious intent— has been addressing himself to the Western world and has shirked his primary responsibility for relating himself to his own culture and people. Consequently, he is not only alienated from his own people at a time when he should be drawing closer to them, he also leaves the job of cultural interpretation to Westerners who do not belong in this role, whatever their good intentions and quality of scholarship. By going between the African scholar/writer and the African peoples, they further deepen the alienation. We must therefore begin to relate ourselves, our literature, and our scholarship to our own people; to the social, political, and cultural realities of Africa. Only in this way can we have claim to any validity. Ironically, it is only after we have achieved communion with our culture and people that we can be of genuine significance to the outside world. I mean seriously, and not as sources of exoticism or vicarious pleasure for a society that is becoming awfully bored with itself.

This should not be interpreted as a rejection of co-operation or assistance from the non-African world. Rather, it is an affirmation that with or without such help, we Africans have a culture to protect and a continent to develop, and that if and when a Western man offers his services or scholarships he must be satisfied with occupying the back seat. African humanism is there to be experienced by all who are interested. It is cultural, not racial, and there is hope that with a little bit of luck the Western man may yet experience it. Peace Corps volunteers and others who have lived in

Africa and have done themselves the favor of letting themselves go, will acknowledge that there is that "something" which becomes a permanent part of their being. That "something" is what we call African humanism. It is essentially what black Americans call "soul." If some might call it "pagan," our answer is Yes, pagan, thank God. But as a cultural humanism it allows for movement across its boundaries. Thus a Western man, through experiencing African culture, can acquire some of its humanism. By the same token, an African, though born into this culture and therefore endowed with its humanism, can lose it though alienation—or Westernization.

As for us African intellectuals, our need for reunion with the main body of our fellow Africans is more than evangelical. After all, it is they who hold the ultimate power by virtue of their numbers: to put it bluntly, it is in our own interest. Though at present we do not relate to the people and so are not relevant to them, we are physically amongst them and must ultimately stand in their way unless we become part of them.

The recent coups d'état have been struggles essentially within the same class. If we fail to relate to the people and the people at last have a chance to see clearly just who is who, there could be a wave of popular uprisings against the alienated classes. If that happens, what will incriminate us will not be our reputations as Western writers, or whether Washington or London thinks we are democratic or Moscow thinks we are communist, or whether our Western colleagues consider us great scholars. What will count is our closeness to the people—how much we are part of them. The "masses" of the people can never be alienated from themselves, for that would be a contradiction in terms. Ironically, the Onitsha market novel will then be recog-

nized as something for the people and Nkrumah's
Consciencism will not. Its language and treatment, by
presupposing a thorough knowledge of Western philosophy, prevent the book from being relevant to the African
people.

In calling for this movement in African thought, literature, and scholarship, I mean to imply that we must
establish our own standards and values through an examination by us of our own humanism and aesthetics. I
hope that our writers, scholars, politicians, and other
"leaders of thought" will respond with the energy and
seriousness the situation demands. I hope too that the
"masses of the people" will respond to the beginnings of
our effort to become closer to them. As for our friends,
there is room for them if they will make adjustments
that are both necessary and inevitable.

8

PLAYBOY INTERVIEW:
JESSE JACKSON

IN THE 19 MONTHS since the murder of Martin Luther King, only one man has emerged as a likely heir to the slain leader's pre-eminent position in the civil rights movement: Jesse Louis Jackson, the 27-year-old economic director of King's Southern Christian Leadership Conference. The Reverend Jackson's first national exposure, in fact, came as a result of his closeness to Dr. King. He was talking to King on the porch of the Lorraine Motel in Memphis when the fatal shot was fired and cradled the dying man in his arms. The very next day, at a Chicago City Council meeting, Mayor Richard Daley read a eulogy that pledged a "commitment to the goals for which Dr. King stood." The Reverend Jackson had flown in from Memphis without sleep to attend the ceremony: he stood up in a sweater stained with Dr. King's blood and shouted to the assembled Chicago political establishment, "His blood is on the hands of you who would not have welcomed him here yesterday."

Jesse Jackson is National Director of Operation Breadbasket of the Southern Christian Leadership Conference.

That gesture demonstrated both the militant indignation and the dramatic flair that mark Jackson's charismatic style. *The New York Times* has written that he "sounds a little like the late Reverend Martin Luther King and a little like a Black Panther." It added that "almost everyone who has seen Mr. Jackson in operation acknowledges that he is probably the most persuasive black leader on the national scene."

Jackson's personality is possibly even more in tune with the present black mood than Dr. King's was, because, as Richard Levine pointed out in *Harper's,* "Dr. King was middle-class Atlanta, but Jesse Jackson was born in poverty in Greenville, South Carolina." Jackson calls himself a "country preacher," but he combines his down-home style with a sharp intellect. He attended the University of Illinois for one year but dropped out in 1960 to attend the Agricultural and Technical College of North Carolina in Greensboro, where the first black sit-in had taken place earlier that year. He was an honor student, quarterbacked the football team and organized civil rights demonstrations. After graduation, Jackson went North to study at the Chicago Theological Seminary, where he devoted most of his extracurricular time to local civil rights work.

It was Dr. King himself who originally spotted Jackson's leadership potential during a massive civil rights drive in Chicago in the summer of 1966 and appointed him to head all of SCLC's economic projects in the North. In the three years since that appointment, Jackson has concentrated most of his efforts on the Chicago-based project called Operation Breadbasket and made that pilot program the most impressive demonstration of black economic and political power in the United States. Breadbasket's organizational methods are now being applied under Jackson's guidance in 15 cities ranging from Los Angeles to Brooklyn.

The project's primary goals are to create jobs for blacks and to encourage them to own and operate businesses. Boycotting, or the threat of it, is Breadbasket's most potent weapon. The effectiveness of this technique was most evident in a breakthrough victory over the huge Atlantic and Pacific Tea Company, which operates 40 stores in Chicago's black ghetto. To avoid the financial loss that a boycott would have caused, the A & P signed a pact guaranteeing jobs for blacks and the distribution of black products on A & P shelves. As *Business Week* reported in a story about Operation Breadbasket, "Nationally, the organization's efforts have resulted in about 5000 jobs and $40,000,000 in annual salaries to Negroes. But the Chicago campaign [against A & P] represents Breadbasket's most significant victory, for it is the biggest settlement with a chain in a single city, and set a precedent for other food-chain negotiations across the country."

The A & P pact was especially significant because—in addition to a guarantee of over 700 jobs for blacks and marketing more black businessmen's products—the company also agreed to use black-owned janitorial and exterminating companies in its ghetto stores, to bank in black-owned banks, to advertise in black media and to have black construction firms build its ghetto stores. Monthly meetings between representatives of A & P and Breadbasket are designed to assure that the company is not shirking. On the personal level, sensitivity seminars attended by A & P executives attempt to awaken management to the existence and effects of prejudice. Similar agreements have been signed with more than half of all the major food distributors in the ghetto.

The Reverend Jackson created an even more far-reaching program last spring, when he initiated the Illinois Hunger Campaign. Believing that hunger is the one issue that could unite the black and white poor, Jackson led a caravan to all of the poverty areas of Illinois, ending with demonstrations at the state capital in Springfield. The pressure this exerted on the Illinois legislature was so great that a planned cut of $125,000,000 in welfare funds was restored at a time when New York and California were making sizable cuts in their welfare payments. An impassioned appeal by Jackson, from the steps of the capitol building, inspired a bill to provide school lunches for all of the needy children in the state. Jackson also extracted a promise from the state legislature to prevail on Washington for special surplus-food allotments for the poor. The Illinois Hunger Campaign was conceived by Jackson as an extension of the Poor Peoples' Campaign begun by Dr. King, and there are plans for similar efforts in other states next year.

No matter what his other commitments may be, Jackson always attends the Saturday-morning meeting of Operation Breadbasket. The location has been changed three times this year, because the congregation continually outgrows its premises, and Breadbasket presently resides in a 6000-seat movie theater on Chicago's South Side. The lobby of the theater is filled with tables displaying black merchandise, and the auditorium itself is hung with signs that exhort the gathering to BUY BLACK PRODUCTS and USE BLACK SERVICES. The first hour of the meeting is devoted to Gospel music by the Operation Breadbasket orchestra and choir, interspersed with the business for the week—either boycotts or special "buy-ins." *Playboy*'s Associate Articles Editor, Arthur Kretchmer, who conducted this interview with Jackson, describes the remainder of a recent meeting.

"After Breadbasket's projects were out of the way, a

frail old lady, whose face was ravaged by time and much else, was given the stage. In a quiet voice, and with great dignity, she briefly described the humiliation she had suffered during an interview with a welfare worker the previous week. Then she said she had come to the meeting to gain the strength that would enable her to block her door in the future. 'They can starve me,' she said, 'but I'll die before they come back with their damn forms and their damn questions.' With that, she slowly raised her fist in the black-power salute and the audience gave her the most sympathetic ovation I've ever heard.

"Then Jackson was introduced—and greeted by ten minutes of standing, clapping, stamping love. He is a big man with an imperial manner. The head is leonine and the facial expression at once fierce and sullen. He was dressed, like a Mod black emperor, in a brilliantly colored *dashiki,* bell-bottom jeans and high-top country shoes. Biologist Desmond Morris has written that a leader never scrabbles, twitches, fidgets or falters, and Jackson qualifies. For over an hour, he delivered a passionate sermon that described the black man's plight in white society. It was filled with street talk, down-home slang and quotations from the Bible—but its effect was Greek tragedy with soul.

"The sermon was punctuated by piano and organ riffs similar to a rhythm section's backing of a good jazz soloist. Halfway into an eloquent plea that blacks not waste their energy fighting among themselves, he called on one of the choir members, Sister Theresa, to sing 'I Can See the Promised Land,' because 'I need it,' he said. At one point in the sermon, he paused, clearly exhausted, and turned to the audience to say, 'Yes, I'm tired.' An old woman's voice called out, 'Take care of him, Lord. We need him too bad for You to let him die.'

"Everyone around Jackson is acutely aware of his poor health. He has suffered this year from traces of sickle-cell anemia and assorted viruses brought on by lowered resistance. He's been hospitalized a half-dozen times but never missed a Saturday at Breadbasket. It is common for a parishioner to greet him with, 'Hello, Reverend Jesse. Are you taking your medicine?'

"After Jackson finished the service, the Operation Breadbasket orchestra played a dozen choruses of a syncopated, soulful 'We Shall Overcome,' while all 6000 people in the audience—a number of whom were white —stood holding hands and swaying back and forth in one of the oldest, most moving rituals of the civil rights struggle. The effect of the morning was catharsis and rejuvenation. I don't think anyone who entered the theater that morning could have left without shedding some of the despair that seems to be afflicting the black liberation movement.

"A few moments later, I had a completely different, but indelible, impression of Jackson's impact. I was waiting to see him in a small dressing room. He was resting in an armchair, talking to a very pretty, shy black girl of about 20 who was standing near him. She said to him, with some embarrassment, 'Reverend, I just want to tell you how much you mean to all of us.' He slowly raised his head and said, 'Hell, that's just a lot of talk. If I was really important to you, you'd take pity on my old tired body and invite me home, so your momma could fix a fine meal for me.' She was immediately flustered and said, 'Oh, Reverend. You're just having fun with me. You don't mean it. You wouldn't come to my house.' He looked at her with a stern expression that he couldn't quite prevent from turning to a smile and said, 'You tell your momma I'm coming over Thursday night. Tell her to do some fixin'.' She looked at him, trying to tell if he were serious, and her eyes widened, her hands began to fuss and her jaw dropped open. Finally, she said, 'Would you *really?* Would you *really* come? If you do, I'll charge my friends admission at the door. A half a dollar to see you and a dollar to touch you!' Jackson looked at the girl and then at me, laughing his appreciation. Actually, on those rare occasions when he's in the city, Jackson is well taken care of by his beautiful 25-year-old wife, Jacqueline—and harassed by his three energetic children."

Because of Jackson's heavy schedule, Kretchmer couldn't get enough time with him until both took refuge in a rural retreat where the "country preacher" was free to explore at length the militant new mood of the black struggle and his own role in it. Since Dr. King's death had seemed for many to signal the end of the nonviolent phase of the civil rights movement—a philosophy Jackson continues to champion—the interview began with that topic.

Playboy: Though the mood of blacks has changed markedly since the death of Martin Luther King, are you still committed, as Dr. King was, to nonviolence as the only way to win racial justice?
Jackson: We will be as nonviolent as we can be and as violent as we must be. We should not choose violence first, because it is an inhumane way of dealing with problems. We also do not have the military resources to deal with the American power structure. There's no sense in facing tanks with a .22 pistol. Our circumstances and terrain would not give us the freedom to use a violent strategy. The ghettos are built like a military

stockade. America never needs to actually come in. The lights can be turned off, the water shut off and the food supply stopped. We could be eliminated in the ghetto without anyone even crossing the railroad tracks to get us.

Playboy: Do you mean to imply that if you did have the military resources, you would wage war against white Americans—

Jackson: I am just pointing out that there is a strong *pragmatic* case for nonviolence. I am philosophically committed to nonviolence because I think it is the creative alternative and should be used as long as it helps protect and sustain life. It is a creative alternative to the Pentagon, for example. Just as there are forces in this world with a design for killing, so must there be forces with a design for healing.

Playboy: Stokely Carmichael and Eldridge Cleaver, among others, say that *unless* blacks create their own design for killing, they are going to be killed themselves. Is this an irrevocable split in the black movement?

Jackson: No. The competition to nonviolence does not come from Stokely or Eldridge; it comes from America's traditions. It comes from little children seeing cowboys solve their moral problems by killing. The competition to nonviolence comes from the military draft, with its nine weeks' training on how to kill. The trouble is that nonviolence is so often defined as refusal to fight, and that is the American definition of cowardice. In fact, marching unarmed against the guns and dogs of the police requires more courage than does aggression. The perverted idea of manhood coming from the barrel of a gun is what keeps people from understanding nonviolence.

Playboy: If your life were endangered, could you use a gun?

Jackson: Yes. Nonviolence does not demand that one develop an absolute, universal commitment to pacifism. That old notion of being in a dark alley and having a man step out with a gun does not apply. Of course, I am going to do whatever I must to get rid of the man *and* his gun. I preach nonviolence because it's the better alternative. In that alley, there *is* no alternative. But peace is the alternative to war, and nonviolence should be seen as the antidote to violence, not simply as its opposite. Nonviolence is more concerned with saving life than with saving face. It is the most sensible way to combat white society's military oppression of blacks.

Playboy: Do you think white America is actually waging war on black America?

Jackson: Yes, it's a war. Sometimes it's waged by a white army in full military gear, as any weapons count among special riot police would show. But it's also a war of attrition, a siege, in which the violence takes other forms. To me, violence is starving a child or maintaining a mother on insufficient welfare. Violence is going to school 12 years and getting five years' worth of education. Violence is 30,000,000 hungry in the most abundant nation on earth. White America must understand that men will steal before they starve, that if there is a choice of a man's living or dying, he will choose to live, even if it means other men die. These are human reactions, and we cannot assume that black people are going to be anything less than human.

Playboy: Is there a point at which you feel violence would be justified?

Jackson: If I saw that there was no other way for us to be liberated, yes.

Playboy: For many white people, the most disturbing incident of potential black violence this year was portrayed by a news picture of armed students at Cornell. What do you think about their use of weapons?

Jackson: They *didn't* use them, except in the symbolic sense of warning groups that had threatened them that they were capable of their own military defense. I have doubts about the enduring success of the technique of military defense, but I appreciate the feelings that brought such a desperate mood into existence.

Playboy: Another group that has endorsed violence as a tactic is the Black Panthers, which J. Edgar Hoover has called "the greatest threat among the black extremist groups to the internal security of the United States." Do you support the Panthers?

Jackson: I'm very sympathetic to the Panthers. They are the logical result of the white man's brutalization of blacks. The remarkable thing about them is that they have not conducted any military offenses. They have not gone to downtown America to shoot up white-owned stores. The Panthers are a defense for justice, just as the Ku Klux Klan is an offense for injustice. That's a qualitative difference between picking up a gun to keep from being brutalized and picking up a gun to *inflict* brutality. As far as Mr. Hoover's opinion goes, I don't think that his perspective is relevant when it comes to the problems that are facing this society— which is surprising, when you consider all the good information he gets. He certainly knows what I'm thinking about and talking about most of the time.

Playboy: Does the FBI keep you under surveillance?

Jackson: Yes. It's admitted tapping Dr. King's phone, and I used to speak with him at least twice a week. The persons he spoke with were also frequently tapped, and I don't imagine they've untapped me, as my activities have increased since his death. But anything they've heard me say, if they come around, I'll be glad to repeat out loud to them. I want to add that I consider Mr. Hoover himself to be one of the greatest threats to our national security. His wire tapping and other surveillance methods violate the principles of democracy. The FBI director doesn't account to anyone, not even to the Attorney General; and, in reality, he heads what is very nearly a secret police.

It's on this subject of abusive police power that the Panthers are profound. No white community in America has a majority of black police, but black communities are militarily occupied by white police. The Panthers are right to say that the white police should be gotten out, just as the Americans were right in saying, "Get the Redcoats out." We are saying, "Get the bluecoats out."

Playboy: Aren't you really saying, "Get the white bluecoats out"?

Jackson: No. We don't want white bluecoats, but we don't want black bluecoats, either. We don't want to be policed by a supreme white authority, even if the agents of the authority are black. We're saying that the black community should police itself: the authority for the police should come from the home area, not from city hall, which is alien to us, has never been sympathetic to us and openly supports the police who oppress us.

Playboy: Do you think, as some radicals seem to, that America is a police state?

Jackson: For black men, it is. Nobody in the black community who's had the experience of being made to spread-eagle over a car for no reason, or because of a simple traffic ticket, would disagree with that. Some black folks disagree, but that's because of their lack of experience. If they just keep on living, they'll confront the reality soon enough. The reality is tyranny, and the tyrant must be opposed. Whether we are called Operation Breadbasket or Black Panthers or niggers, we know who the enemy is. We will gain our freedom by being more willing to die for it than the slavemaster is to die to keep us enslaved.

Playboy: Do you agree with the controversial Panther demand that all black prisoners be released from prison?

Jackson: Yes, but there are probably some black men who have been so broken, whose lives have been so twisted that they would be dangerous to all other men, both black and white, and I suppose they should not be released from confinement, though I would hope that genuine rehabilitation would replace detention. But just as the black community is a colony of white America, and those of us within that colony should be liberated, so should those of us who have been especially victimized by the viciousness of the colonial rules, and tried by the white slavemaster, be released. All of the black community should be liberated, and that includes those behind steel bars as well as those behind economic and social bars.

Playboy: The subject of black crime preoccupies white America and, in the opinion of some commentators, helped elect Richard Nixon President. Many whites feel that their fears of black crime are completely justified, particularly in the light of your previous statement that black prisoners should be freed. How would you respond to that?

Jackson: The Crime Commission appointed by Lyndon Johnson showed that most black crime is against blacks. The white folks who exploit us are as safe as a baby in a womb. The black man's hostility comes from the deprivation and frustration and tension of the ghetto. Most people handle that hostility surprisingly well; and those who don't, take it out on the nearest target—other blacks. Another reason black men hurt other black men is that the punishment is less than when you hurt a white man. The price for hostility against whites is too high. To talk back to a white boss is to be fired. And to make violent gestures against white people is to invite instant death. So the hostility that is bred in the ghetto leads to suffering—but mostly by blacks, not whites.

Playboy: The incidence of property crimes by blacks is very high and is increasing. Do you think the white middle class is wrong to be concerned about protecting its possessions?

Jackson: That property usually belongs to blacks, not whites. It is the ghetto resident whose home is robbed, sometimes two or three times in the same month. Black crimes against property are the result of desperation. I said earlier that a man will steal before he starves. Black crime is crime because of a need; whites commit crimes of *greed.* Black folks do not set up elaborate kid-napings for a million-dollar ransom. The financial value of all of the property crimes committed by blacks in one year doesn't equal the money lost in the famous salad-oil swindle. Blacks are not out for a big score; they are out to stay alive. And when he's caught, the black man can't afford bail and a good attorney. Already wounded and probably crippled by the system, he spends more time than whites inside the jail system, where he is further destroyed by it. His criminality is molded by the police state. I was especially aware of this in the South, where I grew up. The police were an absolute power; they were not merely enforcers of the law; they *were* the law. They could do anything they wanted, because the judges and the legal system were thoroughly racist.

Playboy: Do you have any recollections of personal confrontations with the police when you were young?

Jackson: I remember that they seemed to get a kick out of breaking down the front door if you didn't answer quickly enough. When I was a little kid, we'd run and hide under the house at the sight of a police car. Later on, they locked us up for things like vagrancy or cursing. In time, they would kill a few of the guys I grew up with, and it was always "in the line of duty." There were some humorous incidents, too. One cop in Greenville, South Carolina, became famous for locking up a black man for "reckless eyeballing"; he had been staring at a white woman about 100 feet away. And I remember we weren't allowed to stand around the store windows while they were changing clothes on the white store dummies. My Northern friends get a big kick out of that, but it's symbolic of the awesome pattern of Southern oppression.

My own most frightening experience, though, didn't involve a policeman. There was a store on our street run by a white man named Jack. The customers were all black, and it was a comfortable place. Jack used to play with us kids all the time, and we'd run errands for him. One day, I went in and the store was full of people, but I was in a big hurry, the kind of hurry a six-year-old is always in. I said, "Jack, I'm late. Take care of me." He didn't hear me, so I whistled at him. He wheeled around and snatched a .45 pistol from a shelf with one hand and kneeled down to grab my arm in his other fist. Then he put the pistol against my head and, kneading my black arm in his white fingers, said, "Goddamn it! Don't you *ever* whistle at me again, you hear?" I didn't think he was really going to shoot me, even then; the thing that got to me was that none of the black people in the store did or said anything. My impression of the superpower of whites to do absolutely anything they want and get away with it right in the middle of blacks was a traumatic experience that I've never recovered from.

Playboy: Are such experiences for blacks still part of the Southern heritage?

Jackson: Yes, but less frequently, and I think Dr. King is the reason for the change. The significance of his movement can be seen only against a Southern background. He taught us that even if the police—the law—say you can't sit down, sit down anyway. In most communities until then, there weren't five men who had that kind of courage. He challenged us to stand up to the police we used to run from. In Montgomery, Alabama, the cradle of the Confederacy, he rose up and declared that black men deserve their full rights of manhood. There wasn't enough money to buy him, and there weren't enough jails to hold him. Death itself isn't enough to stop black men from being free, for crucifixion leads to resurrection.

Playboy: One of the seeming ironies of the civil rights movement is that while the Southern black has gone far toward winning freedom, the ghetto black in the North is in an increasingly frustrated mood. How do you explain this?

Jackson: The Southern movement fulfilled some of the hopes it raised. We achieved our goals in the bus boycotts and the freedom rides. The public-accommodation and voting-rights bills were passed. We haven't had corresponding success in the North. The Northern black has seen *some* progress, but his advancement doesn't compare with the advancement of white society. The economy quadruples while blacks creep along with unemployment as high as 35 and 40 percent in some black communities. When the white unemployment rate was 20 percent in 1933, it was a Depression that required massive aid. But the black unemployment rate is ignored.

The most frustrated are those who have worked hardest but remain unrewarded. A black man in Chicago with a master's degree earns less than a white man with a high school diploma. You can't tell a man who has been to college that he's not educated enough to qualify for a job that goes to white high school dropouts. If you do, you castrate him. And the Northern black is more frustrated because the indifference of white colonialism in the North is more vicious than the paternalism of the South. The Northern industrialist doesn't have any emotional relationship with the black; he maintains only economic contact. In the North, you get white smiles while the shops are open, but the hypocritical charade is over when the shops close and whites take the money out of the ghetto. It's no coincidence that those stores are the primary targets in a riot.

Playboy: Los Angeles mayor Sam Yorty once stated on television that he thought riots were caused by the mass media. He said that blacks rioted in imitation of the disruptive behavior they saw on television and that if there had been no television coverage of Watts during the first hours of the trouble there in 1965, there would have been no riot. Do you feel that's true?

Jackson: That's absurd. The riots are expressions of the unheard. The rioters are the mass of black people who invest hard labor on nasty chores—they are floor cleaners, shoeshine boys, hospital attendants—and they find that they have almost no share, no investment, no dividend in a 900-billion-dollar economy. Riots are a reaction to pain and a sense of hopelessness. There are black people whom no President's program has ever reached. My grandmother has lived through every President from 1900 to 1969, and the sum total of their grass-roots programs has not been able to teach her the 26 letters of the alphabet. Riots do not solve problems, but they indicate what those problems are. It is the responsibility of an aching man to tell the truth about his pain. It isn't to his advantage to give the appearance of happiness when he is hurting. In the past, we passively accepted the immoral acts of white society to prove that we were nice, decent folks, but that was our foolishness. Black folks assumed that Pharaoh was going to help them simply because it was the right thing to do. Now we know that Pharaoh's commitment is to property, not to persons. He must be made to do the right thing.

Playboy: It has been alleged by some observers, however, that the riots reveal a kind of death wish on the part of blacks.

Jackson: It's true that there is in the young generation an inclination toward nihilism. To challenge a police headquarters with a handful of bricks is a suicidal act, but it is also a blow for freedom. What the riots really reveal is the beastliness and sadism of white police. Nearly all of the people who died in riots were blacks killed by whites whose ethics dictate that nickels and dimes are more important than flesh and blood.

Playboy: There are whites who say that activists such as yourself foster the riots, that without you, there'd be racial peace.

Jackson: White folks don't want peace; they want quiet. The price you pay for peace is justice. Until there is justice, there will be no peace *or* quiet.

Playboy: At the time of Dr. King's death, many blacks said that white America had lost its last chance to solve the race problem without destroying itself. Do you think that's true?

Jackson: No, I don't, although I was one of the first people to make that statement. It seemed to me then that Dr. King's death ended America's last chance to be redeemed. But it is not for us to determine the chances of redemption. There are still people being born with hope, still people fighting with hope. God has not yet damned this country, though one may wonder how long the wicked will prosper. America at this point is the most violent nation in the world.

Playboy: Isn't that a cliché? Don't other nations have wars and assassinations?

Jackson: Of course. But no other nation wants so clearly to be the world's policeman. No other nation comes down so consistently on the wrong side of every revolutionary movement for liberation from tyranny. Wherever there is a rebellion, our conservative industrialists are helping to end it, whether it's in Angola or Venezuela. Any place we buy oil or rubber, or sell a little Coca-Cola and chewing gum, we've got to protect the old order. We spend $900 per second to kill the Viet Cong but only $77 per person per year to feed the hungry at home. We maintain soldiers in 20 countries around the world, yet we always talk about the Russian threat or the Chinese threat. China does not have a standing army outside of China; Russia has two. Yet we assume that someone's after us, that the "free world" is threatened simply because people want the chance to control their own economic market so they can participate in the world decision-making order. They don't want to go Communist or to crush democracy; they just want to end their serf status; and that's all blacks want here at home.

Playboy: It might seem incongruous to some that you can make this sweeping indictment of America, an indictment that could easily serve as the lead paragraph in one of SDS' revolutionary pamphlets, and yet, as economic director of SCLC and leader of Operation Breadbasket, you are leading blacks who clearly want to buy into the American dream.

Jackson: It's very simple. For all its faults, America is the only country with the capacity to save the world, even at the very moment that we seem bent on destroying it. We can produce more food, medicine, trained and educated people than anyone else. We try to export our killers, but people have stopped wanting them; they would accept our doctors, scientists and creators, but our armies are outdated. We could liberate nations from their poverty and their pestilence if our value system would allow us to do so. The irony is how close we are to being something great. One fifth of our nation is starving, yet we have the capacity to overfeed it. We could end the starvation in India, heal the sickness in Africa. But the tragedy is that we are as close to destroying the world as we are to saving it. We spent 78.4 billion dollars to kill this year but only 12 billion to heal. Those who are silent now, or are neutral now, must make a decision before the opportunity passes forever.

Playboy: Are you encouraged by the young white radicals who seem determined to change America's value system?

Jackson: The issues that move them are qualitatively different from the ones that concern blacks. Many of the radical whites say that materialism is no good, that one must seek a new level of spiritualism. Well, we lived for years with spiritualism but without any materialism. Now we'd like to try to balance the two. Many of the young whites are living on the prerogatives of the materialism they shun. They confront their school in the winter, but in the summer, they go off to Sweden or Hawaii. Their discussions of America's corruption take place over steaks. They spend $5000 a year to attend the schools they shut down. We often have the same moral ideals, but the perspective is very different.

I have also been disappointed that we were unable to get any mass help from young whites on the hunger caravan we recently concluded in Illinois. The students were so radical that feeding starving people didn't constitute revolution to them, because "a man needs to do more than eat." But while they were saying that, they were eating very well. To us, they tend to be superfluous.

Playboy: Weren't the strikes at both Harvard and Columbia concerned mainly with accusations by white students that those schools abuse the black community?

Jackson: I do not mean to condemn their creative protests. They accurately reflect Jesus' position that man cannot live by bread alone. They come from houses with boats and cars and more money than they can spend, yet they find their lives empty. There is beauty in their hearing the heartbeats of other humans. What I'm saying is that there is a lack of depth in their protest, in terms of the black community's real and immediate needs. But I think I must reserve judgment on those whites who are living off the prerogatives of wealth. If they are legitimately concerned, they will take what Daddy leaves and pay back some of that money in reparations to blacks.

Playboy: Do you agree with James Forman's proposal that the churches pay reparations to blacks?

Jackson: Yes, and eventually the demands will not be limited to the churches. The black community in America is an underdeveloped nation, a victim of America's cold war against her own black people. In that war, all of our supply lines have been cut—educational, commercial, political and psychological. We've been the victims of an unjust war and are due reparations from those who launched it. Business owes us reparations, first for enslaving us, then for refusing to give us work or hiring us for only the lowest-paying, most grueling jobs. And even when we have an opportunity to do the same work as white men, we are paid less for it. The labor unions, for whom we fought, owe us reparations for locking us out. The church is also liable, because it has disregarded its own moral imperatives and cooperated in creating and maintaining a racist society.

Playboy: Do you expect these demands to be met?

Jackson: For the most part, no.

Playboy: Then isn't the plea for reparations a rhetorical gesture rather than a serious proposal?

Jackson: The demands are perfectly serious. If they were met, it would mean a great step toward unifying the two separate and unequal societies that the Kerner Commission described after it studied the Newark and Detroit riots. The point is that SCLC and I are not naïve enough to think that the businessmen who control the assets of corporations, labor unions and churches will voluntarily act from some inner moral impetus. America's god is money. God is your ultimate concern, what you give maximum sacrifice for, what you will die for. God is what you worship. The American ideal is maximum profit and minimum person: there is no impulse to share the wealth, to raise up those less fortunate. What counts is the name on the front of the building. Well, I say what counts are the hands that do the work inside.

Playboy: Isn't money also one of Operation Breadbasket's major concerns?

Jackson: Yes. It's a concern because it's a reality. But the essential purpose of Operation Breadbasket is to have blacks control the basic resources of their community. We want to control the banks, the trades, the building construction and the education of our children. This desire on our part is a defensive strategy evolved in order to stop whites from controlling our community and removing the profits and income that belong to black people. Our programs are dictated by the private-enterprise economy in which we find ourselves. In my heart, however, I know that the entire system is a corruption. To me, the earth belongs to everybody; it's just a very successful rumor white folks have going that the earth belongs to them. The earth is the Lord's and no man creates anything that didn't come from other things that God put here. No man really takes anything away, either. No man can claim that he made soil or wool or milk. White folks can make airplanes, but they can't make mountains. They can make syrup but not water. *Genesis* says that the Lord created the earth and everything therein and gave man, not white man, dominion over it and created a dominion sufficient for everyone to be able to survive and prosper. Now the concept of *Genesis* has obviously been destroyed, and it is our concern to rid America of some of her arrogance and control of God's resources by saying that the food belongs to all the people.

Playboy: Do you think farmers and suppliers should give their food away?

Jackson: I don't care how the people get food, as long as they get it. The Government can buy the food and give it away in a large-scale version of the present inadequate surplus-food and food-stamp programs. Or it can give the poor enough money to buy the food themselves.

Playboy: Many middle-class whites think that the poor would only buy booze and guns if they had the money.

Jackson: I challenge anyone with that belief to tour the

reeking, rat-infested tenements of Harlem or Chicago's South Side and count the number of alcoholic welfare mothers. There won't be many. Welfare people do not account for this nation's high number of alcoholics. Nor are most guns bought by the black poor. In a home where the children are eating wall plaster because they are hungry, a gun isn't looked upon as an important commodity. But I don't care if the Government wants to give out food instead of money. I would bless any device it might come up with, as long as it does *something.* The country is producing more food than it needs. There is inherent evil in a system that induces men to plow crops under while others starve.

Not only does the food belong to the people but the industrial profit also belongs to the people. If the employees of General Motors left tomorrow, it would have to stop. If the entire board of directors died tomorrow, nothing would stop. What's indispensable are the laborers, not the directors. The laborers can rise from the ranks and direct their fellow laborers. Because they are the basic need, they ought to reap the basic benefits. But in America, about six percent of the people control the basic wealth, and there's something infinitely demonic about that. It's no wonder that America needs the largest military in the world to protect the wealthiest superrich class from people who would rebel against it. There's no basic conflict among the *peoples* of the world; Russian bus drivers aren't mad at American bus drivers. But the controlling groups are always in conflict with the people—whether it's the Government of the United States, which refuses to adequately protect the poor, or the boards of directors at GM and Ford, which encourage blacks to go into debt to buy automobiles but don't allow blacks to participate in the profitable manufacture and distribution of cars.

Playboy: Can blacks afford to buy automobile agencies?

Jackson: The companies will lend us the money to buy *cars,* which leads to profits for them only. They could lend us the money to buy agencies, but they won't, because that would let us profit also.

Playboy: Aren't there some black car dealers?

Jackson: About 14 dealerships out of 28,000. We are grossly underrepresented in all areas of the economy. There are no black TV stations, for example, and only seven black radio stations. Most of the stations that are beamed toward the black community and play black music are white owned. We can't get FCC outlets, and I'm convinced that there is a conspiracy to keep us from communicating with one another on a mass scale.

Playboy: Do you mean that the Government fears a nationally directed riot?

Jackson: I don't know what they think; all I know is we can't get licenses when we apply.

Playboy: What does Operation Breadbasket intend to do about this sort of economic underrepresentation?

Jackson: We have the power, nonviolently, just by controlling our appetites, to determine the direction of the American economy. If black people in 30 cities said simultaneously, "General Motors, you will not sell cars in the black community unless you guarantee us a franchise here next year and help us finance it," GM would have no choice. We can affect their margin of profit by withdrawing our patronage and resisting the system instead of enduring it.

Playboy: Can this really work? And, if so, why hasn't it been done already?

Jackson: It hasn't been done because we weren't sophisticated enough to see it. This is a step that we haven't been ready to take. But it will certainly be done now, because we are organizing to do it. Black people purchase about 35 to 40 billion dollars' worth of goods each year. We represent the margin of profit in many industries. America depends on our cooperation with her economy, and we shall become the enemies of those businesses and industries that work against our interest by unfair hiring practices, by discriminating against black products, by not making investments in the ghetto to correspond with the profits taken out of it. There is an analogous situation in politics: The black people have not yet realized that *we* can determine who gets elected President: in 1960, it was the South Side of Chicago that turned in the vote that made John Kennedy President. The newspapers all said that Mayor Daley had once again come through with his Cook County machine, but that vote was black. The ghetto, however, has seldom voted in its own self-interest. It has even voted for black politicians who are contemptuous of blacks.

Playboy: Why does the ghetto vote so inefficiently?

Jackson: Because it's so easy to intimidate or con the poor; they have no recourse. On Election Day, the precinct worker comes around and says that if you don't vote his way, he'll have you thrown out of the housing project or he'll have your welfare check canceled. Or, if he's a benign type, he'll buy your vote with a chicken. The poor are also frightened out of coming to freedom meetings. But the poor themselves must learn that food is a right and not a privilege. We are marching to gain a subsidy for 30,000,000 hungry Americans who represent a human resource that is more important than any of the mineral resources that this nation subsidizes.

Playboy: What form would that subsidy take?

Jackson: A guaranteed annual income based upon the Government's own estimate of the amount of money people actually need to live adequate lives. They say that a family of four in a large city in the United States in 1969 requires $5994 per year for minimum maintenance. If that's what's needed, then that's what they should get.

Playboy: Wouldn't that be expensive, especially considering the present high tax burden?

Jackson: The Senate committee on poverty headed by George McGovern stated, after doing field research throughout the nation, that it would cost ten billion dollars per year to feed the poor and fulfill their basic health, clothing and housing needs. I would guess that that's a low estimate. Let's double it, and say that the cost would be 20 billion dollars per year. That's less money than we're spending to kill the Viet Cong. It's less money than we're about to spend on the ABM system. It is less than a third of the defense budget. If we wanted men to live as much as we want to see them die, we could do it without any new taxes.

Playboy: But what motivation does the Government have to subsidize the poor?

Jackson: Out of a spirit of humanity, one would hope, but that is naïve. Our job is to create enough pressure to *force* the Government to act. It is certainly not going to do so on its own. The imbalance of Southern power in the Congress has led to important committees being headed by pathological killers and by men with public commitments to racism. These men—such as Mendel Rivers, Russell Long, Jamie Whitten and Richard Russell—are the black man's burden. The truth is that the Mafia is probably better represented in the Government than blacks are. And numerous other special-interest groups are well taken care of. The situation on the agriculture committees is particularly loathsome to me because of the millions of dollars that are given away to gentleman farmers who don't farm, while children are starving. Contrast that with the Black Panthers' national breakfast program. They are serving thousands of people free food every week, and the only qualification is that the recipient be hungry. If the Panthers can serve breakfast to 3000 children a week in Chicago or 1500 in San Francisco, with their lack of resources, what could those cities' governments be doing if they had the same interest?

Playboy: If you were the mayor of a major American city, what would you do?

Jackson: I would declare the poor communities in a state of emergency and deal with the unemployment rate, the high mortality rate and the high t.b. rate. I would set up medicine tents on the streets, and embarrass the Federal and state governments into opening up their food storehouses. I would declare war on disease and hunger. I would enlarge all the city departments that feed and heal people. The welfare of all the people would be attended to before any new golf courses or monuments or stadiums were built. I would force the Government to call out the National Guard to deal with the existing injustices, which make the ghetto a permanent disaster area. There's no reason why the Army couldn't be coming down the street with bayonets, looking for slum landlords. The Army would force trade unions to allow the minority groups in. And those who did not pick up the garbage would themselves be picked up. An Army like that wouldn't have any trouble getting volunteer soldiers because it would be engaged in a *relevant* war.

Playboy: Is that statement a reference to Vietnam?

Jackson: Let me just say that Vietnam is not a relevant war. It is a war in which the black poor are paying with their lives to protect the investments of a small, rich elite whose Asian investments are threatened by Hanoi.

Playboy: Whatever interests are being served in Vietnam, do you think that you, as a citizen, have the right to pick the wars in which you will fight and those in which you won't?

Jackson: Of course I have that right. I must reserve the right to decide which wars are just. And I would not fight in a war that I thought was unjust. Nor would I approve of anyone else doing so.

Playboy: Would you encourage drafted blacks to refuse to go to Vietnam, even if it means jail for them?

Jackson: Yes. And whites, too. Fighting in Vietnam is a step back into slavery for blacks, and into barbarism for whites. The road to jail has often been the road to freedom. Many men—Gandhi, Jomo Kenyatta, Dr. King—have learned that.

Playboy: Although a disproportionate number of blacks have died in Vietnam, there have been few blacks active in the peace movement. Why?

Jackson: To blacks, the peace movement is a luxury that presupposes you have the time to save somebody aside from yourself. Blacks are just too occupied with their own survival. They have not even been sophisticated enough to know that they can oppose murder. A black man can be easily seduced; it's a revolution for him to go from one meal a day to three. Sometimes I think that blacks are so locked away from information that we could be duped into fighting in South Africa for apartheid, if America told us to do it. We certainly were down there shooting our Dominican brothers. I saw televised scenes of Dominicans lined up against a wall while black GIs held guns on them. But this is not because of ignorance but because of cultural suffocation and improper education.

Playboy: Malcolm X once proposed that the UN send observers into the American black community to determine if blacks were being treated humanely. Do you think that's a practical idea?

Jackson: Only for symbolic purposes; the UN doesn't have any power and is subject to the American veto.

Playboy: Wouldn't exercising the veto prove so embarrassing to the U. S. that it would refrain from doing so?

Jackson: I doubt it. And the countries that one might expect to pressure America into dealing humanely with its black minority—the countries of Africa—are themselves too dependent on America's trade and financial aid to wish to antagonize her. It is not in the enlightened self-interest of those countries to rise up in indignation when we're shot up in Detroit or Watts, because we don't affect their essential relationship with the world markets or the World Bank.

Playboy: Both Malcolm and Dr. King worked to mobilize a world-wide conscience against racism before they were struck down. Do you share the view of some that both murders were part of a plan to deprive blacks of their leaders?

Jackson: Not a single elaborate conspiracy, but it's clear that as we have moved closer to America's nerve center, closer to a position where we could vote men out of office, the killings have increased. And I don't think America has done anything to indicate that she is on the side of Dr. King rather than of his killers.

Playboy: You used the plural. Don't you think that James Earl Ray acted alone?

Jackson: I would be surprised if it wasn't a conspiracy involving many others.

Playboy: Do you have any evidence to support that belief?

Jackson: I think the circumstances were very suspicious. As you know, I was with Dr. King when the assassin's bullet was fired. We were talking with Operation Breadbasket's music director, Ben Branch, about songs for the next day's rally. Dr. Abernathy, Andy Young, James Bevel and Bernard Lee were very near. When Dr. King was shot, I hit the ground, along with the others. We scrambled toward the steps where he was and I looked back over my shoulder, because I was afraid that more shots were going to be fired. I saw so many police coming *from the direction of the shot* that I actually threw up my hands, thinking that the shot had come from one of them and that I was going to be killed, too. There were hundreds of police in the area, some jumping from the hill where the shot had come from. I tried to tell them that the bullet came from that way.

Now, the hotel that Ray was in—if Ray was the killer—is next door to the fire department. With the shot having been fired and all those police in the area, the usual thing during an emergency in a Southern town would be for a siren to go off that stops the lights and traffic on Main Street, where the hotel is. It was six o'clock in the afternoon, the busiest time for traffic, and it all could have been brought to a halt. But no siren went off, traffic wasn't stopped and Ray escaped through downtown Memphis. The distance he subsequently traveled indicates to me that he didn't do it by himself and that he may have had some very highly placed help. But, of course, finding Dr. King's killers is secondary to getting at the roots of America's violent atmosphere—an atmosphere in which you conform or are broken, in which you take your subordinate place in the industrial hierarchy or are destroyed.

Playboy: What do you think Dr. King would be doing if he were alive today?

Jackson: Dr. King would still be dealing with the problem of finding a job for everybody; he would still be raising the questions of medical care for everybody, of a full-employment economy. He would still be on the basic issues, still be pointing out the stupidity of the war. He would be in general conflict with Nixon. He would still, as we say, be on the case.

Playboy: Will there ever be another black leader as important as Dr. King?

Jackson: I don't think so, though, of course, no man can say. But it was Dr. King who crossed the frontier, who made a permanent break with the past. I grew up in the period from 1955 to 1965, and that time was dominated by his courage and strength, as opposed to the previous mass docility of black men. Dr. King was a surprise for a lot of whites who had conned themselves into believing that Negroes were really inferior. He was intelligent, moral, eloquent and courageous. The contrast of his eloquence with the lack of it in those whites he was forced to deal with gave us a rallying point. Even more important was the way he stood up to white military power in the South. Dr. King wasn't afraid of the cop's billy stick, guns or dogs. He overcame the stigma of jail cells; in fact, he *dignified* the jail cell and wrote great words from it. He was willing to die for black people, and finally did die, not on some lofty mountainside or in the company of ambassadors but kissing garbage men, trying to set them free.

Playboy: In the weeks before he died, did Dr. King express any particular optimism or pessimism about the future of the movement?

Jackson: He expressed both. SCLC was at that time involved in making its decision about the Poor Peoples' Campaign in Washington, D. C., that ultimately led to Resurrection City. Many of Dr. King's friends and some board members said that we should not go to Washing-

ton because of the possibility of a riot. The final decision was his. He was going through a bad time and he
showed it at one of the last staff meetings he would ever
attend. He was despairing that morning and Andy
Young tried to tell him to relax, that things were going
to get better. And Dr. King told Andy, "Don't say
'Peace, peace' when there is no peace. The country is
swinging to the right and our President is obsessed with
the war. Maybe I ought to turn around," he said. But
then he stopped; and when he continued, his voice was
more firm. "But we've gone too far to turn around.
There were dark days during the sit-ins, and in Selma
and Birmingham. We've come too far."

Then he changed again. "But I'm still disturbed by
the division in the country. Maybe I ought to just fast.
And when I get to the point of death, perhaps we could
have a summit meeting of blacks. Maybe that would
bring us together." But then he seemed to resolve the
argument in his mind. He said, "I've seen where we've
got to go. We are going to fight the good fight; we are
going to liberate our brothers and raise up the poor.
We're not going to turn around. It's all very clear to me
now." And I think Dr. King at that moment was as sure
as he had ever been of the ultimate victory of his movement. Once you've been to the mountaintop, it doesn't
matter if James Earl Ray is in the bushes waiting for
you.

Playboy: Do you share Dr. King's vision?

Jackson: In my stronger moments, I have no doubts.
I'm even able to love those who persecute me. There
must be some force that's committed to redemption,
even though it's painful. The alternative is that we will
destroy ourselves—"die together as fools," as Dr. King
said once. He and Gandhi and Jesus reached a spiritual
state that liberates the self. Dr. King did not represent

ordinary men. That's what made people love him so much. But what finally happens to the extraordinary men is what happened to Jesus. We admire them but we don't follow them, and finally we kill them because they become such a threat to us.

Playboy: In what way?

Jackson: Most of us cannot live up to the ideal of the noble and virtuous. Such men make us aware that we must settle for the real and the expedient. We are diminished by their purity, which is a threat to our self-esteem. The idealist keeps our consciences awake, but the pressure on our conscience is so great that it can be relieved only by murder.

Playboy: Dr. King was criticized for placing too much emphasis on conscience. David Halberstam wrote that Dr. King left Chicago in 1966, for example, because he could not inspire a moral consciousness, and Mayor Daley was able to dissipate his campaign with high-sounding but unspecific resolutions. Do you think that Dr. King was too concerned with the moral rather than the tactical aspects of the civil rights movement?

Jackson: No, I think that even as recently as 1966, Dr. King was correctly analyzing his problem as the need to change the psyche of the black man. You couldn't impress black folks unless you impressed white folks first. Dr. King had to make the movement as large as possible in white eyes to get respect for blacks. I think that we are inclined to lose perspective on how much things have changed since 1955. There was no black consciousness then. Dr. King was dealing with "Negroes"—put quotes around that—whose minds, desires, ambitions and images were white inspired. Aretha Franklin couldn't have made it in 1955. It was Dr. King who moved the "Negro" farther and farther out; and the farther he got from that white shore, the blacker he became.

Dr. King had the most national influence of any black leader, and his concern was to change national policy. The strategy was always to form a coalition of conscience between the black community and a segment of the white community. An issue had to be defined along moral lines, because the white community will split on the basis of moral against immoral, liberal against conservative. Without that white help, there is no chance for us to have an impact on national policies. Dr. King used to point out that there is not a black college in the country that could remain open six months on black contributions. That's a reality we must face. Even now, there is no civil rights organization of any consequence that functions on black money.

Playboy: Does Operation Breadbasket accept white money?

Jackson: SCLC accepts any money, and it finances us. But we get more black money out of Chicago than any other civil rights organization has ever gotten out of the black community.

Playboy: What does SCLC think of white participation in the leadership of Breadbasket and other programs?

Jackson: We discourage it. We need and want to encourage the technical and financial aid of whites in the civil rights movement, but we should make our own decisions. Whites should spend their physical energy liberating *white* America, because white folks need someone to help them understand blacks or they're going to continue to be paralyzed by their paranoia. Whites suffer from nightmares and irrational anxiety. When a black family moves onto a white street, the white girls are not magically impregnated by a black boy. Those fears are unreal. But whites do not allow enough communication with blacks to learn the truth. So other white folks must defend our humanity, even though our skin color is different and our hair grows differently and we have a different heritage.

Playboy: Why is there a preoccupation now with black studies and Afro styles?

Jackson: The so-called natural movement is simply trying to say that I may not know who I am psychologically and historically, but I'm not going to be defined by white folks any longer. I want to see how I'd look if I just grew. If I didn't use anything white folks gave me to fancy myself up with, what would I look like? Most of us have never given ourselves a chance to find out. We're in search of our existence as a new people—Afro-American. White people forced us to suppress our beauty: now we want to glorify it. The fact that our natural selves conflict with the comfortable, stereotyped white image of the black man is not our problem.

Playboy: But this new emphasis on blackness seems to lead to some paradoxical situations. In spite of the need for expanded opportunities for blacks to attend college, a number of strikes were initiated last year by black college students who demanded black-studies programs at their schools. Are black-studies programs so important that it's worth closing down school to get them?

Jackson: I think so. History plays a large role in a people's growth. The white man took away our history because it was one more way for him to control us. Without a group identity, we had no group loyalty; we were separated from our past to make it easier to control us in the present. It is one thing to see ourselves as a people only 300 years old, born as slaves and moving toward freedom. But, in fact, our forebears date back to the origin of man, and we have always been a creative and productive people: we were enslaved, but now we are returning to freedom—and it's good to come back home. We need the pride and dignity of knowing that we are part of a great continuum. Anthropologists say that mankind originated in Africa. We are the people who carved out the great civilizations of Kush, Songhai, Ghana and Mali. We smelted iron; we mined copper and gold. For us to know this is to know that we can look forward to a great destiny.

Playboy: It's the idea of exclusively black studies that bothers many white people. Other ethnic groups don't have special study programs, do they?

Jackson: But they do, and the schools recognize them as such. If you are Italian, for instance, your history courses will cover the entire history of early Rome and then Renaissance Italy, and they will stress the worth of the Italian contributions. But no ancient-history courses emphasize the blackness of the great early civilizations. And American-history courses generally ignore the black man. If the schools had done their job, they wouldn't have the problems they are now confronted with—and richly deserve.

Playboy: Many athletes and entertainers—Bill Cosby, for example—have adopted Afro hair and clothing styles; but aside from this sort of symbolic identification, do you think successful blacks have been as involved as they should be with the movement?

Jackson: I think the symbolism is important; it shows a new sensitivity. The black athletes and entertainers who are wearing natural hair styles and Afro clothes are specifically defying the white measurement apparatus. But the fact is that the black artist has never been as far away from the black community as the white press sometimes portrays him. Every black man, for example, knows where Sammy Davis' heart is. The black entertainer moves into a white community because the houses are bigger and better there. He is just taking advantage of a new freedom. Historically, the black athlete and entertainer have been in a precarious position where, if they overidentified with the racial situation, they couldn't play in the major night clubs, couldn't get into a movie or were blackballed from a league. Black athletes who take a militant position on the race problem endanger their jobs, even though teams are dependent on their participation. Jackie Robinson broke into baseball in 1945. In 1969, blacks dominate the game. The stars of the National Basketball Association are nearly all black, as are many in the National Football League. But we'd be doing even better in sports if there were not still some discrimination there.

Playboy: What kind of discrimination?

Jackson: Before I entered college, I was offered a contract to pitch for the Chicago White Sox. They wanted to give me less money to sign than the white boys I was striking out. I'm sure that's generally true, and many black boys can't afford to leave the farm or the factory to try to make it with a team. More indicative of the racism still alive in sports is the fact that in all of major-league baseball, there isn't one black executive or manager.

Playboy: If a black baseball player clearly shows himself to be managerial material, don't you think he'll get a shot at a manager's job?

Jackson: What does that mean? Is every white manager "managerial material"? Then how come they're always being fired? In America, a white man, no matter how dumb, is expected to boss a black man; but no black man, no matter how highly qualified, is allowed to give orders to a white man. If a white ballplayer like Eddie

Stanky is argumentative and aggressive, he's considered fiery. Therefore, he's a managerial prospect. But Jackie Robinson was fiery as hell, only they called it arrogance. He was an "uppity nigger." When Robinson left baseball, his accumulated knowledge about running bases, pitching, hitting and fielding went with him. It was a waste of a great baseball mind.

Playboy: You seem to be saying that unless a black man is docile, he can't survive; yet the mood of young blacks—including you—is anything but docile. Haven't the times changed?

Jackson: We have changed; I don't know about the times. White society still tries to impose a different code of behavior on blacks than on whites. What to me is an expression of confidence is to white folks an expression of defiance. The country is so used to black people smiling and bowing and acting unsure of themselves that when whites meet someone who confronts them and challenges their standards, they make harsh judgments. Now things are changing so fast that the hostility of white society toward a black man may lead to respect for him from the black community. For a white man to embrace you is for a black man to hold you suspect.

Playboy: You have been accused of cynically manipulating that new mood in your personal choice of dress and hair style. Do you think that if you didn't wear sideburns and a *dashiki,* but dressed conservatively and looked somewhat like a young Martin Luther King, that you could make it as a black leader today?

Jackson: Style—whether it's Afro or Ivy League—isn't crucial. Hell, there are kids around who look like Ché Guevara, but they still need their mommas to get them across the street. Because of all the losses we have suffered, black people are looking for *winners;* that's the only way to get their respect. And a winner is someone who successfully defies white America. The reason Joe Louis will always be respected in the black community is that at a time when other blacks couldn't even talk back to white people, Joe Louis was beating them up, knocking them down and making them bleed. When I do a TV show, I'm aware that every black watching is scoring me against the white opposition, as if I were in a fight. Every black man who has won the loyalty of his community has indicated some expression of defiance for the white man. Malcolm X is a good example. He could look Whitey straight in the eye and tell him he was lying. And Malcolm showed that even the most brutalized experience could be overcome.

Playboy: You obviously don't agree with those who felt that Malcolm was a disruptive force.

Jackson: Malcolm had become an apostle of peace after his trips to the Near East. America has a knack for killing her men of peace, while men of war continue to thrive. Malcolm's death also pointed up the futility of thinking in exclusively white-black terms. Blacks killed Malcolm, just as a black man betrayed Marcus Garvey and a black woman once tried to stab Dr. King. Black is not always good, just as white is not always bad. We confirmed that lesson at Resurrection City, where white Appalachians shared the mud with us while some blacks on U Street were asking The Man to run us out of town. And it was a black woman who started many of Adam Powell's troubles.

Playboy: The consensus among white liberals is that Adam Powell deserved his fate—and that he was a hindrance to the civil rights movement. Do you disagree?

Jackson: Absolutely. First of all, and to set the record straight, as head of the House Education and Labor Committee, Adam Powell was responsible for passing

over 60 pieces of significant social legislation—more
than any other of his virtuous colleagues have ever
done. But Adam is even more important, for a depressed black psyche, as a defier of white rules. Something happened to my dad in World War Two that
illustrates this. He was serving in France and Strom
Thurmond came to speak to his all-black regiment. The
Senator's message was that they were there to fight the
War, that they were not to bother any women; they
were to know their place. In other words, it was all right
for my father to risk his life to serve America, but he
was still a nigger. So when Adam Powell walked down
the halls of Congress with two white women on his arm,
just the outrageous defiance of it gave us gratification.
The appeal of that defiance will never be lost.

Playboy: That story touches on the strong sexual aspect
of racism. Both Malcolm X and Eldridge Cleaver have
expressed elaborate theories in which white sexual fears
are cited as a fundamental cause of race hatred. Do you
agree?

Jackson: Although sex is a crucial underlying cause of
prejudice and racial hatred, it is not relevant to the
black liberation movement. We will not allow the white
man's sexual problem to stand in the way of our freedom.

Playboy: Can you just ignore it?

Jackson: Let me explain it with some awful history. In
the South, when a slave ran away—thereby expressing
his manhood and independence—and he was caught,
the punishment for his first offense was whipping or
branding. If he ran away again, which was the clearest
way for him to assert himself, his punishment was likely
to be castration. The slave was told that he was inferior,
less than human and completely unappealing to the
white woman; but The Man still castrated him. That

says a lot about the psychosexual dilemma of the Southern white male. The other part of that dilemma was that because of his fear of black men, the white man had to desensitize white women. The white woman had to spiritually kill herself. For a white woman to see Jim Brown and not think of him as an attractive male means that the nerves are dead within her being. She dehumanized herself, because white men wanted it that way. But when the white man destroyed his relationship with his women, he got his satisfaction from the pursuit of money. So the white man perverted himself and his women.

If some great psychoanalyst had emerged 300 years ago, he might have solved some of the white man's problems and prevented the brutalization of blacks by whites. But we were not rescued, and the intervening 300 years have served to diminish the importance of sexual antagonisms and replace them with a more crippling form of racism. Today, racism is integrated into the ideology of capitalism. I said that the sexual aspect is irrelevant because even if sexual tensions disappeared tomorrow, capitalism would still require a racist ideology in order to maintain a cheap labor base. Racism provides a mechanism by which the slavemaster assured that society will have a ready supply of inferiors who can serve as slaves. Racism is as important to America's domestic colonialism as it was to foreign colonialism; it is an excuse to exploit and enslave a people because they have been defined as inferior. Colonialism is not built upon emotions; it is built upon behavior patterns that are designed to get a profit.

Playboy: Do you think, as some revolutionaries do, that capitalism will have to be destroyed in order to end racism?

Jackson: It is futile for us to think about ending racism;

that is a psychological problem that seems beyond our attempts to affect it. We are fighting to end colonialism —oppression and exploitation. That requires power. The civil rights movement is a lifetime struggle for power. A man who is impotent, no matter how courteous and pleasant looking he is, is told to wait in the lobby. But if you have power, you can be an illiterate boor with tobacco juice running down your face and they will open the door for you. As I said earlier, we are going to organize to exert power on the big corporations. We are going to see to it that the resources of the ghetto are not siphoned off by outside groups. Right now, black exterminating companies don't even get the contracts to kill the ghetto's rats. But that's going to change. If a building goes up in the black community, we're going to build it. And we're going to stop anyone else from building it. If we can't get into those construction unions, they're not going to get into our neighborhoods.

Playboy: But other neighborhoods don't control their business according to ethnic separation. They try to become part of what is traditionally called the American melting pot.

Jackson: I hear that melting-pot stuff a lot, and all I can say is that we haven't been melted. We've been getting burned on the bottom of the pot. We don't want anything that's different from the experience of the other ethnic groups. If you go into an Irish neighborhood, most of the businesses are run by Irishmen. The same is true in a Chinese or Jewish or Italian neighborhood. The difference between all of them and us is that they are all separate and independent groups, while we are separate and *dependent.* We want to control the vital elements of our lives: the school boards, the churches, the businesses, the police. The other groups are separate and control themselves, but they are separate and control *us* as well. That is a colonial situation. And the slums will exist as long as the colonists continue to turn a profit on them. As in any other revolution, we must fight for our independence.

Playboy: But Dr. King once said that his aim was to "break open the city," so that ultimately there would be no separate black and white communities. Have you forsaken that goal?

Jackson: No. But we recognize that a major part of the black community must first gravitate around itself, as other ethnic groups have done. In these areas, where our living together provides collective security, we ought to have the right to control it. But just as we have the private right to stay where we choose, we should also have the public right to participate in the public arena the way other people do. A man should choose where he wants to live, based on his income, or the fact that a house is close to his job, or because there's a good school nearby; he should not be refused because of his color. He should not be afraid of being bombed out by white bigots or of being harassed by police when he returns from work.

Playboy: Aren't the open-housing laws changing this?

Jackson: No. There is still segregation. In Chicago, blacks are 30 percent of the population, but they live on ten percent of the land. That congestion is inhuman and a prime target for exploitation by slumlords. People are cramped in body and spirit, and those who can't afford it are paying more for the space in which they live. We are locked away from the resources of the community. Black children who are sick are untended and left to play in their own filth in understaffed, ill-equipped hospitals. Four- and five-year-olds who were lucky enough to enter Head Start programs substantially raised their learning capacity, only to have it fall again as soon as they entered public school. Yet the teachers call the children incompetent. We have no choice about schools and hospitals, because public mobility is denied us. When a white mother decides to move because her neighborhood doesn't serve the needs of her children, the broker asks her where she would like to live; when a black mother faces that problem, she *knows* where she can live—and where she can't. In white communities, there are about 3000 people per square mile; in the ghetto, there are 30,000 people in each square mile. The overcrowding produces bent and perverted people. They are made to suffer so much pain that they feel no need to conserve themselves or their neighborhoods, so they decide to destroy. These are the unheard—until they riot.

Playboy: The majority of those who have participated in riots are in their teens or early 20s. Why?

Jackson: These kids have an awful lot of reasons for hating America. Their experiences with the dominant culture are nearly all negative: whether it be in school or a courtroom or applying for a job, they are being either deprived or discriminated against. This sense of resentment is acute, and it's just a matter of time before they give up on themselves and this country. Many of them already have. If Richard Nixon really cared about America's future, he'd be showing up at Operation Breadbasket meetings and offering to join us in the fight to reclaim these kids' minds and souls, because they are going to have a large effect on that future. He might at least give us equal time and attention with the moon shot.

Playboy: Weren't you impressed by the moon landing as a scientific achievement?

Jackson: The only thing that moon shot did for me was

turn my stomach. I was in a migrant worker's shack in Georgia a few weeks before the launch. It was about 115 degrees inside in the daytime. It had no toilet—not even an outhouse. No refrigerator, no running water. There was greasy butcher's paper over the space where there should have been windows. The shack was temporary residence for a family of four and they actually paid rent for it. If they hadn't rented it, they wouldn't have been allowed to work the harvest. They were all hungry. The kids' bodies were bloated and discolored. And they suffered from worms. This was *good* time for these people. When the harvest ends, they have to move on and they have nowhere to go. That Sunday night of the moon walk, in my mind's eye, I could see those poor, broken people walking four miles to the company store to watch the two astronauts jump around. Each step Armstrong took cost enough money to feed that family for 100 years.

America has spent 57 billion dollars since 1957 for the ego gratification of planting her flag on top of everyone else. One *tenth* of that was spent in the same period to inadequately feed the hungry. The psychological state of this nation is revealed by the fact that the men whose egos are swelled by putting a flag on a dead rock would not feel the slightest sense of accomplishment from the more humane task of feeding hungry people.

Playboy: Are you encouraged by Nixon's proposals about black capitalism?

Jackson: Not very much. It is a limited vision to make a few people rich, whereas SCLC's Poor Peoples' Campaign proposes a decent economic base for *all* people. Dr. King died talking about raising the level of dignity for all men. The difference between Dr. King and Mr. Nixon is the difference between a prophet and a politician. I don't believe the Government has plans for the extensive development of the black community. If it did, then the Job Corps would not have been curtailed recently. Even more serious is the Government's lack of understanding of the problems of the potential black businessman and its failure to develop programs to help him.

Playboy: White businessmen object to such demands on the grounds that blacks don't deserve Government considerations that aren't extended also to whites.

Jackson: The Government aids white businesses all the time—in the areas in which they are endangered. It subsidizes airlines and railroads. It sets up tariffs, to protect textile businesses from cheap foreign imports. The black man is endangered as a businessman because of his substandard education, and the Government should be offering technical and advisory services to blacks.

Playboy: What kind of services?

Jackson: There are some basic areas where the black businessman can use Government help. One is feasibility studies that will tell a man if his idea is sound. Another, of course, is capital, which should be lent according to the soundness of a business idea, rather than withheld reflexively in accordance with impossibly strict notions of what constitutes "a bad risk." If a black man came up with the idea for the next generation's Xerox, he probably couldn't get the money to develop it. Next, the Government should help him get his foot in the market's door, so that the black man can at least have a fair chance. This is one area in which Operation Breadbasket has been very successful; we've gotten chain stores such as Jewel and A & P to give shelf space to black products. Then the Government should provide real vocational training. Even if a black kid, who never intends to go to college, graduates from high school, he can't fix the wiring in the house, can't run a machine, can't lay a brick.

And the vocational training should apply also to those who are already running a black business. We helped increase a black man's business from $12,000 to $160,000 in four months. But he couldn't grow with it. He had to pull his business back down to the size of his mind; he had to feel the money, count it in his hands. He couldn't handle a balance sheet, couldn't write notes for working capital before his receipts came in. That man can't go to Harvard Business School—but if the Small Business Administration and President Nixon were serious, there'd be an operation Head Start for the black entrepreneur. The way it is now, a black with talent has to choose to work in the security of a big white company. And his sapped spirit will never produce anything on its own. Black businesses, on the other hand, are a step on the road to freedom. Black products are a focus for a pride in black ability. We can't just consume what the white folks decide to make for us. Consumption leads to fatness, but production leads to freedom. A producer is free to make decisions, but a man who only consumes is a prisoner whose decisions are made by others.

Playboy: Breadbasket's aims, if fulfilled, seem likely to create more middle-class blacks. Do you think there will be strong class divisions between black middle and lower classes as the former get farther away from the ghetto?

Jackson: I don't think we will have significant class divisions. No matter how wealthy he gets, the black man can rarely buy a house where he wants to; he is still subject to the whim of any white policeman who doesn't like his looks; he is still going to be tried, if accused of a crime, by a jury of his white nonpeers. And these facts bind him firmly with his destitute brother.

Playboy: How do you feel about the young militants' derisive notion that every successful black is an Uncle Tom?

Jackson: I think it's important to be sensitive to who Uncle Tom is. Uncle Tom is not our enemy. He grew up in the ghetto; he went to bad schools. He's a successful black hustler who bends and smiles before the white man in order to provide for his children He's not a man who sits around thinking up ways to hurt black people. There's nothing wrong with a Southern boy who grew up in a shack with an outhouse wanting a real home. The jobs we once picketed to get are now being derided as Uncle Tom jobs. But the black *bourgeoisie* is still very close to the roots, if for no other reason than the fact that in the colonial system, he can't get too far. Blacks don't move to white society for joy, fulfillment, good music or tasty meals. They move to get away from bad schools and apartments where the trash isn't collected. They aren't moving away from blacks but from the rats.

Playboy: Are you saying that there's no disunity among blacks?

Jackson: There *is* an unfortunate division among blacks now that is set off by a certain self-righteousness, a competition for being the blackest. But we must never forget that Nat Turner was middle class, as were Frederick Douglass and Dr. King—and even Stokely Carmichael. We will not be trapped into glorifying ignorance and poverty. That will not improve the lives of black people.

Playboy: Do you agree with young radicals who feel that blacks who are assimilated into the economy will become new cogs in the corporate machine?

Jackson: We want to create a new value system that will produce a generation of black liberators, not exploiters. You can't ask a black man not to work because America's value system is perverted. But I would hope that when the black man gets a job in a company that is part of the military-industrial complex, he will organize in a union that is as concerned with basic values as it is with decent wages. Instead of producing war matériel for an unjust and immoral war, the union could pressure the company into producing goods that will help and heal people. The virtuous and vicious aspects of our economy are interrelated. We produce more food and clothing—and guns—than we need; we have the capacity to save more people from malice and disease than any other nation in the history of the world, and to *kill* more people than any other nation in the history of the world. No one attacks our ability to build X-ray machines or washing machines. Our national priorities are the real problem.

Playboy: Can blacks change them?

Jackson: This is the challenge of Operation Breadbasket. The businessmen we help, for example, are discouraged from getting rich and leaving the ghetto. We develop profit sharing; we try to make it *our* company as much as the owner's. We encourage a dialog between owner and employee, and we encourage participatory democracy.

Playboy: Can Breadbasket help blacks outside the ghetto as well as within it?

Jackson: Yes. Let me give you an example of how it can work—a case of real soul power, where blacks had the integrity to stick out a crisis and aid one another

over thousands of miles. When the most recent Voting
Rights Bill was passed, black Alabama farmers found
that they weren't able to find markets for their products
anymore. Whites were retaliating for their new political
power. On top of that, George Wallace prevented them
from borrowing money, so they couldn't expand economically, because of the combined pressures of racism
and capitalism. There were 1500 of them—all farming
small plots. Instead of quitting, they formed the South-
west Alabama Farmers' Cooperative. They planted and
harvested their crops and then brought them to Chicago. We at Breadbasket then went to the supermarkets
in the ghetto and told the owners that they would either
put the brothers' products on the shelves or face boycotts. They accepted the produce. The brothers in Alabama could farm there and have an open outlet in
Chicago. We were able to do this out of a sense of
"peoplehood." That's my kind of black nationalism—
blacks helping one another on a national scale.

Playboy: Isn't it one of the great fears of Southern
whites that blacks—who outnumber them—will usurp
their place in society if they ever win enough economic
and political power?

Jackson: The problem here is that the poor white and
the poor black have mutual fear. Poor blacks fear that
if poor whites aren't eliminated, they won't be able to
eat, and the poor whites feel just the same way in reverse. The historical difference is that poor whites in the
South have controlled the police and the military and
have thereby maintained power over the blacks. We in
the Poor Peoples' Campaign believe that the basic anxiety of whites is an irrational fear of extermination—a
fear that can be removed with a guaranteed income,
with guaranteed medical care and education. Dr. King
was firm in his resolve that black power must be sec-

ondary to peoples' power. When the economic base of all the people is raised, racism will decline. As the Poor Peoples' Campaign gets stronger, racism will lose its hold on the consciousness of the white poor.

Playboy: Do you honestly think, as Dr. King did, that there's going to be a movement of the poor that will include whites, blacks, Puerto Ricans, Mexicans and Indians?

Jackson: It's inevitable. If our good sense doesn't connect us through affirmation, then America's greed will lock us together by negation. False racial pride has divided the lower class, but we must stop defining and separating ourselves because of skin color. We should define ourselves by our economic position and shift the fight from a horizontal confrontation of poor black versus poor white to a confrontation of "have" versus "have not." Dr. King could have been the suture that connected the various bones of the bottom classes. Just two weeks before his assassination, there was a meeting of a dozen representative ethnic groups in SCLC's Atlanta office. That was the beginning of something really new, and it is continuing. For just one example, Dr. Abernathy marched with Cézar Chávez and Operation Breadbasket supports the grape strike as if it were our own project, by boycotting and picketing Jewel Tea and other stores where California table grapes are sold.

Playboy: But do you really think that the white poor are going to join you?

Jackson: The white poor have always been distracted from demanding their rights; they've been too embarrassed to admit their deprivation. They've nourished themselves on the meager psychic diet of racism. But during the Illinois Hunger Campaign, we offered poor whites food and they digested it. In East St. Louis, Illinois, a white man named Hicks addressed a congregation of hunger marchers. Mr. Hicks has nine children and works five and six shifts of day labor a week but still can't make enough to feed his family or even to put a shack over their heads. Mr. Hicks and his family were taken in by black folks. They shared equally, and it was the first time in his life, he said, that he felt any sense of security. There are a lot more Mr. Hickses out there who just haven't realized yet that they don't have to suffer alone, that a massive cooperative effort by the poor class is the only answer. United in a class struggle, we can force the redistribution of wealth in America.

Playboy: The idea of class war, hot or cold, has always been associated with the theories of socialism. Do you think of yourself as a socialist?

Jackson: I adhere to the ideals of my religion—that the earth is the Lord's and its food was intended for all men. The trend of the world today—in Sweden, Guinea and Britain, for example—is toward some form of democratic socialism, where men eat because the ground is fertile. America stands in conflict with that trend by allowing a few people to control and distribute the food, rather than letting people eat because they are living. The truth, of course, is that this same America, where socialism is such a dirty word, is already operating in a sophisticated state of socialism for the rich, while the poor live in a crude state of classic capitalism.

Playboy: Please explain that.

Jackson: The people in this society who follow the Protestant ethic and work long hours by the sweat of their brow are the poor. They work at the hardest jobs and often still don't get enough money to pass the poverty level. Even when they try to break out, it's an attempt to start a street-corner business, where the rules of classic capitalism prevail. The poor storekeeper, for example, doesn't control his market through advertising; he can't float a bond issue and use other people's money to run his business. But the rich man has socialism. We've got 6536 farmers in this country who receive $25,000 not to work. That's socialism. The campuses expand, chopping pieces of land out of black neighborhoods, with the financial help of the National Education Act. Even wealthy schools for rich men's sons are state supported. The interstate highway program, none of which benefits those who can't afford a car, is 90 percent Federally financed. There wouldn't be a trucking industry without Government help. The list is endless and includes the oil companies and their depletion allowance, the railroads, the airlines and airports, the power companies. The rich talk about tax shelters and tariff protections, while the poor talk about sweat and blood.

Playboy: But isn't welfare a form of socialism for the poor?

Jackson: As it now stands, welfare is a form of humiliation. It is demeaning and dehumanizing. Men use money; welfare recipients use stamps. Men have privacy; welfare recipients have no privacy and can be visited any time of day or night. Their most intimate relationships can be called into question by people who are indifferent to them. Instead of abusing the poor, this nation has to understand that the welfare recipient is a product of the success of our economy. The unskilled black man whose job has been lost to technology today will be joined shortly by the unskilled white man whose job will be lost to the next technological advance. Either we see these men as having been freed by technology, perhaps to fulfill a creative role, or we see these men as having worked hard only to find themselves enslaved in poverty by the same technology. Whichever perspective one has, we must evolve a subsidy that will preserve these precious human lives, not destroy them as welfare has.

Playboy: Were you encouraged by President Nixon's new welfare proposals?

Jackson: I was thoroughly *dis*couraged. I watched Nixon the night he delivered that welfare address. My anger was tempered only by my incredulity at the immensity of his con job. He lied for nearly an hour and didn't even crack a smile. He asked the country to think of him as a great humanitarian, but we weren't fooled. Behind all those promises is the single fact that the states are going to retain control of most of the Nixon program. When the states had the power, black people couldn't vote, couldn't ride in the front of a bus, couldn't drink from any public water fountain, couldn't use any john they wanted. Now Nixon says to Thurmond and Stennis, "Take care of them poor folks." Right this minute, there are 40 states violating the welfare laws. We don't need a redistribution of welfare-disbursement stations in this country; we need a redistribution of wealth. The President challenged the poor to go to work, without saying what he would do to improve the lot of those who *can't* work. I'll be encouraged when the President challenges the rich to show their humanity and grant to the poor their basic rights as human beings.

Playboy: The white lower middle class is becoming quite vocal about its opposition to welfare in any form for those they characterize as too lazy to work. What's your reaction?

Jackson: The fact is that the poor work the hardest and have always done so. We made cotton king, cooked other people's food when we had none of our own, stooped to clean bathrooms. Now we are unskilled, because the schools don't teach us, because less money is spent on the education of blacks than is spent on whites. A state of despair has set in for those in the black community who have been told no too often, and perhaps they can never be healed. When white people say they know a man on welfare who is too lazy to work, I say that may be so. But the man they see is a dried-up prune. I ask them, "Did you see that man when he was a boy? Did you see him when he said, 'Momma, do you have a piece of bread?' Did you see him before hope was snuffed out by despair?" The white middle class is paying less tax money to support welfare mothers than it is to support the farm industry. I don't hear them complaining about that. The bulk of their tax money goes to subsidizing the rich and fighting wars abroad— wars fought by the sons of welfare mothers, not by the middle-class kids who go to college. The middle class invests in America with its tax dollars, but the poor have to invest their lives.

Playboy: Is it possible to raise a family on the funds provided by welfare? Many claim it isn't.

Jackson: Let me put it this way: If I give you 22 cents for a meal, you know pretty well what you're going to get to eat. I thought I knew what poverty was all about until I went on our hunger campaign. I saw children eating red clay. Doctors call it pica when people who don't get sufficient food eat things that have the appearance of food. I saw a mother give her child saltine and onions for breakfast and send her off to school on that. I saw a white mother with four kids, one of whom, a boy, had leukemia. He drank all the milk the family was allotted on a food-stamp supplement, and it wasn't enough even for him. She took him everywhere in a little wagon, the kind kids play with. He was frail and helpless, and the mother was exhausted; the entire family looked bloodless and frightened, as if they would never have a moment's joy. I can understand why they might feel that way, living as they must with the fact that there is a ceiling on the welfare allotment but no ceiling on the rent or the food prices or the amount of tragedy a family can suffer. The insufficient welfare funds are especially damaging to babies. Eighty percent of the brain develops during the three months immediately before birth and the first three years of life. The minds of welfare children, who cannot get enough to eat, are stricken early.

Playboy: Why don't welfare allowances provide adequate support?

Jackson: Welfare allotments tend to be about one third of the minimal standard of living as defined by the Government. In Texas, New York and California this year, even that meager appropriation was cut. Furthermore, rents and food prices are higher in poor areas than in middle-class areas, so the poor must spend more, even though they have less. The result of this deprivation is that the black child goes to school without breakfast, cannot afford lunch at school and cannot look forward to a decent supper at night. His hunger is such a distraction that he is not motivated to learn. All of these elements combine to place him farther and farther behind in school. He has no goals, no hero images, no sense of purpose or identity. He is physically weaker than his white contemporaries and probably sickly, because he doesn't get medical care.

Playboy: Earlier, you referred to the dominance of professional sports by black athletes. That doesn't fit with the image of physical weakness you just presented.

Jackson: Some men will thrive even in a prison camp, so it isn't surprising that you'll find an occasional black youth who overcomes his poverty. But the important reason for the dominance of black athletes is that a high proportion of black men—both those who ate well and those who didn't—directed themselves toward athletics because the field was more open to them than any other. More blacks tried to be boxers because there was no point in trying to be a bookkeeper or a mathematician. A black man whose mind might have had great aptitude for math wouldn't have been trained by a ghetto school. It made more sense for him to try to be a ballplayer, even a third-rate one, because it was so unlikely that he'd have a fair chance to be anything else.

Playboy: A persistent part of the white stereotype of the black man is that he runs faster and jumps higher than whites. But some anthropologists have claimed recently that there actually are genetic differences between white and black. Will this new evidence worsen the relationship between white and black?

Jackson: It won't affect us. The black man has never needed to believe that there are differences; that's a white man's problem. Our natures are the same. Our urges and drives as people are the same. Mankind has one father, and that's time. It has one mother, and that's nature. Both of these life processes are sound and consistent and universal. The third process is brotherhood, which is all messed up, because white folks have tried to withdraw from it. The eternal existential dilemmas of fate and death, guilt and condemnation, emptiness and meaninglessness are the same for all men. But our relationship, based upon distorted information peddled by white folks who reject the humanity of others, has been perverted.

Playboy: What are the psychological and cultural differences between white and black, if any?

Jackson: Slavery is our cultural heritage and it should

have been a thoroughly destructive one. But instead of
seeing ourselves as slaves from Africa brought over to
serve the lusts and wants of white people, a providential
way of seeing our slavery is that we are missionaries
sent from Africa by God to save the human race. Who
else is in a position so close to the Pentagon, the greatest threat to the world's existence? Who else is in a
position to literally redirect the most powerful economy
on earth? Who else in the world is in the enemy's
kitchen and his schoolroom? We are, perhaps, the only
ethnic group in the world that has the power to redirect
the destiny of white America. Neither China nor Russia
nor France nor England could do it. I don't look for
white folks to give me any direction. My experience has
taught me that white people are spiritually impotent, by
and large, because all they've really produced is a lot of
goods and services and a lot of death.

Playboy: That's a sweeping condemnation. Would you
say that the late Norman Thomas, to name one of many
men, was spiritually impotent?

Jackson: No, he was certainly a spiritual man, and you
could find others. The point is that such a man is not
representative of the white American culture. In fact,
the secondary roles that genuinely humane white people
are forced to play is indicative of what I'm trying to say.
Black society chooses to be led by its prophets, white
society by its hustlers. The men of highest sensibility in
white society find themselves rebelling from it—just as
blacks must rebel. America is known not for her capacity to love and heal but for her capacity to organize and
kill. America has an aristocratic, military definition of
man. American men judge themselves by their wealth,
status and power, not by their intelligence, compassion
or creativity. That's why the idea of looking for racial

equality here is a farce. To become equal to white folks would be to become part of the greatest tradition of killing in the history of the world.

Playboy: That might sound to some not only like a blatant overstatement but like a proclamation of black supremacy.

Jackson: I don't know what it sounds like, but I know what the record will indicate. There is no evidence of Africa invading Europe, of her early advanced civilizations killing or enslaving other nations. Historically, blacks have not been the aggressors in war, not even here in America. We did not mobilize to go to war for our long-overdue justice, but there have been wars of injustice waged against us. The profound men in this culture have been black—Frederick Douglass, for example, who was more pertinent than Lincoln on the subject of slavery and the liberation of mankind. And the crusader for justice in Mississippi was Medgar Evers, not Jim Eastland. In New York, Malcolm was pertinent, not Nelson Rockefeller, who did not bat an eye when he approved the welfare cuts. The one who cried out for peace in the world and meant it was not the white leader, President Johnson; it was the black leader, Dr. King. During the past 15 years, Dr. Abernathy has been more relevant than any American President. Blacks have striven for moral dignity and, by contrast with America's state of immorality, we appear to be moral supremacists, not black supremacists.

Playboy: The war in Biafra seems every bit as brutal as any other war. Black life there seems to be as cheap to blacks as you say it is to whites in this country.

Jackson: The Nigerians and Biafrans are fighting with white men's weapons. They are fighting a war that is based on a white man's division of Africa, and the cause of the division was an earlier economic colonialism. The war is an unfortunate aberration and the signs of white meddling are everywhere in it.

Playboy: During the 1968 teachers' strike in New York City, there was evidence of deep-rooted black hostility toward Jews. Is anti-Semitism consistent with your claim of black moral supremacy?

Jackson: In the first place, there were really few examples of black anti-Semitism, and these examples were blown out of all proportion by the teachers' union, which benefited by the dissemination of fear. More significantly, though, I don't think you can characterize blacks as anti-Semites. We have never been obsessed with the Jew as Christ killer. But our relationship with the Jew has changed as the black movement has changed. When blacks began to confront the Southern white power structure, most of which was WASP Baptist and Methodist, Jews gave us great support, both financial and moral, and a real kinship developed. But once the movement moved North and the problem was defined not just in terms of social segregation but in terms of economic colonialism, the Jew began to be revealed as landlord and shopowner. Of course, he is more conspicuous than the Protestant, because his name is likely to identify his ethnic background. And he is also more sensitive: It is much easier to embarrass or humiliate a Jew than either a Protestant or a Catholic, because, unlike the others, the Jew immediately identifies with suffering.

As blacks have emerged, the Jew has been there as teacher and shopkeeper, and there has been an inevitable friction. But I think the mood of the blacks is more one of anti-colonialism than of anti-Semitism. For blacks cannot afford to be anti-people; no matter who the people are, they must be anti-evil. I think the Jews who are most concerned about anti-Semitism, however, should keep in mind that blacks have not exploited Jews *at all*. We have not owned anything in the Jewish community—no clothing stores, banks, food stores. The Jewish community, like most others, has a left and a right wing—some who operate in a tradition of justice and others who violate that tradition. Rather than develop a persecution complex, perhaps it ought to expend some of the energy it spends complaining about black anti-Semitism on the Jewish merchants who are known to be exploiters and tend to pull the reputation of the Jewish community down.

Playboy: Jews, along with Irish, Italian and other immigrant groups, are often held up as an example that the blacks, if they were industrious enough, could emulate. The premise is that those groups were poor and lived in ghettos but were able to overcome that experience and join the American mainstream. Why hasn't that happened to blacks?

Jackson: First, those groups came here voluntarily and were always free. We came here involuntarily and are still not wholly free. The other immigrant groups are white and could lose their identity and merge with the majority when it was necessary; with a few technical skills or a decent education, it was a simple matter for them to bypass prejudice. Their families were not destroyed and their sense of historical continuity was preserved. Most importantly, they did not suffer the tremendous color stigma of the white man.

Historically, there was a conspiracy to hold us down. We were enslaved, then locked into plantations, as we are now locked into ghettos. When America finally released our physical bonds in 1865, it was as if we had been in jail for 200 years and were let out without a road map or a dime to go to the city. There was no attempt to help us overcome the psychological or economic hardships of slavery. Many blacks didn't survive; and of those who did, most had to pervert their natures —become invisible men, as Ralph Ellison wrote, become hidden, for it was too dangerous to assert one's real identity, one's manhood. No other ethnic group was faced by a hostile white society that wanted to castrate it both physically and psychologically.

Playboy: Then today's black militance is a quest to resurrect that manhood.

Jackson: One thing that I have to say right off is that there's nothing to be learned from the white man's idea of manhood. An American man is identified by his weapon, by what he controls. American men are obsessed; they are gratified by making money they can't even spend, which is a kind of emptiness of the soul. Real manhood should be defined by the ability to help and to heal, by an extension of the mind, by knowledge exerting its power over ignorance. Real manhood comes from helping others be free, by breaking the bonds of slavery.

Playboy: Do you mean that metaphorically?

Jackson: Only partly. Many of us have internalized slavery and behave like slaves, responding to the slave-master when he calls. In some communities, we must fight our own people because they maintain the slave institutions. They are still in awe of Pharaoh and are afraid to confront him. That is a form of slavery. The slave psychology works on a subtle level that warps the black mind. It has been drummed into blacks that whites are the creators and producers and thinkers. Blacks whom we might have respected were taken from us. George Washington Carver's image is one of a docile creature—an old man in a laboratory, bowing to a white child. The fact is that he developed over 300 elements from the peanut and almost singlehandedly revived the Southern economy. A black man, Daniel Hale Williams, was the first open-heart surgeon. There are many, many other examples, but the point is that blacks never knew about them. It was easy to preserve the image of the dull-witted, slow-talking and -thinking black bumbler. There is still a need among blacks for white validation of their efforts. If Tommie Smith and John Carlos had a race tomorrow and both broke their records for the 220-meter dash, and the race were held on a black campus, where all the judges were black, black people wouldn't believe it—and neither would whites. But if it were a white track meet, there'd be no problem. As for our churches, they gave up their soul— and I mean that in both senses—to copy white church styles. That's why at Operation Breadbasket meetings, which are deeply based in religion, we have a band and a Gospel choir and consciously try to capture the rhythm of our people.

Playboy: Is the slave psychology the reason for your own fieriness and emotionalism when you address a black congregation?

Jackson: Certainly. I am seeking converts—not necessarily to religion, although there's that, too. But I want to make my people realize their own selfhood. I begin each service with a chant that says, "I am *somebody.*" It also says, "I may be poor and I may be on welfare, but I am *somebody.*" Because black people have to learn that they have rights just because they're alive. They've got to stop putting themselves down because of an induced inferiority complex. The slave psychology was apparent when Dr. King came out against the Vietnam war. He had all the credentials you could ask for: Nobel Prize winner, an international leader, a scholar and a Ph.D. But blacks said he had a lot of audacity; he's a preacher and should confine himself to civil

rights. But when Robert Kennedy and Senator Mc-
Govern took the same position, then it was all right.
And after Memphis, when SCLC's James Bevel expressed Dr. King's contempt for capital punishment, he
was scorned by the black community. He said Dr. King
would have wanted James Earl Ray rehabilitated, would
have said to fight hatred but spare the hater. Bevel also
pointed out the irony of trying to obtain justice by
sacrificing a two-bit waiter for a billion-dollar black
prophet. But blacks said he was crazy. Then Ted Kennedy said that Sirhan's life should be spared because his
brother Robert was against capital punishment. The
black community immediately cited Teddy as a great
man of justice who didn't become vindictive in the face
of personal tragedy. This is a painful indication of our
self-contempt. We must stop looking to whites to validate our worth: we must look within for beauty and
strength and courage.

Playboy: Your own self-confidence, as contrasted with
Dr. King's humility, seems to be of formidable dimensions, and you've been accused of messianic impulses.
Do you see yourself as the next great national black
leader?

Jackson: First of all, Dr. King was not humble: he was
forthright and audacious. He was killed for challenging
white power. As for me, I am confident of my abilities
as a social analyst, but I have no illusions of grandeur.
My job is to proclaim liberty, to preach unity, to bind
up broken hearts. I am just taking care of my assign-
ment. Besides, anyone in public life in this violent society who would make such long-range plans is a fool.

Playboy: You certainly expose yourself to the risk of
assassination as much as any man. Do you think that
you may be subconsciously seeking martyrdom?

Jackson: I want to live. I've got no hang-up with that.

But a man must be willing to die for justice. Death is an inescapable reality, and men die daily, but good deeds live forever. An assassin believes that you can kill the dream by killing the dreamer; that is an error.

Playboy: Would you have any special message to leave with black people if you were killed?

Jackson: Yes. Don't send flowers. Don't come around with your tears. Picket. Go to P. T. A. meetings. Fight for higher wages. If I die tonight and you wake up tomorrow, make the most of it.

Playboy: You've been quite sick a few times this year, once with a form of anemia, and also with some very debilitating viruses. Yet you hardly let up on your activities, rarely sleep and constantly drive yourself toward exhaustion. Why?

Jackson: Because I have a sense of urgency about what has to be done. It is not the thought of death so much as it is the crying need for justice. Perhaps both facts motivate me simultaneously. I do feel that I have to fulfill my work in an appointed time. I would like to sleep, but ideas come to me in the night and wake me. I think I'm drawing my stamina from a spiritual source that has been allotted to me; for that reason, I have no choice but to keep on driving. You can't devote the energy necessary to confront Pharaoh unless you are spiritually consumed by the need for liberation. But that is social consciousness, not a messianic need to be worshipped. There are some aspects of glory attached to having the privilege to lead, but none of the agony ever gets publicity, because television cameras don't record people tossing and turning in their beds at night.

Playboy: Inasmuch as the Southern Christian Leadership Conference is basically a religious group, it's understandable that religion plays a large role in your life.

But what appeal can the church have for a cynical 20-year-old kid from the ghetto?

Jackson: The black church is relevant because it has provided a home for our rebellion. It has cherished our people. The white church, on the other hand, worships *worship,* not Christ nor love nor brotherhood. God is very sick here; the God of justice and liberty is almost nonexistent. Christianity is universal, but the American flag flies higher than the cross in American churches; and when wartime comes, universal love goes out the window. If Americans had a true God consciousness, they could not leave the church on Sunday and shield their eyes from the hungry.

But there is extraordinary relevance in the actual teaching of Christ. If you love people, you will not destroy them in war; if you love deeply, you will distribute the goods of the earth that the Father provided, so that people will be fed and housed. That is the Jesus I identify with. His was a program for feeding the hungry, clothing the naked and giving company to the lonely.

Playboy: In the past, some critics have regarded Christianity as an impediment to black liberation; blacks were supposed to have been content to get their reward in heaven. Did you consciously evolve this activist approach to Christianity?

Jackson: My religious philosophy can be summed up in an old Southern story about two farmers. One farmer was most concerned about his duty to God. He attended church every day and worked his fields in the afternoon. His neighbor never attended church and never paid any attention to religious rituals. The first farmer was just eking out a living; the second farmer was getting twice the harvest from a lot the same size. Finally, the first farmer said to the second, "Brother, I don't understand. I've been working this land and doing my duty for God and asking His help. I go to church each day. Yet I can't get ahead at all. You never take care of your religious obligations, yet you're getting all the bounty. What am I doing wrong?" The second farmer answered, "I don't know what you're talking to God all the time for. He doesn't know anything about farming. This place didn't produce *anything* when He had it all to Himself." That's the whole thing. God made it but man has to go out and do it.

Playboy: In our interview with Dr. King four years ago, he said the aims of SCLC were removing the barriers of segregation, disseminating the creative philosophy of nonviolence and total integration of the Negro into American life. How much have things changed since then?

Jackson: Four years ago, SCLC was a Southern movement primarily concerned with social segregation. Blacks were defined as less than human and were not allowed to participate in public. We were "boys" and our goal was to be recognized as men. That drive was aimed at creating a moral consciousness, and one of our slogans was "Save the soul of America." I think that one of the reasons for impatience among blacks today, and the reason for the appeal of violence, is that we never before knew just how awful the secrets locked in America's soul really were. We didn't know then that America would bomb a people to pieces and side with the oppressors in order to preserve her financial investments. We didn't know then that the Northern liberal had better manners than Bull Connor but that his institutions were no less thoroughly racist. And we didn't know then that the capitalists who slandered us with cries of "Communist" were living high off the Government hog, while we were starving in the streets.

This education of ours has led to a change of mood. Our first concern now is not white America's soul; it is black America's body. We are justified in our impatience, because that body is hungry. When Moses had his illumination and realized that he could confront Pharaoh, the Bible says that Moses had to take his shoes off, because now he was on holy ground and the bushes were burning. Actually, the bushes were not burning; Moses was burning. His eyes were aflame—the skin had come off them. Black people today are burning; the skin is off their eyes. The movement is now in a resistance phase and we will no longer cooperate with the white slavemaster. Either we are going to live or America is going to die. The ghetto experience has not been a satisfying or a useful one, but it has given us inner resources —the ability to do much with very little.

I read in the white press how black people are dispirited and confused. White editorial writers claim that the civil rights movement is fragmented. That is not true; the movement is very together: The NAACP, which just saved the Voting Rights Bill, is doing its thing in Southern courts; the Urban League is doing its thing in industry; the Panthers are feeding kids in the streets: SCLC just had a political victory in Greene County, Alabama; Operation Breadbasket is thriving. It is white America that is at the crossroads. If she does not join us in the resurrection of her soul, in the fulfillment of her dream for all her people, then I foresee a day when little children in a schoolroom on the moon read in the history books about an empire that crumbled because all her power and might of arms could not cure the immoral greed that diseased her spirit.

9

TOWARD AN OVERALL ASSESSMENT OF OUR ALTERNATIVES

Robert S. Browne

AWARE AND CONCERNED Brothers and Sisters—It is with great humility that I have accepted this invitation to deliver the keynote address for this important conference on Black Economic Development. We are all aware in what a critical period we black people in America now find ourselves. In the richest nation which the world has ever known, we find ourselves in a position of relative impoverishment. In a nation which boasts of its democratic processes, we find ourselves relatively powerless. In a nation which worships education as the magic key to success, our children are going unlettered. In an era of global nationalism, we are a people without a nation.

Obviously I have only begun to enumerate a few of the ways in which we are a disadvantaged people in this society. And indeed, there is nothing which I have

Robert S. Browne teaches Economics at Fairleigh Dickinson University and is Director of the Black Economic Research Center. Professor Browne delivered this paper as the keynote speech at the National Black Economic Development Conference held in Detroit in April 1969.

stated which Frederick Douglass, or Booker T. Washington, or Dr. Du Bois could not have declared with equal validity 69 or more years ago, as we entered upon this cataclysmic twentieth century. Indeed, they did make many of these very observations to groups not unlike this one. But I feel there is a difference today— not merely the obvious difference that for us today is real whereas they are history—but a qualitative difference which derives from the differing mood of black people generally. I sense that today's blacks, and especially the younger ones, are a new breed of black person. I sense that the old passivity and dependency psychology has been replaced by a psychology of independent action and I sense that the old gradualism has been replaced by a new urgency. And I also suspect that the several hundred people in this auditorium enjoy a capacity for implementation which far surpasses that of any audience which Douglass or Washington or Du Bois ever addressed.

It might of course be argued that the obstacles to black achievement have increased at least as much as has our potential for achievement. I would not agree however. Our oppressors are probably no more vicious than they ever were; naturally their desperation can be expected to increase as they feel more threatened by our successes in fighting free from their grasp, but this is inevitable. Meanwhile, the general world situation has evolved in a manner more favorable to our cause. We have sympathetic allies in every corner of the globe, and modern communications insures that world opinion remains constantly apprised of the major happenings in our noble struggle.

However, lest I mislead you into thinking that my address will be cast in an optimistic vein, allow me to move on to some more sobering considerations. The subject of my talk is "the need for formulating an economic plan for Black people." What is an economic plan? The term initially gained its popularity from its usage by the Soviet Union.

In 1928, about a decade after the 1917 revolution, the Soviet Union announced that it was launching a 5 year plan for economic development. Since that time it has undertaken several more such plans, and the practice has been widely copied by other Socialist countries as well as by many non-socialist countries such as India and many of the smaller nations. Indeed, such plans have become a regular part of the economic development process for a growing number of nations. Although differing in some details, the heart of these economic plans is the setting forth of specific goals to be achieved by a certain date, and some plan for attaining these goals. Goals are likely to be such things as: achieving a certain level of industrial productivity in designated categories, a certain level of agricultural production, a certain volume of exports, a certain rise in per capita income, lowering illiteracy by "x" percent, training "x" number of teachers, graduating so many doctors, etc. Obviously, such a plan must be internally consistent if it is to succeed, i.e., a large increase in agricultural production cannot be achieved unless plans are also made for producing (or importing) the necessary fertilizer, farm equipment, etc. Considerable research and data collection must precede the making of any economic development plan so that the goals will in fact be within the realm of possibility.

Does such an economic plan have meaning for black people in America? It seems to me that the answer is both yes and no. The answer is no because this type of a plan assumes the existence of a nation which has title to a cluster of contiguous resources and which exercises sovereignty over both itself as a community and over its members, who must feel themselves to be a part of this community. This sovereignty may be exercised either by consent or by coercion, but it must be effective if there is to be a nation. In effect, there must be a government with the power to govern. Short of this there can be no sovereignty, no nation, no economic development plan in the customary sense of the word.

Black America clearly fails all of these tests. The concepts of gross national product, imports and exports, agricultural or industrial output, etc., are not only not measurable for the black community; they have no meaning. In a rather crude fashion we can measure black purchasing power, the capitalization of black owned business establishments. And with extreme difficulty we might succeed in measuring black savings and black land ownership. Next year the census bureau will presumably attempt to measure the magnitude of the black population and will view with alarm its rate of increase, but I suggest that these magnitudes at present have little meaning in a national sense. It may be quite useful to get these measurements—indeed, urgent to do so—but the mere gathering of such data will not create the necessary conditions for nationhood or for an economic development plan. We are not yet a consciously cohesive community; we do not have sovereignty over ourselves as individuals; we do not have sovereignty over ourselves as a community. That is to say, we cannot draw up final rules for governing ourselves, for taxing ourselves, for conducting foreign relations and trading, for law enforcement, for property rights, for immigration and emigration, nor can we establish our own monetary unit. No, we are far from enjoying the basic prerogatives of nationhood, and despite the presence at this conference of some distinguished brothers who are doing ground-breaking work along these lines, I sense that this conference is not primarily to be concerned with the question of whether national sovereignty is desirable for blacks or how it can be achieved.

Rather, it seems to me, we have been brought here to discuss the more modest question of what is achievable by black people within the existing limitations of our *not* enjoying national sovereignty. That is, given the reality that we are, for the moment, inseparably attached to the larger, white, capitalistic American society, what are the most promising techniques which we can utilize to maximize black well-being.

Admittedly, this is a much more modest objective than the building of a black nation. It is clearly not an objective which will bring black people a major degree of control over their destinies. But it may put some additional bread on their tables and ease some chronic illnesses and therefore it is probably worth doing. For the achievement of this more limited objective I think that the concept of an economic plan can have considerable significance—obviously not the classical type of economic planning appropriate to an independent nation, but it is of the utmost importance that black people sit down and take inventory of where we are, where we hope to get to, and what series of steps seem most likely to get us there. Clearly, this conference did not convene in order to discuss simple band-aids which might be applied to some of the more painful sores on the black community. As a matter of fact, the white establishment has not been ungenerous with its band-aids—but any child knows that a band-aid is of little help when the limb is broken and bleeding profusely. Surgery may be necessary but short of that, major treatment is certainly called for. The task then of this conference, it seems to me, is to begin to prescribe that treatment. I am even hesitant to suggest that the conference should spend very much time diagnosing our malady, for we have been diagnosed thousands of times and I suspect that there is little new to be said on that count.

Essentially, the illness is that black people have no handle on the basic levers or sources of power in this country which I conceive to be six in number: (1) Accumulations of private wealth,—if you want to know who these families are I refer you to the May, 1968, issue of *Fortune* magazine, where most of them are listed together with an estimate of their assets. (2) Some 200 major corporations, most of whose annual incomes far exceed the budgets of most of the nations of Africa. The annual revenues of General Motors Corporation are larger than the gross national product of all but the top 15 of the nations of the world. (3) The military-industrial complex, centered in the Pentagon and obviously overlapping with the 200 largest corporations which I have just cited. (4) The federal and state governmental apparatus. (5) The federal legislative apparatus. (6) The crime syndicate. In deference to our host city I might add a close seventh—organized labor.

We lack access to these levers of control because of a combination of reasons, the main one being of course the history which we have experienced in this country. When the country was being divided up and raped, we were slaves. Indeed, we were part of the very property which was being divided and raped—literally. So we didn't get in when the melon was being cut and now almost the only way to get a really significant hunk of it is to wrest it away from someone else. We also lack access because we are numerically too small a group, and too dispersed, to have been able to seize control of any one of these levers. This lack of access to the instruments of power, supplemented by white America's vicious racial prejudice toward black people, has led to our perpetual impoverishment, our self-hatred and psychological insecurity, our poor educational attainment, and our social disorganization.

If this diagnosis is correct, and I suspect that it is a diagnosis to which most blacks would subscribe, the question then arises: Should our attack be focussed on the causes of the malady or on the symptoms? Do we focus on raising black peoples' wages, enlarging their education and skills, overcoming their psychological insecurities, and building up their social organization? Or do we focus on the causes of our poverty and degradation, namely, our powerlessness, our lack of access to the levers of power in the society?

There will be a natural tendency to respond by saying "Attack the causes, not the symptoms." This is obviously what we usually do in medicine and I am quite sympathetic with this view. If only surface manifestations are changed while the underlying causes are left intact there is always the likelihood of a re-eruption of the malignancy. Realistically speaking, however, I see very limited possibility for our grasping the levers of control in this society. True, we have an excellent potential for exercising a sort of negative power, a limited veto so to speak, over how the white establishment uses its power. And we should work toward building this sort of negative power, essentially I suppose via the electoral process but not forgetting that our brothers in the streets have been rather creative about devising other techniques as well.

If we were to decide to go after the causes of our oppression, the sole avenue which might offer some hope for our grabbing a tenuous hold onto one lever of control, and an avenue which could serve a dual purpose of also helping us toward achievement of black nationhood, would be for blacks to capture control of one or more state governments. Unlike control of a municipality, control of a state government not only offers tremendous opportunities for developing an extensive corps of black technicians but also provides black people with a somewhat viable economic unit from which to build a tangible sense of community and of cultural autonomy. Where today are the black men who can design, build, and operate giant bridges, hydro-electric installations, water works and sewage disposal plants, massive port facilities, and other basic elements of the physical infra-structure of a modern society? If there are such people, and they can't be many, they are lost in a vast white ocean. There is no identifiable corps of blacks with these capabilities. Perhaps as a result, we have few blacks studying these skills. I have never forgotten how, in 1961, at the height of the Lumumba era, I was asked by an official of the Congolese government if I could recommend about 60 black mining engineers to come to the Congo to take over the direction of the Katanga mines from the Belgians. I hardly need to tell you that I was unable to produce even one such person. Indeed, as far as I could determine, there was no record of any blacks having finished from the Colorado School of Mines, which is perhaps the major institution for such study in this country. Mining engineering is of course only symbolic for an entire range of very basic technical activities which it would rarely occur to a black youngster to pursue, but which black possession of a state government might offer some access to. Hopefully, the Cleveland and Gary experiences, though they may be mere tokens of black control, and other black-run municipalities soon to come, will provide vitally needed opportunities for our black youth to gain some new skills and experiences. But a city is a relatively limited economic unit; it is usually not a viable financial unit these days; and physically a city is an extremely vulnerable unit in that it raises no food and is totally dependent on outsiders for its external communications. Thus it could not serve even as a symbolic homeland for black people—nor could a series of such enclaves. For me, the currently popular "parallel economy" concept takes on meaning not with black control of a series of geographically separated communities or cities but only with black control of a unit at least as large as a state. One avenue of effort by this conference then might be to explore the feasibility of a legal black takeover of one of the 50 states. Such a program would require extensive research and planning; it would require channeling millions of dollars into a concentrated voter registration drive in the designated state; the quiet buying up of large properties and the provision of an economic base for attracting black immigrants, etc. The New Towns provision of the Housing Act of 1968 might be of some use here, but needless to say, once the whites realized what was happening the resistance would be substantial. And let me reiterate that such an effort, although I put if forth as a form of direct thrust for real power in America, would—even if highly successful—represent the accretion of only a modest amount of additional power for blacks. But it would enormously enhance our capability for further advance.

Let us, however, return to our consideration of whether we are better off to focus our attack on the causes of our disadvantage or on the symptoms. Can we launch an effective, direct attack on black poverty, black illiteracy, black insecurity despite our exclusion from the national power structure? I feel that we can. Our achievements will be of limited scope and will certainly not bring into being The Black Nation. But in putting some more bread on the table, in bringing us a greater degree of self-reliance, it will justify itself. It is in this sense that the numerous local development projects, small business programs, job training, consumer education, vocational guidance, school improvement and other community programs are all helpful. I believe such limited goals to be achievable because they do not threaten the superestablishment, the six power centers which I earlier specified. Achieving these limited goals may require expropriating some local landlords and businessmen, it may undermine some petty white racketeers and party hacks, it may deny some government-salaried jobs to some white middle class professionals, and it may weaken some racist union locals. But none of these groups are part of the national power structure anyway. The superestablishment, recognizing that blacks must be placated in some way, will be prepared to sacrifice the small fry local white exploiters so that it may continue uninterrupted with its global strategies. Thus we are presented an opportunity and a danger. The opportunity is to utilize our wits to exploit this willingness of the national power structure to meet some of our demands at the expense of the local exploiters. The danger is that we may find ourselves unwitting collaborators in a system which does long run damage to our self-interest. It is a tricky bag in which we niggers find ourselves.

Certainly we must assume control of our communities. Certainly we must acquire ownership and control of income producing properties, and most especially those located within our communities. The real estate, the businesses, the public facilities, must belong to the community in some form or another. Racketeering, prostitution, the numbers—if they are to continue—

must be put into the hands of the community. Education must be made more effective for black children. We must develop some industry. A larger portion of tax revenues must flow through our hands. I will not dwell on this because I suspect most everyone here agrees. But the implications of some of these demands cut many ways. Fifty per cent of federal tax revenues currently go into military expenditures. We are already getting a healthy share of the portion of these expenditures which go for enlisted men's salaries. Do we want to increase this share? Do we want to lobby Washington to award a few defense contracts to the black community so that we can make tanks and napalm to be used on black Africans—and on us? Do we want more of our black brothers in the State Department and the CIA if in fact it means that they will be flying about the world carrying out the Pentagon's repressive policies toward non-white nations?

What I am suggesting is that any significant economic development which we achieve will come about largely through political maneuvering, and we must therefore be very together and know exactly what we are doing. There is considerable resistance among black intellectuals to the concept of black capitalism and strong support for some sort of communal or cooperative ownership. This is desirable I think, but there is a risk of exaggerating the importance of such institutional differences.

In a capitalist, imperialist society, is a cooperatively owned Standard Oil Company likely to be any less exploitative than a privately owned one? If so, is it likely to succeed for very long? To repeat what I suggested earlier; the amount of self-determination which we can achieve while remaining a part of white, capitalistic American society is extremely limited and we should clearly understand this. Otherwise, there is likely to be great disappointment. It is probably true that black control of our communities may provide us a much broader power base than we now have from which to attempt to make a leap to the power table. But it is far from being a guarantee that we can successfully make such a leap.

I do not bring you answers; if so, the Conference could be just about winding up now. Rather, I bring you questions . . . questions which you must wrestle with today and tomorrow, and perhaps for some time to come. I have purposely avoided detailing specific actions which we might take, such as forming black construction unions, demanding a guaranteed income, channeling black savings into the community, and many other tasks which you will certainly be taking up in your workshops.

In developing plans for dealing with these specifics, however, may I point out that an economic plan is not a plan unless it comes to grips with the question of priorities. A shopping list of desirable things to be done is not a plan. To be a useful guide, the plan must have, first of all, clearly defined goals. Fanon, incidentally, in his revolutionary writings, placed great stress on the importance of being clear about your goals and being certain that the populace clearly understands the goals. Secondly, a development plan must have an overall logic, it must recognize the interdependence of each part with every other, it must state what is to be done first, what next, etc. Developing such a plan is an enormous task. It can't be completed in a week or a month, and in a sense such plans are never really completed because they must be flexible enough to change as the dynamics of the situation change. For blacks in America the question of an economic plan is further complicated by the fact that no group is likely to be given a mandate to draw up such a plan. Personal and institutional jealousies as well as valid ideological factionalism within the black community insures that no development plan will be accepted as satisfactory by all segments of the black population. It is a source of some distress to me that the head of one major national black organization intimately involved in economic development work complained to me that he had not been invited to attend this conference. I do not know if he was telling me the truth, but I do feel strongly that at this stage we should be inclusive. Nevertheless, this conference will have made an unprecedented contribution to black economic development if it seriously explores some of the grand issues which must necessarily be raised by such a planning effort.

For instance, it is believed that black people in the South have been selling their land holdings—sometimes rather substantial ones—and moving to cities; an action which is perhaps justified from the point of view of the individual but which may be contrary to the best interests of black as a group. Such questions demand exploration and research. If it appears that such actions are in fact harmful to us then we might need to develop a fund to purchase such land and to decide its disposition on the basis of some rational black program. In exploring such an undertaking one should consider what resources blacks already have which might be useful. For example, there are a half dozen or more land grant Negro colleges in the South: Prairie View, Alcorn, A&T, Tennessee A&I, etc. What are these schools doing with regard to rural black populations? What should they be doing? What can we get them to do, and how? All such questions can be meaningfully explored as part of a black economic development plan.

On yesterday afternoon another national conference on black economic development opened in New York—organized by white academic and money interests. I attended yesterday's deliberations, which were participated in by about 30 white and 30 black persons from around the country. Obviously, a bi-racial conference of that nature has certain built-in inhibitions, a principal one being that black economic development cannot be discussed separately from black political development, and blacks don't easily discuss this with whites.

But within its limitations, the conference was instructive. One of the brothers who was there but who was also invited to be here summed up his dilemma by saying that he couldn't decide whether it was more instructive to listen to the folks who had the dough or to those who were trying to get it away from them. (Actually, we need people to do both.) The spectrum of black opinion at that conference is probably less broad than this audience here. But I did meet two or three beautiful cats whom I had never heard of before, and there are probably more whom I didn't meet. The same thing has already began to happen to me here. I am really struck by the endless numbers of sharp, dedicated, together black guys who are appearing as if from nowhere. This suggests to me an additional benefit of an economic plan.

It is possible that the arduous task of forging an economic plan for black people, which would necessarily involve the intense interaction of most of these brothers with one another, could begin to produce the degree of unity which we so desperately need for the next stages of our liberation process.

In conclusion then, I suppose that the meat of my address has been that the first step in black economic development is not economic at all, but political. There is no question of "pulling ourselves up by our boot-straps." We have no bootstraps. We are starting with so few economic resources of our own that our tactic must be to utilize cleverly what strength we do have, namely, the political force of 25 million potentially united black minds, for extracting some economic resources from those who do have them. In many cases, of course, the resources morally belong to us anyway. But obtaining control of them will not be easy. A commitment even prior to the political one is implied in my statement, however, for I referred to our political force being based on 25 million potentially united black minds. Achieving a substantial degree of unity is an obvious prerequisite for rendering the political force effective as a lever for extracting resources. As Harold Cruse well said: our revolution must take place on three levels: cultural, political and economic. As this conference proceeds with its discussions focussed on economic issues I feel certain that the cultural and political—which is to say ideological—factors will inescapably impose themselves into your framework. It is inevitable and essential that they do so. But ideology is divisive as we all know, and can paralyze us totally. Therefore, as we begin this important work here this weekend I feel it to be of foremost importance that we recognize the tremendous implications of what we are about and that we approach our task soberly, humbly, and with a spirit of tolerance and black love.

I would urge that each of us concentrate our efforts on discovering what are the short run tasks that we can find common agreement on—irrespective of the fact that the brother who is pushing any particular program may indeed be our bitter personal rival or ideological opponent. Although we have had rather tragic experiences with black spokesmen and black cabinets in the past—whether Booker T. Washington, Mary McLeod Bethune, or the Civil Rights Leadership Conference—I can't help but feel that a great deal could be gained were we able to develop a united position on at least some aspects of how we would like to see government and private money used in the black community. This would be at least the beginnings of an economic plan.

Brothers and Sisters, what you do here this weekend may significantly influence where black people go from here. Shoulder your responsibilities well! UHURU!

10

THE CHURCH AND THE
THIRD WORLD

João Da Veiga Coutinho

CAN THE CHURCH cope with the consciousness of the
Third World? In the dialogue between rich and poor
which must come in the wake of decolonization, is the
body of Christians able to play any significant role?
Note that the question is asked about the "Church," not
about individual Christians. It is occasioned by the
efforts of the hierarchy to play a role in this dialogue
and to involve the laity in the increasingly turbulent
confrontation. The Church is visibly trying to adjust its
behavior to the new mood of the poor. Taking its cue
from secular agencies, in its programs for the underpriv-
ileged it is shifting its policies from service to self-help.
Simultaneously, an intellectual change seems to be oc-
curing among some theorists who are beginning to in-
voke justice rather than charity as the basis of the
Church's commitment. This new attitude, it is suggested, is not only more in keeping with changed rela-

*João Da Veiga Coutinho is a staff member of the Center
for the Study of Development and Social Change, Cambridge, Massachusetts.*

tionships among men and nations, but with the Gospel itself.

At this point one suspects that there has been some mystification. If, in the name of the Gospel, charity is being shelved and justice put in its place, the question arises: has not something happened to the notion of charity? And if it has, is not the same fate likely to overtake the idea of justice? The object of the present article is to take these questions seriously and to examine these suspicions.

INTRODUCING THE CHARACTERS

Since we are speaking of "Church" and "Third World," we must first make clear what these terms mean in the present context. It is also necessary to describe what went into the making of the consciousness of both partners in the proposed dialogue.

By "Church" I mean Christian people of any denomination, who may be organized in a variety of institutional forms, all of them issued from a historical experience of the Gospel. My main concern is with the Western Church: the Catholic Church, its Protestant offshoots and the many evangelical groupings. The reason why I am more concerned with the Western Church than with its Eastern counterpart will, I hope, become clear as we proceed. The Western Church, as here referred to, is a complex of institutions which are by no means homogeneous but have a certain affinity. All of them adhere to certain values and claim to promote them; all frame questions in recognizably similar ways, all share in varying degrees in a certain tradition and experience. In the framework of this article, it is this experience, more than anything else, that gives the

"Church" its unity and suggests the questions with which I began. This is the experience of what is known today as the First World.

As I intend to speak of it, therefore, the Church is both the mass of Western or Western-trained Christians and the institutions which govern their lives and have conditioned their mentalities. It is thus both what is called the "official" and the "unofficial" Church. "Official" here includes the hierarchized roles and functions *and* the traditional institutionalized structures of thought, feeling and behavior that it is the task of authority to maintain and perpetuate. "Unofficial" refers to the mass of the faithful insofar as they are governed and molded by the official authority and institutions. The faithful are here considered precisely as mass, as large numbers, because, as we said at the outset, the question which concerns us is not asked about individuals. For the individual is not in every case a mere unit in the mass nor is he entirely determined by the institutions, as the mass commonly is.

The "Third World" is no more homogeneous than the Church. At first glance it comprises that part of the planet which is not included in the North Atlantic region (Western Europe and North America) or in the Eastern European region of the Soviet Union and its socialist allies. It would include therefore not only the remainder of what some persist in calling the "free world" but regions and peoples not usually so considered—for example, China and Cuba.

This, however, is an unsatisfactory way of describing the Third World. For one thing, Australia and New Zealand, which are clearly a part or extension of the First World, would not fit in this scheme. Nor would Spain or Portugal or certain regions of Western Europe and North America which, although located in the First

World, should more properly be classified with the Second or Third. A further difficulty would be presented by Japan which, for reasons I am about to explain, should be considered part of the Second.

The truth is that the three worlds, though in a very important sense contained within territorial boundaries, are not in fact geographical entities but realities of a different order. They represent various stages of a worldwide disturbance which began at a given point in time and space and is spreading to the whole planet. There are pockets of the Third World in predominantly First and Second World environments, and vice-versa.

Just as the "Church" is given whatever unity it has by a common historical experience, the Third World, in spite of its bewildering diversity, can be seen as one in its relation to the disturbance just mentioned. The Third World is made up of those regions and peoples of the earth who are farthest behind in catching up with this phenomenon. The disturbance is not only planetary in extent but total in scope. It cannot be described exclusively in economic, political, social, cultural or psychological terms, for it includes all these. It has sometimes been called an ecological disturbance resulting from a technical revolution. This means a disturbance in the age-old equilibrium of man's relation to his environment, which has brought about not only a greater mastery of man over the environment but a consequent alteration both of the environment and of man's consciousness of himself.

In studying this occurrence at least two sets of data must be distinguished: the processes by which the mastery of the environment was achieved, and certain patterns of human control (or control over human beings) which accompanied and facilitated them.

The first set includes the vastly increased access to

and utilization of resources, the greatly refined methods of detection, analysis and processing of these resources; the expansion of the horizon of human investigation and endeavor, in scientific research, geographical exploration, trade and communication; and the internalization of time, by which I mean the perception that time is not a sacred and immutable succession of seasons but a process which can be understood, utilized, controlled and predicted. This internalization of time has enabled man not only to rediscover history but to seize an evolutionary movement in nature; to arrive at a new understanding of society as a gradual accumulation of man-made artifacts, and of the human psyche itself as the product of a lived personal-historical experience. This first set of data is therefore made up of mental and manual or mechanical techniques. Their application has resulted in an enormous increase of wealth and power, and in the well-known phenomena of industrialization, urbanization and large-scale mobilization and organization of men. These in turn have upset the old arrangement of norms, roles, statuses, work habits and modes of family and community living.

The other set of data concerns the particular structures of wealth, power and ideas within which the above-mentioned processes have taken and are taking place. It gives the answer to questions dealing not with how wealth is expanded but by whom it is controlled; not how human power is increased but who wields it and on whose behalf; and what ideas are shaped not only to understand the whole process but to legitimize it.

Now the occurrence we are talking about took several centuries to mature in a certain part of the world and then to spread to the whole planet, at first slowly but in the past several decades at an increasing tempo. As it spread, touching all parts of the world, already-existing states tried to take advantage of the technical innovations, and to protect themselves from the mechanisms of control. Hence one can easily see what is meant by the First, the Second, and the Third World. The First World is where the process originated. It has contributed most decisively to its development, is at present profiting most from it, and is therefore most interested in maintaining existing patterns of thought and control. The Second World comprises those (few) countries which, at somewhat different times but far ahead of the rest, were able to take advantage of the techniques while escaping the mental, political or economic control of the First World. Of this Second World, the Soviet Union and Japan are the most typical examples. However different they are in other ways, Japan and the Soviet Union have this in common: they both succeeded in utilizing the new techniques and in obtaining a share of the resulting wealth and power while escaping the political control of, and rejecting or significantly modifying the ideas prevalent in, the First World.[1]

A difference of opinion is possible as to which countries belong to the Second World, but there can be none about the Third. The Third World consists of those nations and human groups that have so far been unable to achieve mastery of techniques or any significant share in the power and wealth deriving from them. The chief reason for this is that the Third World was under the domination of the First, which controlled the techniques themselves and dictated the conditions and ideological framework within which they could be employed. What is known as decolonization is the relinquishing by the First World of the more overt and blatant forms of control over the Third. This makes it somewhat easier for the Third World to assimilate the needed knowledge and techniques but does not enable it to modify the patterns of control. Power and wealth remain in the hands of the First World, shared to some extent by the Second, and the relationship between them is an intricate game of competition and collusion. A fermentation seems, therefore, to be occurring in the realm of ideas throughout the Third World: struggling to acquire the skills needed to derive some benefit from the technological revolution, but unable to free itself from the stranglehold of the power and wealth of the long-dominant nations, the Third World appears to be readying itself to change its fundamental assumptions. "Dialogue" has suddenly become a common word in current vocabulary and one begins to understand the eagerness of the Church to listen to the Third World.

THE EMERGENCE OF THE THIRD WORLD

The Church, as I have described it, had its institutions and its consciousness shaped by the experience of the First World. The Church has itself shaped that experience and helped in part to articulate it. Institutions are structures not only of roles and functions but of regulative symbols which give meaning both to the life of the body as a whole and to large numbers of members. By consciousness I mean chiefly the understanding that the Church has of itself. That consciousness was shaped largely in opposition to what constitutes the major part of the Third World—the Islamic world and the world of the "pagans."[2] The question therefore is: how well is the Church now prepared to meet that world's self-understanding? The mere fact of its historical connection with the First World would not necessarily incapacitate the Church for understanding the Third World; at least in the eyes of the faithful, the

Church is no mere projection of the First World. There are, nevertheless, certain aspects of the Church's experience which justify raising the question.

A thorough reflection on this theme would be long and arduous. However, the dimensions of this essay are more modest, working from a clear point of departure —the notion of *emergence.*

The Third World is commonly spoken of in the First as the emerging world. The term itself is value-neutral and is in fact employed in a variety of contexts, but when applied to the Third World it carries a certain emotional connotation. The phenomenon of emergence can be the object of keen, dispassionate intellectual interest but this particular phenomenon is hardly ever looked at in that way. Emergence can even be a delightful thing to watch, as when Venus is said to have emerged from the waters, but the emergence of the Third World is admittedly not that kind of phenomenon. The thing has some of the awesomeness of a large-scale natural occurrence, as when a land mass surfaces from the sea or when a ridge begins to loom above the horizon. But unlike these natural phenomena, the emergence of the Third World does not allow the onlookers to be mere curious, though impressed, spectators. The more alert feel that they are involved. In fact, the immediate reaction is frequently panic. The emergence is perceived as a threat, or, to say the least, as a problem.

Why a threat? The Third World is said to be emerging into history, into history as such and into a particular history—Western Christian history, which according to some is the only history there is. The Third World was non-historical, which does not necessarily mean that it had no history or historical records, but mainly that it was unwilling or unable to pay much attention to them for purposes of self-understanding. It was a world without reflective self-awareness. What is new today, what the phenomenon of emergence is all about, is that this unselfconscious world is becoming self-conscious. Having been "discovered" by the First World—which also gave it its own sense of history, the Third World now insists on being "recognized" by it. Its emergence into history is, therefore, tantamount to a challenge to that very history; hence the threatening character of the phenomenon.

The threat is often understood in military terms. That is, the vanguard or advance units of the Third World—which according to context and circumstances are placed in China, in Latin America, or in the ghettoes of U. S. cities—are thought to be planning an armed expedition against the ramparts of the privileged First World, an expedition in which eventually the whole Third World is to take part. This notion is not simply a hallucination, for the emergence we are talking about is accompanied by a widespread and sometimes quite audible growl. Moreover, the same image has been utilized by China to give meaning and shape to the phenomenon. Nevertheless, the fear is older and more deeply rooted than the image. In any case, the leaders of the privileged world are preoccupied with the threatened ramparts; walls are strengthened and extended, and new systems of defense are put into operation. The Church is no stranger to this fear of "pagan invasions"; for centuries it had to be alert to such expeditions and to organize counter-expeditions of its own. In fact, its very existence and self-image have, as already suggested, been largely conditioned by such opposition to an enemy, whom it has usually characterized, to its own satisfaction, as the enemy of Christ.

Again, the Third World is perceived as a potential rival and competitor for the limited resources of the planet. A good portion of these resources are located in the Third World itself but so far that world has been unable either to gain effective political control over them, or to exploit them to its best advantage, due to lack of skills or financial power. The struggle for the control of these resources is but another aspect of the military conception of the phenomenon of emergence. This economic aspect of the problem has till recently been masked from the Church, which has seen it only as a matter of better distribution of products and not sufficiently as a matter of self-direction and autonomy, not only in the ownership of the resources but in the process of their utilization.

There is a third aspect to the threat. Although absolute technical superiority ensures for the foreseeable future the domination of the First World over the Third, the sheer numbers of the latter are seen to be alarming. Their demographic exuberance, therefore, must be substantially reduced or at least contained. For large numbers are imagined to be mobs, and mobs are notoriously irrational. When mobs are spearheaded by a hard nose packed with sophisticated weapons—say, nuclear missiles—then the prospect is not to be taken lightly. The population problem thus adds its own contribution to the military view.

This military threat, based on an economic struggle and reinforced by the alleged unpredictability of hungry multitudes, is further heightened by the fact that the whole phenomenon is fraught with ideological implications. It is here, the Church feels, that its greatest threat lies and at the same time, its greatest challenge. In fact, however, the Third World does not hold a uniform ideology, though it tends to have a common consciousness. Ideologies are accepted or rejected—often uncritically— to the extent that they help or hinder the sharpening of that self-consciousness. The Third World (or at least the more alert elements in it) lives in an environment dominated not only by the power and wealth of the First World but also by that world's intellectual products. It manages to speak in the language of its former masters but is essentially motivated by a passion of its own, which often produces unexpected twists and turns in the symbolic system. Its over-riding passion is nationalism, or an acute consciousness that it is made up of human groups possessing distinctive historical and cultural characteristics hitherto neglected, despised or destroyed by the First World and often by its disciples of the Third World itself. This awareness is accompanied by a moral indignation at thus being ignored, despised and injured. This passion drives the Third World to search restlessly for its past, to reawaken a memory long lost or bewitched; it is thus goaded into a ceaseless questioning of the norms, ideas and institutions of the First World, and of the latter's rendering of history, in the process of which its own self-image or identity is to re-emerge from its ruins. In this task of demolition the Third World is so far equipped principally with tools fashioned by the First World itself and then largely rejected by it. The first of these is Marxism. Marxism is for the Third World not a complete philosophy of life or explanation of history, but primarily an analytical tool for understanding the recent historical process and the present structure of power and ideas.

It is more difficult to define the other instrument of demolition. Some have called it the Western ethical code and have congratulated themselves on having bestowed it upon the Third World. The "Christian conscience" would be a better name, if one immediately made clear that it has no clear institutional subject. It is neither the conscience of the First World, the Third

World, nor that of the institutional Church. None of them lives by it but all somehow find themselves exposed to its judgment, and because of this paradoxical reality the Church is inextricably implicated in the quarrel between the Third and the First Worlds quite apart from any decision on its part.

THE CONSCIOUSNESS OF THE CHURCH

In this argument between the First and the Third Worlds the Church seems to have defined for itself the role of *meditator*. This is by no means an easy role, for it involves the reconciliation not only of the "best interests" of the opposing parties (presumed to be objectively determinable) but also of their respective self-images— that is, the self-image of the possessors and of the dispossessed, of the established and the disestablished, of the powerful and the powerless, of Dives and Lazarus. How well the Church is equipped for that task is a question to which there are no grounds for giving a categorical answer, positive or negative. One can only speculate and point out dangers and temptations inherent in the undertaking.

The Church, it must be remembered, was the cradle of the First World. And although this world (the "West") is defined by historians as that which was born on the break-up of what is known as the medieval Church or Christendom, one must not for that reason believe that either the contemporary Church or the First World have altogether outgrown the presiding image of that period: the image of a unified and expanding "Christian" commonwealth. The First World has rejected much that was considered "Christian" in the medieval Church but has retained under many guises the notion of a Christian civilization as an existing historical reality of which it is the guardian and prototype. The Western Church and the First World still rest, therefore, on the same foundations laid in medieval times, however modified and travestied these have been in subsequent centuries. This is why the Church has tried and continues to try to come to some understanding of and with the First World; it can never deny a substantial identity with it. It supports and draws support from First World institutions even while often displaying but little insight into its problems.

In the European world of Socialism (which is often thought to be identical with the Second World but which in reality contains fragments of all three), the Church has been the object of radical rejection, the extent and meaning of which are still being debated both within the Church and in parts of the Socialist world itself. The rejection is not unprecedented, since the First World, in its revolutionary periods, also asserted itself against both the Church's world-view and its quasi-political structures. That the break between the Church and the Socialist world need not be definitive is suggested by the new Christian-Marxist ecumenism, in which both sides rediscover their common foundations.

My concern, however, is with the Third World, where the role of the Church seems most problematic. Here, for the first time, something not born of a Christian experience—a "pagan" consciousness and an anti-Christian memory—combined with a heretical Christian tool and vaguely invoking a Christian "conscience" never quite operative in the "Christian" world, faces a Church which is itself struggling to define its identity in contemporary history.

The Church has been active in the Third World for

many centuries. It went there in a double capacity: as an institution of the Western World and as an independent force entrusted with the task of making the gospel of Christ heard by the nations and the charity of Christ visible to all men. Mission meant evangelization and service. The missionary Church was at one and the same time an instrument of Christ and an instrument of the West, supporting and supported by the expansion of the West, though at times critical of it.

In its encounter with the Third World the mission of evangelization found an unexpected difficulty: the "nations," the *gentes,* found it difficult to come to terms with an alien consciousness. The moment had come for the Western Church to put itself to the test of criticism by another self. The moment, however, was brief. The other self was not yet conscious enough to oppose its own self-image to the intruding one. Defeated in military combat, its consciousness turned totally inward and no longer had to be taken into account. The evangelization of the "nations," initiated by the First World and which should have involved dialogue with the culture and traditions of these nations—that is, with the instruments of their self-consciousness—never took place. What did take place in its stead was the "Christianization" of groups or pockets of the Third World, torn from the traditional consciousness and assimilated into an alien one or left without any; and, later, a relentless criticism of the refractory consciousness in the name of "conscience" which was nowhere quite visible in the institutional world. It is this ceaselessly invoked but structurally inoperative "conscience" which was eventually to be turned by the Third World against the First, and is now about to be turned against the Church.

The defeated "nations" having withdrawn from dialogue (to which they had not been invited), there remained the mission of charity or service. The poor will always remain with you, Christ had said—or, as some would insist, had promised. Mission would concentrate its powers of evangelization and service on the poor. [Very soon the call to "preach to all nations" was understood as the duty "to evangelize the poor."] As the "nations" themselves kept getting poorer and poorer, the identity of the two sayings of Jesus became more and more plausible: mission simply meant mission to the poor.

How the poor were evangelized has been for some time the subject of much debate and soul-searching: what concerns me here is the way they were served. The idea of service has of late also come into disrepute. This is due to a widespread feeling—among servers and served—that service, as so far rendered, implies and perpetuates a situation of inferiority and dependence, an asymmetry that the served are no longer willing to tolerate. Therefore, in place of service (from others), self-help (from oneself) is advocated. The Church accordingly shows much eagerness to promote self-help. Is the Church, however, equipped to promote self-help? The reason the question is raised is that a Church which never quite understood service is not likely to understand self-help. There is no self-help without self-awareness, and the Church today is in danger of not understanding the conditions for self-help any better than it grasped the conditions for true service.

A symptom of this danger is the equivalence which is supposed to exist between service and charity, on the one hand, and self-help and justice on the other. Just as self-help is now preferred to service, so justice seems to be preferred to charity. This is a sign that mystification has occurred in the very notion of charity.

This change in the attitude of the Church to the

Third World, and to the world of the poor in general, is most evident in writers and speakers of Christian inspiration who deal with what is known as aid or assistance to the "underdeveloped." These men and women want to convince their well-meaning publics that relations between rich and poor have changed (how or why is never made quite clear), that henceforth these relations should be governed by justice and not charity. They go on to say that help should not be *given* to the poor but that the poor should be helped to help themselves. This, the speakers declare, is an advance over previous attitudes as well as more in keeping with a new relationship.

The most striking thing is the alacrity with which charity is abandoned in favor of justice. Justice is the new name, charity is outmoded. No tears are shed for the passing of charity, no regret shown for its inability to be present in the contemporary world. Justice is not being advocated on the ground that charity is the norm of the Kingdom, and therefore of the future, whereas justice should be the norm of the present world. No, it is simply suggested that the attitude of charity is to be shed because it is more Christian to do so. This may well be. The point is that nothing indicates that the speakers know that charity means love.

How did the idea of charity, which means love, become so distorted in the Western world that it had eventually to be rejected and replaced with something quite different? Such an inquiry would help explain many things; indeed, an examination of the vicissitudes of "charity" would be as interesting as the study of the notion of authority has been. The two notions are not unrelated, at least in Christian history. I surmise that the problem began when the Church took over the civilizing task of the Roman Empire and was entrusted with the education of masses of barbarians. The Church was doubtless not unmindful of the fact that charity was meant to be the new, specifically Christian norm of ordinary behavior toward people—any people. But the Romans had an idea about the humanizing power of law, so the Church set about codifying Christian behavior into law. Before the elaboration of the natural law, the law most readily available to Christians in the Biblical tradition was the Law of Moses, the Ten Commandments. The commandments thus became the basis of a supposedly "Christian" code of morality. Wherever the law was not specific, the norm was to be mercy. Mercy would intervene where law failed to prescribe. So, alongside the Ten Commandments, there were to be Fourteen Works of Mercy. On these two sets of norms Christian civilization was built. Mercy has indeed been an extremely fruitful source of works, giving birth to all our "charities" and welfare services, but in the process it has come to define charity itself.

Mercy, not law—like "charity," not justice—is a norm which seems eminently suited to situations in which one deals with the sick, the ignorant, the erring— in short, to all cases in which the relationship is not, and is not expected to be, mutual, to cases in which one is unable or unwilling to assume a perfect equality between partners, to cases in which there is a donor and a receiver, one of whom is above the other. It seems therefore a norm perfectly suited to the relationship between the rich and poor. But the inability or unwillingness to assume equality has a series of predictable effects. The donor gives, not because the recipient "deserves" anything, but for other reasons of his own. The receiver is a mere object of mercy. Indeed, the gesture of the giver is not really addressed to him at all. The real transaction takes place between the donor and God.

The deed is, as it is said, done for God. The receiver is mere occasion. In such a situation the receiver exists for the sake of the giver and for his standing before God. The receiver is in this way effectively obliterated as consciousness—that is to say, as person. The literature of charities as well as of missions is full of examples which can illustrate this simple process.

In the dealings between rich and poor, therefore, charity, regarded as something other than justice, ends up by creating or maintaining a relationship and a mentality which render justice itself impossible. The history of the welfare systems of the Western world, all authentic products and the legitimate pride of Christian civilization, would provide ample material for testing this hypothesis. Justice at least requires that the other be regarded as other, as a person different from but similar to oneself and in his own right. When, in dealing with the poor, "charity" replaces justice, a time comes when "charity" itself has to be discarded, to make room for justice.

Nevertheless, there *is* another way of understanding charity which avoids these embarrassing results. In this case, charity would not be something other than justice but that which makes justice possible, the "soul" of justice, that which inspires justice and undertakes to achieve it. Such a charity would understand that justice does not come from law but is a work of love. Genuine charity does not place itself above the receiver, claiming to do things for God and not for men. In a certain way it acts like God—that is, it acts, it loves because God has first loved men. But it knows that giver and receiver are equally in need of the love and mercy of God (that is, are equally under His judgment) and have both equally received it. That is why they are able to love each other. They are equal.

This would seem to be the foundation of Christian morality. Nevertheless, this conception of charity, though not unknown even among Western Christians brought up on the Ten Commandments, has never regulated the dealings of the Church with the Third World.

THE CHURCH FACE TO FACE WITH THE THIRD WORLD

The Church, then, tends to approach the problem of justice to the world of the poor without adequate criticism of its historical understanding of charity. This may be the reason for the alacrity with which charity is abandoned in favor of justice, and the absence of shock and scandal at such alacrity. But this only produces an almost inevitable repetition of the process of mystification. For in this apparently new approach, the Church talks of justice but thinks of "charity" in the old way. Justice itself is conceived as a gift, unconcerned with the person—that is, with the consciousness of the receiver. Justice is talked of as aid, as assistance, as help; it is not conceived of as something due, but as the fruit of the actor's generosity, something he does for his own sake, not for the other's. No more than the rich, therefore, does the Church seem able to confront the consciousness of the poor.

These apparently theoretical remarks have immediate political implications, since all kinds of evasions are likely to ensue from such an attitude to justice. Out of many possible examples three should be singled out for purposes of illustration. In dealing with the plight of the poor in general and the poor nations in particular, care is being taken not to offend the rich. The rich are not to be told how, by their past and current actions, they may be responsible for that plight and for the inability of the poor to break out of it. The book of history is not to be reopened, nor is the past to be raked up. The idea of *reparation* for a wrong done—if ever mentioned—is quickly buried under apologies for the benefits of the old order, an order which is said to be passing and therefore need not be spoken of. The wrongs of colonialism, for example—or of slavery—are attributed to the imperfection of human action, *all* human action, rather than to any particular attitudes or structures. These attitudes and structures, when spoken of, are conceived of as incidental, not decisive. The rich, in this way, are called upon to do their duty without the meaning of that duty ever being first specified. All delicacy is employed to encourage them to do that indeterminate duty while preserving their riches, their dignity and their self-respect, to the extent of being told, as by Pope Paul VI in Bogota—if one is to believe the press—that they are the vanguard of the poor.

In the same spirit, the poor are exhorted not to judge the rich but to learn their ways—that is, to acquire their skills and adopt their values. This seems to be the problem facing the Latin American Church summoned to pronounce itself on the subject of "conscientizacao." The word, and the thing, that has to do with the process by which the poor acquire a self-consciousness, raises the problem regarding the meaning of the education of the masses. The masses are to be made to understand the contemporary world and their part in it. Are they to be taught only the norms and skills of the dominant minority, or are they also to be given an insight into the odds stacked against them, to be brought face to face with such issues as class structure, exploitation, conflict, resistance, revolution? The Church has not so far found it in itself to give a clear answer.

Besides the question of reparation for a wrong, justice demands attention to the patterns of action at work between classes and nations, usually included under the rubric "international trade patterns." As already mentioned, the Church has tended to think of these problems in terms of the regulation of prices and the distribution of wages and profits, and not enough in terms of ownership of the resources and self-direction in their utilization. Although its performance in this matter has been somewhat better than in any other area of our subject, the Church has usually contented itself with general principles illustrated with second-rate information. It has been unwilling to undertake an independent inquiry into facts and has indulged in gestures and pronouncements whose chief merit has been their propaganda value. The problems of the Middle East and those of Black Power, for example, if studied together under a common perspective, might enable the Church at least to sharpen its vision.

My third example is the question of violence. The poor are exhorted to shun violence, not because it is futile, dangerous or inopportune, but because it is unchristian. Probably for the first time in about seventeen centuries of Christian history, violence in the pursuit of social, economic or political goals is authoritatively declared to be unchristian. And it is the poor, not the rich, who are reminded of that. Whether there can be a "theory" or "theology" of organized violence in keeping with the total message of the Gospel is a question I need not enter into at this point. But the fact remains, and needs to be emphasized, that historically the Church has not only condoned but preached the use of violence; it condoned the violence of the State and aroused the violence of the "people of God." The only known "theories" of violence produced by the Church (which, incidentally, have never been repudiated but are often combined into a single theory) are the "theories" of the "just war" and the "holy war." The just war theory, whatever its original intentions, has, with the connivance of the Church, regularly served the ends of the established and the powerful. The holy war theory was intended—and is still used—to mobilize the energies of the "Christian" people against the "enemies of God" or of Christ. The poor alone are not to be allowed any such theological support for their aggressivity. It is, however, just possible that, faced with the demand for a "theology of revolution," the Church may finally rethink its previous theories—that is, it may re-examine its whole relationship with the State, with the keepers of the established power and wealth and the guardians of the prevalent symbolic system, and finally revise its own self-image as a quasi-political "people."

This brings us to our final remarks. The Church faces the Third World, the world of the poor, burdened with an outworn legacy of many centuries. Left to itself, the Church would probably not be able to shake off or even to criticize that legacy clearsightedly. Challenged by the poor, the Church is forced to rethink itself. The dependence of the Church on the established order is a hangover from the times when the Church thought itself to be and was in fact an order of some kind, not merely the inspirer but the actual manifestation of that order. That order was embodied in the idea of Christendom, of a fully organized Christian body which, after its breakup, left behind the idea of a Christian civilization. The new idea was equally understood in political terms and had therefore to be defended against enemies and expanded into the darkened regions of the world. This was the Christian man's burden, the precursor of the white man's burden, for "Christianity" so understood is nothing but the ideology of the white man. The Church is the originator of both and bears in its mind as in its body the scars of their expeditions.

If this is true, the Church is to be seen as having understood charity and justice not only in terms of the dichotomy of law and mercy but even more as a political body concerned with its own survival or well-being. A church which thinks of itself in political terms is unlikely to see justice in what threatens its existence and is prone to identify charity with what helps its own expansion. A disturbing thought follows from this: as long as the Church maintains its present self-image and organization, it is likely to be the accomplice of the enemies of justice and charity. Therefore, the tentative answer to my initial question seems to be that the Church will be able to cope with the consciousness of the Third World only to the extent that it can disengage itself from its present outmoded institutional settings and adopt the shape of what many have called a "prophetic community," judging itself and history in terms of an eschatological promise and hope. It can also be expected that nothing better than an intimate contact with the world of the poor and the powerless will enable it to achieve this necessary transmutation.

✑ NOTES

1. The subsequent career of Japan and its present situation are not within the scope of this article and are not, in the author's opinion, a refutation of his judgment.

2. Even Latin America, though classified as "Christian," is, it must be remembered, populated mainly by the direct or indirect descendents of the peoples of the old pagan kingdoms who, although ruled and controlled by the descendents of the Christian *conquistadores*, have refused to assimilate their thought-patterns and norms.

11

THE ADULT LITERACY PROCESS AS CULTURAL ACTION FOR FREEDOM

Paulo Freire

EVERY EDUCATIONAL PRACTICE IMPLIES A CONCEPT OF MAN AND THE WORLD

EXPERIENCE TEACHES US not to assume that the obvious is clearly understood. So it is with the truism with which we begin: All educational practice implies a theoretical stance on the educator's part. This stance in turn implies—sometimes more, sometimes less explicitly—an interpretation of man and the world. It could not be otherwise. The process of men's orientation in the world involves not just the association of sense images, as for

Paulo Freire is presently Special Consultant to the Office of Education, World Council of Churches, Geneva, Switzerland. This article, which appeared in the Harvard Educational Review, *is part of a longer essay written while the author was a Fellow at the Center for the Study of Development and Social Change. The remainder of the essay is published in the August 1970 issue of the* Review. *Translated by Loretta Stover. Copyright © 1970 by the Center for the Study of Development and Social Change, 1430 Massachusetts Avenue, Cambridge, Massachusetts, 02138.*

animals. It involves, above all, thought-language; that is, the possibility of the act of knowing through his praxis, by which man transforms reality. For man, this process of orientation in the world can be understood neither as a purely subjective event, nor as an objective or mechanistic one, but only as an event in which subjectivity and objectivity are united. Orientation in the world, so understood, places the question of the purposes of action at the level of critical perception of reality.

If, for animals, orientation in the world means adaptation to the world, for man it means humanizing the world by transforming it. For animals there is no historical sense, no options or values in their orientation in the world; for man there is both an historical and a value dimension. Men have the sense of "project," in contrast to the instinctive routines of animals.

The action of men without objectives, whether the objectives are right or wrong, mythical or demythologized, naive or critical, is not praxis, though it may be orientation in the world. And not being praxis, it is action ignorant both of its own process and of its aim. The interrelation of the awareness of aim and of process is the basis for planning action, which implies methods, objectives, and value options.

Teaching adults to read and write must be seen, analyzed, and understood in this way. The critical analyst will discover in the methods and texts used by educators and students practical value options which betray a philosophy of man, well or poorly outlined, coherent or incoherent. Only someone with a mechanistic mentality, which Marx would call "grossly materialistic," could reduce adult literacy learning to a purely technical action. Such a naive approach would be incapable of perceiving that technique itself as an instrument of men in their orientation in the world is not neutral.

We shall try, however, to prove by analysis the self-evidence of our statement. Let us consider the case of primers used as the basic texts for teaching adults to read and write. Let us further propose two distinct types: a poorly done primer and a good one, according to the genre's own criteria. Let us even suppose that the author of the good primer based the selection of its generative words[1] on a prior knowledge of which words have the greatest resonance for the learner (a practice not commonly found, though it does exist).

Doubtlessly, such an author is already far beyond the colleague who composes his primer with words he himself chooses in his own library. Both authors, however, are identical in a fundamental way. In each case they themselves decompose the given generative words and from the syllables create new words. With these words, in turn, the authors form simple sentences and, little by little, small stories, the so-called reading lessons.

Let us say that the author of the second primer, going one step further, suggests that the teachers who use it initiate discussions about one or another word, sentence, or text with their students.

Considering either of these hypothetical cases we may legitimately conclude that there is an implicit concept of man in the primer's method and content, whether it is recognized by the authors or not. This concept can be reconstructed from various angles. We begin with the fact, inherent in the idea and use of the primer, that it is the teacher who chooses the words and proposes them to the learner. Insofar as the primer is the mediating object between the teacher and students, and the students are to be "filled" with words the teachers have chosen, one can easily detect a first important dimension of the image of man which here begins to emerge. It is the profile of a man whose consciousness is "spatialized," and must be "filled" or "fed" in order to know. This same conception led Sartre, criticizing the notion that "to know is to eat," to exclaim: *"O philosophie alimentaire!"*[2]

This "digestive" concept of knowledge, so common in current educational practice, is found very clearly in the primer.[3] Illiterates are considered "undernourished," not in the literal sense in which many of them really are, but because they lack the "bread of the spirit." Consistent with the concept of knowledge as food, illiteracy is conceived of as a "poison herb," intoxicating and debilitating persons who cannot read or write. Thus, much is said about the "eradication" of illiteracy to cure the disease.[4] In this way, deprived of their character as linguistic signs constitutive of man's thought-language, words are transformed into mere "deposits of vocabulary"—the bread of the spirit which the illiterates are to "eat" and "digest."

This "nutritionist" view of knowledge perhaps also explains the humanitarian character of certain Latin American adult literacy campaigns. If millions of men are illiterate, "starving for letters," "thirsty for words," the word must be *brought* to them to save them from "hunger" and "thirst." The word, according to the naturalistic concept of consciousness implicit in the primer, must be "deposited," not born of the creative effort of the learners. As understood in this concept, man is a passive being, the object of the process of learning to read and write, and not its subject. As object his task is to "study" the so-called reading lessons, which in fact are almost completely alienating and alienated, having so little, if anything, to do with the student's socio-cultural reality.[5]

It would be a truly interesting study to analyze the reading texts being used in private or official adult literacy campaigns in rural and urban Latin America. It would not be unusual to find among such texts sentences and readings like the following random samples:[6]

A asa é da ave—"The wing is of the bird."
Eva viu a uva—"Eva saw the grape."
O galo canta—"The cock crows."
O cachorro ladra—"The dog barks."
Maria gosta dos animais—"Mary likes animals."
João cuida das arvores—"John takes care of the trees."
O pai de Carlinhos se chama Antonio. Carlinhos é um bom menino, bem comportado e estudioso—"Charles's father's name is Antonio. Charles is a good, well-behaved, and studious boy."
Ada deu o dedo ao urubu? Duvido, Ada deu o dedo a arara. . . .[7]
Se vocè trabalha com martelo e prego, tenha cuidado para nao furar o dedo.—"If you hammer a nail, be careful not to smash your finger."[8]
"Peter did not know how to read. Peter was ashamed. One day, Peter went to school and registered for a night course. Peter's teacher was very good. Peter knows how to read now. Look at Peter's face. [These lessons are generally illustrated.] Peter is smiling. He is a happy man. He already has a good job. Everyone ought to follow his example."

In saying that Peter is smiling because he knows how to read, that he is happy because he now has a good job, and that he is an example for all to follow, the authors establish a relationship between knowing how to read and getting good jobs which, in fact, cannot be borne out. This naiveté reveals, at least, a failure to perceive the structure not only of illiteracy, but of social phenomena in general. Such an approach may admit that these phenomena exist, but it cannot perceive their relationship to the structure of the society in which they are found. It is as if these phenomena were mythical, above and beyond concrete situations, or the results of the intrinsic inferiority of a certain class of men. Unable to grasp contemporary illiteracy as a typical manifestation of the "culture of silence," directly related to underdeveloped structures, this approach cannot offer an objective, critical response to the challenge of illiteracy. Merely teaching men to read and write does not work miracles; if there are not enough jobs for men able to work, teaching more men to read and write will not create them.

One of these readers presents among its lessons the following two texts on consecutive pages without relating them. The first is about May 1st, the Labor Day holiday, on which workers commemorate their struggles. It does not say how or where these are commemorated, or what the nature of the historical conflict was. The main theme of the second lesson is *holidays*. It says that "on these days people ought to go to the beach to swim and sunbathe . . ." Therefore, if May 1st is a holiday, and if on holidays people should go to the beach, the conclusion is that the workers should go swimming on Labor Day, instead of meeting with their unions in the public squares to discuss their problems.

Analysis of these texts reveals, then, a simplistic vision of men, of their world, of the relationship between the two, and of the literacy process which unfolds in that world.

A asa é da ave, Eva viu a uva, o galo canta, and *o cachorro late*, are linguistic contexts which, when mechanically memorized and repeated, are deprived of their authentic dimension as thought-language in dynamic interplay with reality. Thus impoverished, they are not authentic expressions of the world.

Their authors do not recognize in the poor classes the ability to know and even create the texts which would express their own thought-language at the level of their perception of the world. The authors repeat with the texts what they do with the words, i.e., they introduce them into the learners' consciousness as if it were empty space—once more, the "digestive" concept of knowledge.

Still more, the a-structural perception of illiteracy revealed in these texts exposes the other false view of illiterates as marginal men.[9] Those who consider them marginal must, nevertheless, recognize the existence of a reality to which they are marginal—not only physical space, but historical, social, cultural, and economic realities—i.e., the structural dimension of reality. In this way, illiterates have to be recognized as beings "outside of," "marginal to" something, since it is impossible to be marginal to nothing. But being "outside of" or "marginal to" necessarily implies a movement of the one said to be marginal from the center, where he was, to the periphery. This movement, which is an action, presupposes in turn not only an agent but also his reasons. Admitting the existence of men "outside of" or "marginal to" structural reality, it seems legitimate to ask: Who is the author of this movement from the center of the structure to its margin? Do so-called marginal men, among them the illiterates, make the decision to move out to the periphery of society? If so, marginality is an option with all that it involves: hunger, sickness, rickets, pain, mental deficiencies, living death, crime, promiscuity, despair, the impossiblity of being. In fact, however, it is difficult to accept that 40 percent of Brazil's population, almost 90 percent of Haiti's, 60 percent of Bolivia's, about 40 percent of Peru's, more than 30 percent of Mexico's and Venezuela's, and about 70 percent of Guatemala's would have made the tragic *choice* of their own marginality as illiterates.[10] If, then, marginality is not by choice, marginal man has been expelled from and kept outside of the social system and is therefore the object of violence.

In fact, however, the social structure as a whole does not "expel," nor is marginal man a "being outside of." He is, on the contrary, a "being inside of," within the social structure, and in a dependent relationship to those whom we call falsely autonomous beings, inauthentic beings-for-themselves.

A less rigorous approach, one more simplistic, less critical, more technicist, would say that it was unnecessary to reflect about what it would consider unimportant questions such as illiteracy and teaching adults to read and write. Such an approach might even add that the discussion of the concept of marginality is an unnecessary academic exercise. In fact, however, it is not so. In accepting the illiterate as a person who exists on the fringe of society, we are led to envision him as a sort of "sick man," for whom literacy would be the "medicine" to cure him, enabling him to "return" to the "healthy" structure from which he has become separated. Educators would be benevolent counsellors, scouring the outskirts of the city for the stubborn illiterates, runaways from the good life, to restore them to the forsaken bosom of happiness by giving them the gift of the word.

In the light of such a concept—unfortunately, all too widespread—literacy programs can never be efforts toward freedom; they will never question the very reality which deprives men of the right to speak up—not only illiterates, but all those who are treated as objects in a dependent relationship. These men, illiterate or not, are, in fact, not marginal. What we said before bears repeating: They are not "beings outside of"; they are "beings for another." Therefore the solution to their problem is not to become "beings inside of," but men freeing themselves; for, in reality, they are not marginal to the structure, but oppressed men within it. Alienated men, they cannot overcome their dependency by "incorporation" into the very structure responsible for their dependency. There is no other road to humanization—theirs as well as everyone else's—but authentic transformation of the dehumanizing structure.

From this last point of view, the illiterate is no longer a person living on the fringe of society, a marginal man, but rather a representative of the dominated strata of society, in conscious or unconscious opposition to those who, in the same structure, treat him as a thing. Thus, also, teaching men to read and write is no longer an inconsequential matter of *ba, be, bi, bo, bu,* of memorizing an alienated word, but a difficult apprenticeship in naming the world.

In the first hypothesis, interpreting illiterates as men marginal to society, the literacy process reinforces the mythification of reality by keeping it opaque and by dulling the "empty consciousness" of the learner with innumerable alienating words and phrases. By contrast, in the second hypothesis—interpreting illiterates as men oppressed within the system—the literacy process, as cultural action for freedom, is an act of knowing in which the learner assumes the role of knowing subject in dialogue with the educator. For this very reason, it is courageous endeavor to demythologize reality, a process through which men who had previously been submerged in reality begin to emerge in order to re-insert themselves into it with critical awareness.

Therefore the educator must strive for an ever greater clarity as to what, at times without his conscious knowledge, illumines the path of his action. Only in this way will he truly be able to assume the role of one of the subjects of this action and remain consistent in the process.

THE ADULT LITERACY PROCESS AS AN ACT OF KNOWING

To be an act of knowing the adult literacy process demands among teachers and students a relationship of authentic dialogue. True dialogue unites subjects together in the cognition of a knowable object which mediates between them.

If learning to read and write is to constitute an act of knowing, the learners must assume from the beginning the role of creative subjects. It is not a matter of memorizing and repeating given syllables, words, and phrases, but rather of reflecting critically on the process of reading and writing itself, and on the profound significance of language.

Insofar as language is impossible without thought, and language and thought are impossible without the world to which they refer, the human word is more than mere vocabulary—it is word-and-action. The cognitive dimensions of the literacy process must include the relationships of men with their world. These relationships are the source of the dialectic between the products men achieve in transforming the world and the conditioning which these products in turn exercise on men.

Learning to read and write ought to be an opportunity for men to know what *speaking the word* really means: a human act implying reflection and action. As such it is a primordial human right and not the privilege of a few.[11] Speaking the word is not a true act if it is not at the same time associated with the right of self-expression and world-expression, of creating and re-creating, of deciding and choosing and ultimately participating in society's historical process.

In the culture of silence the masses are "mute," that is, they are prohibited from creatively taking part in the transformations of their society and therefore prohibited from being. Even if they can occasionally read and write because they were "taught" in humanitarian—but not humanist—literacy campaigns, they are nevertheless alienated from the power responsible for their silence.

Illiterates know they are concrete men. They know that they do things. What they do not know in the culture of silence—in which they are ambiguous, dual beings—is that men's actions as such are transforming, creative, and re-creative. Overcome by the myths of this culture, including the myth of their own "natural inferiority," they do not know that *their* action upon the world is also transforming. Prevented from having a "structural perception" of the facts involving them, they do not know that they cannot "have a voice," i.e., that they cannot exercise the right to participate consciously in the socio-historical transformation of their society, because their work does not belong to them.

It could be said (and we would agree) that it is not possible to recognize all this apart from praxis, that is, apart from reflection and action, and that to attempt it would be pure idealism. But it is also true that action upon an object must be critically analyzed in order to understand both the object itself and the understanding one has of it. The act of knowing involves a dialectical movement which goes from action to reflection and from reflection upon action to a new action. For the learner to know what he did not know before, he must engage in an authentic process of abstraction by means of which he can reflect on the action-object whole, or, more generally, on forms of orientation in the world. In this process of abstraction, situations representative of how the learner orients himself in the world are proposed to him as the objects of his critique.

As an event calling forth the critical reflection of both the learners and educators, the literacy process must relate *speaking the word* to *transforming reality,* and to man's role in this transformation. Perceiving the significance of that relationship is indispensible for those learning to read and write if we are really committed to liberation. Such a perception will lead the learners to recognize a much greater right than that of being literate. They will ultimately recognize that, as men, they have the right to have a voice.

On the other hand, as an act of knowing, learning to read and write presupposes not only a theory of knowing but a method which corresponds to the theory.

We recognize the indisputable unity between subjectivity and objectivity in the act of knowing. Reality is never just simply the objective datum, the concrete fact, but is also men's perception of it. Once again, this is not a subjectivistic or idealistic affirmation, as it might seem. On the contrary, subjectivism and idealism come into play when the subjective-objective unity is broken.[12]

The adult literacy process as an act of knowing implies the existence of two interrelated contexts. One is the context of authentic dialogue between learners and educators as equally knowing subjects. This is what schools should be—the theoretical context of dialogue. The second is the real, concrete context of facts, the social reality in which men exist.[13]

In the theoretical context of dialogue, the facts presented by the real or concrete context are critically analyzed. This analysis involves the exercise of abstraction, though which, by means of representations of concrete reality, we seek knowledge of that reality. The instrument for this abstraction in our methodology is codification,[14] or representation of the existential situations of the learners.

Codification, on the one hand, mediates between the concrete and theoretical contexts (of reality). On the other hand, as knowable object, it mediates between the knowing subjects, educators and learners, who seek in dialogue to unveil the "action-object wholes."

This type of linguistic discourse must be "read" by anyone who tries to interpret it, even when purely pictorial. As such, it presents what Chomsky calls "surface structure" and "deep structure."

The "surface structure" of codification makes the "action-object whole" explicit in a purely taxonomic form. The first stage of decodification[15]—or reading— is descriptive. At this stage, the "readers"—or decodifiers—focus on the relationship between the categories constituting the codification. This preliminary focus on the surface structure is followed by problematizing the codified situation. This leads the learner to the second and fundamental stage of decodification, the comprehension of the codification's "deep structure." By understanding the codification's "deep structure" the learner can then understand the dialectic which exists between the categories presented in the "surface structure," as well as the unity between the "surface" and "deep" structures.

In our method, the codification initially takes the form of a photograph or sketch which represents a real existent, or an existent constructed by the learners. When this representation is projected as a slide, the learners effect an operation basic to the act of knowing:

they gain distance from the knowable object. This experience of distance is undergone as well by the educators, so that educators and learners together can reflect critically on the knowable object which mediates between them. The aim of decodification is to arrive at the critical level of knowing, beginning with the learner's experience of the situation in the "real context."

Whereas the codified representation is the knowable object mediating between knowing subjects, decodification—dissolving the codification into its constituent elements—is the operation by which the knowing subjects perceive relationships between the codification's elements and other facts presented by the real context—relationships which were formerly unperceived. Codification represents a given dimension of reality as individuals live it, and this dimension is proposed for their analysis in a context other than that in which they live it. Codification thus transforms what was a way of life in the real context into "objectum" in the theoretical context. The learners, rather than receive information about this or that fact, analyze aspects of their own existential experience represented in the codification.

Existential experience is a whole. In illuminating one of its angles and perceiving the inter-relation of that angle with others, the learners tend to replace a fragmented vision of reality with a total vision. From the point of view of a theory of knowledge, this means that the dynamic between codification of existential situations and decodification involves the learners in a constant re-construction of their former "ad-miration" of reality.

We do not use the concept "ad-miration" here in the usual way, or in its ethical or esthetic sense, but with a special philosophical connotation.

To "ad-mire" is to objectify the "not-I." It is a dialectical operation which characterizes man as man, differentiating him from the animal. It is directly associated with the creative dimension of his language. To "admire" implies that man stands over against his "not-I" in order to understand it. For this reason, there is no act of knowing without "ad-miration" of the object to be known. If the act of knowing is a dynamic act—and no knowledge is ever complete—then in order to know, man not only "ad-mires" the object, but must always be "re-ad-miring" his former "ad-miration." When we "re-ad-mire" our former "ad-miration" (always an "ad-miration" *of*) we are simulatneously "ad-miring" the act of "ad-miring" and the object "ad-mired," so that we can overcome the errors we made in our former "ad-miration." This "re-ad-miration" leads us to a perception of an interior perception.

In the process of decodifying representations of their existential situations and perceiving former perceptions, the learners gradually, hesitatingly, and timorously place in doubt the opinion they held of reality and replace it with a more and more critical knowledge thereof.

Let us suppose that we were to present to groups from among the dominated classes codifications which portray their imitation of the dominators' cultural models—a natural tendency of the oppressed consciousness at a given moment.[16] The dominated persons would perhaps, in self-defense, deny the truth of the codification. As they deepened their analysis, however, they would begin to perceive that their apparent imitation of the dominators' models is a result of their interiorization of these models and, above all, of the myths of the "superiority" of the dominant classes which cause the dominated to feel inferior. What in fact is pure interiorization appears in a naive analysis to be imitation. At bottom, when the dominated classes reproduce the dominators' style of life, it is because the dominators live "within" the dominated. The dominated can eject the dominators only by getting distance from them and objectifying them. Only then can they recognize them as their antithesis.[17]

To the extent, however, that interiorization of the dominators' values is not only an individual phenomenon, but a social and cultural one, ejection must be achieved by a type of cultural action in which culture negates culture. That is, culture, as an interiorized product which in turn conditions men's subsequent acts, must become the object of men's knowledge so that they can perceive its conditioning power. Cultural action occurs at the level of superstructure. It can only be understood by what Althusser calls "the dialectic of overdetermination."[18] This analytic tool prevents us from falling into mechanistic explanations or, what is worse, mechanistic action. An understanding of it precludes surprise that cultural myths remain after the infrastructure is transformed, even by revolution.

When the creation of a new culture is appropriate but impeded by interiorized cultural "residue," this residue, these myths, must be expelled by means of culture. Cultural action and cultural revolution, at different stages, constitute the modes of this expulsion.

The learners must discover the reasons behind many of their attitudes toward cultural reality and thus confront reality in a new way. "Re-ad-miration" of their former "ad-miration" is necessary in order to bring this about. The learners' capacity for critical knowing—well beyond mere opinion—is established in the process of unveiling their relationships with the historical-cultural world *in* and *with* which they exist.

We do not mean to suggest that critical knowledge of

man-world relationships arises outside of praxis, a verbal knowledge. Praxis is involved in the concrete situations which are codified for critical analysis. To analyze the codification in its "deep structure" is, for this very reason, to reconstruct the former praxis and to become capable of a new and different praxis. The relationship between the *theoretical context,* in which codified representations of objective facts are analyzed, and the *concrete context,* where these facts occur, has to be made real.

Such education must have the character of commitment. It implies a movement from the *concrete context* which provides objective facts, to the *theoretical context* where these facts are analyzed in depth, and back to the *concrete context* where men experiment with new forms of praxis.

It might seem as if some of our statements defend the principle that, whatever the level of the learners, they ought to reconstruct the process of human knowing in absolute terms. In fact, when we consider adult literacy learning or education in general as an act of knowing, we are advocating a synthesis between the educator's maximally systematized knowing and the learners' minimally systematized knowing—a synthesis achieved in dialogue. The educator's role is to propose problems about the codified existential situations in order to help the learners arrive at a more and more critical view of their reality. The educator's responsibility as conceived by this philosophy is thus greater in every way than that of his colleague whose duty is to transmit information which the learners memorize. Such an educator can simply repeat what he has read, and often misunderstood, since education for him does not mean an act of knowing.

The first type of educator, on the contrary, is a knowing subject, face to face with other knowing subjects. He can never be a mere memorizer, but a person constantly readjusting his knowledge, who calls forth knowledge from his students. For him, education is a pedagogy of knowing. The educator whose approach is mere memorization is anti-dialogic; his act of transmitting knowledge is inalterable. For the educator who experiences the act of knowing together with his students, in contrast, dialogue is the seal of the act of knowing. He is aware, however, that not all dialogue is in itself the mark of a relationship of true knowledge.

Socratic intellectualism—which mistook the definition of the concept for knowledge of the thing defined and this knowledge as virtue—did not constitute a true pedagogy of knowing, even though it was dialogic. Plato's theory of dialogue failed to go beyond the Socratic theory of the definition as knowledge, even though for Plato one of the necessary conditions for knowing was that man be capable of a *"prise de conscience,"* and though the passage from *doxa* to *logos* was indispensable for man to achieve truth. For Plato, the *"prise de conscience"* did not refer to what man knew or did not know or knew badly about his dialectical relationship with the world; it was concerned rather with what man once knew and forgot at birth. To know was to remember or recollect forgotten knowledge. The apprehension of both *doxa* and *logos,* and the overcoming of *doxa* by *logos* occurred not in the man-world relationship, but in the effort to remember or rediscover a forgotten *logos.*

For dialogue to be a method of true knowledge, the knowing subjects must approach reality scientifically in order to seek the dialectical connections which explain the form of reality. Thus, to know is not to remember something previously known and now forgotten. Nor can *doxa* be overcome by *logos* apart from the dialectical relationship of man with his world, apart from men's reflective action upon the world.

To be an act of knowing, then, the adult literacy process must engage the learners in the constant problematizing of their existential situations. This problematizing employs "generative words" chosen by specialized educators in a preliminary investigation of what we call the "minimal linguistic universe" of the future learners. The words are chosen (a) for their pragmatic value, *i.e.*, as linguistic signs which command a common understanding in a region or area of the same city or country (in the United States, for instance, the word *soul* has a special significance in black areas which it does not have among whites), and (b) for their phonetic difficulties which will gradually be presented to those learning to read and write. Finally, it is important that the first generative word be tri-syllabic. When it is divided into its syllables, each one constituting a syllabic family, the learners can experiment with various syllabic combinations even at first sight of the word.

Having chosen seventeen generative words,[19] the next step is to codify seventeen existential situations familiar to the learners. The generative words are then worked into the situations one by one in the order of their increasing phonetic difficulty. As we have already emphasized, these codifications are knowable objects which mediate between the knowing subjects, educator-learners, learner-educators. Their act of knowing is elaborated in the *circulo de cultura* (cultural discussion group) which functions as the theoretic context.

In Brazil, before analyzing the learners' existential situations and the generative words contained in them, we proposed the codified theme of man-world relationships in general.[20] In Chile, at the suggestion of Chilean educators, this important dimension was discussed concurrently with learning to read and write. What is important is that the person learning words be concomitantly engaged in a critical analysis of the social framework in which men exist. For example, the word *favela* in Rio de Janeiro, Brazil, and the word *callampa* in Chile, represent, each with its own nuances, the same social, economic, and cultural reality of the vast numbers of slum dwellers in those countries. If *favela* and *callampa* are used as generative words for the people of Brazilian and Chilean slums, the codifications will have to represent slum situations.

There are many people who consider slum dwellers marginal, intrinsically wicked and inferior. To such people we recommend the profitable experience of discussing the slum situation with slum dwellers themselves. As some of these critics are often simply mistaken, it is possible that they may rectify their mythical clichés and assume a more scientific attitude. They may avoid saying that the illiteracy, alcoholism, and crime of the slums, that its sickness, infant mortality, learning deficiencies, and poor hygiene reveal the "inferior nature" of its inhabitants. They may even end up realizing that if intrinsic evil exists it is part of the structures, and that it is the structures which need to be transformed.

It should be pointed out that the Third World as a whole, and more in some parts than in others, suffers from the same misunderstanding from certain sectors of the so-called metropolitan societies. They see the Third World as the incarnation of evil, the primitive, the devil, sin and sloth—in sum, as historically unviable without the director societies. Such a manichean attitude is at the source of the impulse to "save" the "demon-possessed" Third World, "educating it" and "correcting its thinking" according to the director societies' own criteria.

The expansionist interests of the director societies are implicit in such notions. These societies can never relate to the Third World as partners, since partnership-presupposes equals, no matter how different the equal parties may be, and can never be established between parties antagnoistic to each other.

Thus, "salvation" of the Third World by the director societies can only mean its domination, whereas in its legitimate aspiration to independence lies its utopian vision: to save the director societies in the very act of freeing itself.

In this sense the pedagogy which we defend, conceived in a significant area of the Third World, is itself a utopian pedagogy. By this very fact it is full of hope, for to be utopian is not to be merely idealistic or impractical but rather to engage in denunciation and annunciation. Our pedagogy cannot do without a vision of man and of the world. It formulates a scientific humanist conception which finds its expression in a dialogical praxis in which the teachers and learners together, in the act of analyzing a dehumanizing reality, denounce it while announcing its transformation in the name of the liberation of man.

For this very reason, denunciation and annunciation in this utopian pedagogy are not meant to be empty words, but an historic commitment. Denunciation of a dehumanizing situation today increasingly demands precise scientific understanding of that situation. Likewise, the annunciation of its transformation increasingly requires a theory of transforming action. However, neither act by itself implies the transformation of the denounced reality or the establishment of that which is announced. Rather, as a moment in an historical process, the announced reality is already present in the act of denunciation and annunciation.[21]

That is why the utopian character of our educational theory and practice is as permanent as education itself which, for us, is cultural action. Its thrust toward denunciation and annunciation cannot be exhausted when the reality denounced today cedes its place tomorrow to the reality previously announced in the denunciation. When education is no longer utopian, *i.e.*, when it no longer embodies the dramatic unity of denunciation and annunciation, it is either because the future has no more meaning for men, or because men are afraid to risk living the future as creative overcoming of the present, which has become old.

The more likely explanation is generally the latter. That is why some people today study all the possibilities which the future contains, in order to "domesticate" it and keep it in line with the present, which is what they intend to maintain. If there is any anguish in director societies hidden beneath the cover of their cold technology, it springs from their desperate determination that their metropolitan status be preserved in the future. Among the things which the Third World may learn from the metropolitan societies there is this that is fundamental: not to replicate those societies when its current utopia becomes actual fact.

When we defend such a conception of education— realistic precisely to the extent that it is utopian—that is, to the extent that it denounces what in fact is, and finds therefore between denunciation and its realization the time of its praxis—we are attempting to formulate a type of education which corresponds to the specifically human mode of being, which is historical.

There is no annunciation without denunciation, just

as every denunciation generates annunciation. Without the latter, hope is impossible. In an authentic utopian vision, however, hoping does not mean folding one's arms and waiting. Waiting is only possible when one, filled with hope, seeks through reflective action to achieve that announced future which is being born within the denunciation.

That is why there is no genuine hope in those who intend to make the future repeat their present, nor in those who see the future as something predetermined. Both have a "domesticated" notion of history: the former because they want to stop time; the latter because they are certain about a future they already "know." Utopian hope, on the contrary, is engagement full of risk. That is why the dominators, who merely denounce those who denounce them, and who have nothing to announce but the preservation of the status quo, can never be utopian nor, for that matter, prophetic.[22]

A utopian pedagogy of denunciation and annunciation such as ours will have to be an act of knowing the denounced reality at the level of alphabetization and post-alphabetization, which are in each case cultural action. That is why there is such emphasis on the continual problematization of the learners' existential situations as represented in the codified images. The longer the problematization proceeds, and the more the subjects enter into the "essence" of the problematized object, the more they are able to unveil this "essence." The more they unveil it, the more their awakening consciousness deepens, thus leading to the "conscientization" of the situation by the poor classes. Their critical self-insertion into reality, *i.e.,* their conscientization, makes the transformation of their state of apathy into the utopian state of *denunciation* and *annunciation* a viable project.

One must not think, however, that learning to read and write precedes "conscientization," or vice-versa. Conscientization occurs simultaneously with the literacy or post-literacy process. It must be so. In our educational method, the word is not something static or disconnected from men's existential experience, but a dimension of their thought-language about the world. That is why, when they participate critically in analyzing the first generative words linked with their partial experience; when they focus on the syllabic families which result from that analysis; when they perceive the mechanism of the syllabic combinations of their language, the learners finally discover, in the various possibilities of combination, their own words. Little by little, as these possibilities multiply, the learners, through mastery of new generative words, expand both their vocabulary and their capacity for expression by the development of their creative imagination.[23]

In some areas in Chile undergoing agrarian reform, the peasants participating in the literacy programs wrote words with their tools on the dirt roads where they were working. They composed the words from the syllabic combinations they were learning. "These men are sowers of the word," said Maria Edi Ferreira, a sociologist from the Santiago team working in the Institute of Training and Research in Agrarian Reform. Indeed, they were not only sowing words, but discussing ideas, and coming to understand their role in the world better and better.

We asked one of these "sowers of words," finishing the first level of literacy classes, why he hadn't learned to read and write before the agrarian reform.

"Before the agrarian reform, my friend," he said, "I didn't even think. Neither did my friends."

"Why?" we asked.

"Because it wasn't possible. We lived under orders. We only had to carry out orders. We had nothing to say," he replied emphatically.

The simple answer of this peasant is a very clear analysis of "the culture of silence." In "the culture of silence," to exist is only to live. The body carries out orders from above. Thinking is difficult, speaking the word, forbidden.

"When all this land belonged to one *latifundio*," said another man in the same conversation, "there was no reason to read and write. We weren't responsible for anything. The boss gave the orders and we obeyed. Why read and write? Now it's a different story. Take me, for example. In the *asentiamiento*,[24] I am responsible not only for my work like all the other men, but also for tool repairs. When I started I couldn't read, but I soon realized that I needed to read and write. You can't imagine what it was like to go to Santiago to buy parts. I couldn't get orientated. I was afraid of everything— afraid of the big city, of buying the wrong thing, of being cheated. Now it's all different."

Observe how precisely this peasant described his former experience as an illiterate: his mistrust, his magical (though logical) fear of the world; his timidity. And observe the sense of security with which he repeats, "Now it's all different."

"What did you feel, my friend," we asked another "sower of words" on a different occasion, "when you were able to write and read your first word?"

"I was happy because I discovered I could make words speak," he replied.

Dario Salas reports,[25] "In our conversations with

peasants we were struck by the images they used to express their interest and satisfaction about becoming literate. For example, 'Before we were blind, now the veil has fallen from our eyes'; 'I came only to learn how to sign my name. I never believed I would be able to read, too, at my age'; 'Before, letters seemed like little puppets. Today they say something to me, and I can make them talk.'

"It is touching," continues Salas, "to observe the delight of the peasants as the world of words opens to them. Sometimes they would say, 'We're so tired our heads ache, but we don't want to leave here without learning to read and write.' "[26]

The following words were taped during research on "generative themes."[27] They are an illiterate's decodification of a codified existential situation.

"You see a house there, sad, as if it were abandoned. When you see a house with a child in it, it seems happier. It gives more joy and peace to people passing by. The father of the family arrives home from work exhausted, worried, bitter, and his little boy comes to meet him with a big hug, because a little boy is not stiff like a big person. The father already begins to be happier just from seeing his children. Then he really enjoys himself. He is moved by his son's wanting to please him. The father becomes more peaceful, and forgets his problems."

Note once again the simplicity of expression, both profound and elegant, in the peasant's language. These are the people considered absolutely ignorant by the proponents of the "digestive" concept of literacy.

In 1968, an Uruguayan team[28] published a small book, *You Live as You Can (Se Vive como se Puede)*, whose contents are taken from the tape recordings of literacy classes for urban dwellers. Its first edition of three thousand copies was sold out in Montevideo in fifteen days, as was the second edition. The following is an excerpt from this book.

The Color of Water

Water? Water? What is water used for?

"Yes, yes, we saw it (in the picture)."

"Oh, my native village, so far away. . . ."

"Do you remember that village?"

"The stream where I grew up, called Dear Friar . . . you know, I grew up there, a childhood moving from one place to another . . . the color of the water brings back good memories, beautiful memories."

"What is the water used for?"

"It is used for washing. We used it to wash clothes, and the animals in the fields used to go there to drink, and we washed ourselves there, too."

"Did you also use the water for drinking?"

"Yes, when we were at the stream and had no other water to drink, we drank from the stream. I remember once in 1945 a plague of locusts came from somewhere, and we had to fish them out of the water . . . I was small, but I remember taking out the locusts like this, with my two hands—and I had no others. And I remember how hot the water was when there was a drought and the stream was almost dry . . . the water was dirty, muddy, and hot, with all kinds of things in it. But we had to drink it or die of thirst."

The whole book is like this, pleasant in style, with great strength of expression of the world of its authors, those anonymous people, "sowers of words," seeking to emerge from "the culture of silence."

Yes, these ought to be the reading texts for people learning to read and write, and not "Eva saw the grape," "The bird's wing," "If you hammer a nail, be careful not to hit your fingers." Intellectualist prejudices and above all class prejudices are responsible for the naive and unfounded notions that the people cannot write their own texts, or that a tape of their conversations is valueless since their conversations are impoverished of meaning. Comparing what the "sowers of words" said in the above references with what is generally written by specialist authors of reading lessons, we are convinced that only someone with very pronounced lack of taste or a lamentable scientific incompetency would choose the specialists' texts.

Imagine a book written entirely in this simple, poetic, free, language of the people, a book on which interdisciplinary teams would collaborate in the spirit of true dialogue. The role of the teams would be to elaborate specialized sections of the book in problematic terms. For example, a section on linguistics would deal simply, though not simplistically, with questions fundamental to the learners' critical understanding of language. Let me emphasize again that since one of the important aspects of adult literacy work is the development of the capacity for expression, the section on linguistics would present themes for the learners to discuss, ranging from the increase of vocabulary to questions about communication—including the study of synonyms and antonyms, with its analysis of words in the linguistic context, and the use of metaphor, of which the people are such masters. Another section might provide the tools for a sociological analysis of the content of the texts.

These texts would not, of course, be used for mere mechanical reading, which leaves the readers without any understanding of what is real. Consistent with the nature of this pedagogy, they would become the object of analysis in reading seminars.

Add to all this the great stimulus it would be for those learning to read and write, as well as for students on more advanced levels, to know that they were reading and discussing the work of their own companions. . . .

To undertake such a work, it is necessary to have faith in the people, solidarity with them. It is necessary to be utopian, in the sense in which we have used the word.

◢ NOTES

1. In languages like Portuguese or Spanish, words are composed syllabically. Thus, every non-monosyllabic word is, technically, *generative*, in the sense that other words can be constructed from its de-composed syllables. For a word to be authentically generative, however, certain conditions must be present which will be discussed in a later section of this essay. [At the phonetic level the term *generative word* is properly applicable only with regard to a sound-syllabic reading methodology, while the thematic application is universal. See Sylvia Ashton-Warner's *Teacher* for a different treatment of the concept of generative words at the thematic level.—Editor]

2. Jean Paul Sartre. *Situations I* (Paris: Librairie Gallimard, 1947), p. 31.

3. The digestive concept of knowledge is suggested by "controlled readings," by classes which consist only in lectures; by the use of memorized dialogues in language learning; by biblographical notes which indicate not only which chapter, but which lines and words are to be read; by the methods of evaluating the students' progress in learning.

4. See Paulo Freire, "La alfabetizacion de adultos, critica de su vision ingenua; compreension de su vision critica," in *Introducción a la Acción Cultural* (Santiago: ICIRA, 1969).

5. There are two noteworthy exceptions among these primers: (1) in Brazil, *Viver e Lutar*, developed by a team of specialists of the Basic Education Movement,

sponsored by the National Conference of Bishops. (This reader became the object of controversy after it was banned as subversive by the then governor of Guanabara, Mr. Carlos Lacerda, in 1963.) (2) in Chile, the ESPIGA collection, despite some small defects. The collection was organized by Jefatura de Planes Extraordinarios de Educación de Adultos, of the Public Education Ministry.

6. Since at the time this essay was written the writer did not have access to the primers, and was, therefore, vulnerable to recording phrases imprecisely or to confusing the author of one or another primer, it was thought best not to identify the authors or the titles of the books.

7. [The English here would be nonsensical, as is the Portuguese, the point being the emphasis on the consonant *d*.—Editor.]

8. The author may even have added here, ". . . If, however, this should happen, put a little mercurochrome."

9. [The Portuguese word here translated as *marginal man* is *marginado*. This has a passive sense: he who has been made marginal, or sent outside society; as well as the sense of a state of existence on the fringe of society.—Translator.]

10. UNESCO: *La situación educativa en América Latina*, Cuadro no. 20, page 263 (Paris, 1960).

11. Paulo Freire, *op. cit.*

12. There are two ways to fall into idealism: The one consists of dissolving the real in subjectivity; the other in denying all real subjectivity in the interests of objectivity." Jean Paul Sartre, *Search for a Method*, trans. Hazel E. Barnes (New York: Vintage Books, 1968), p. 33.

13. See Karel Kosik, *Dialectica de lo Concreto* (Mexico: Grijalbo, 1967).

14. [*Codification* refers alternatively to the imaging, or the image itself, of some significant aspect of the learner's concrete reality (of a slum dwelling, for example). As such, it becomes both the object of the teacher-learner dialogue and the context for the introduction of the generative word.—Editor]

15. [*Decodification* refers to a process of description and interpretation, whether of printed words, pictures, or

other "codifications." As such, decodification and decodifying are distinct from the process of decoding, or
word-recognition.—Editor.]

16. Re the oppressed consciousness, see: Frantz Fanon,
The Wretched of the Earth (New York: Grove Press,
1968); Albert Memmi, *Colonizer and the Colonized*
(New York: Orion Press, 1965); and Paulo Freire,
Pedagogy of the Oppressed (New York: Herder &
Herder, 1970).

17. See Fanon, *The Wretched;* Freire, *Pedagogy.*

18. See Louis Althusser, *Pour Marx* (Paris: Librairie Fran-
çois Maspero, 1965); and Paulo Freire, *Annual Report:
Activities for 1968, Agrarian Reform, Training and
Research Institute ICIRA, Chile,* trans. John Dewitt,
Center for the Study of Development and Social
Change, Cambridge, Mass., 1969 (mimeographed).

19. We observed in Brazil and Spanish America, especially
Chile, that no more than seventeen words were necessary for teaching adults to read and write syllabic
languages like Portuguese and Spanish.

20. See Paulo Freire, *Educacao como Pratica da Liber-
dade* (Rio de Janeiro: Paz e Terra, 1967). Chilean
Edition (Santiago: ICIRA, 1969). French Edition
(Paris: Sintese, 1968).

21. Re the utopian dimension of denunciation and proclamation, see Leszek Kolakowski, *Toward a Marxist
Humanism* (New York: Grove Press, 1969).

22. "The right, as a conservative force, needs no utopia;
its essence is the affirmation of existing conditions—a
fact and not a utopia—or else the desire to revert to
a state which was once an accomplished fact. The Right
strives to idealize actual conditions, not to change them.
What it needs is fraud not utopia." Kolakowski, *op. cit.,*
pp. 71–72.

23. "We have observed that the study of the creative aspect
of language use develops the assumption that linguistic
and mental process are virtually identical, language
providing the primary means for free expansion of
thought and feeling, as well as for the functioning of
creative imagination." Noam Chomsky, *Cartesian Linguistics* (New York: Harper & Row, 1966), p. 31.

24. After the disappropriation of lands in the agrarian reform in Chile, the peasants who were salaried workers

on the large latifundia become "settlers" (*asentados*) during a three-year period in which they receive varied assistance from the government through the Agrarian Reform Corporation. This period of "settlement" (*asentamiento*) precedes that of assigning lands to the peasants. This policy is now changing. The phase of "settlement" of the lands is being abolished, in favor of an immediate distribution of lands to the peasants. The Agrarian Reform Corporation will continue, nevertheless, to aid the peasants.

25. Dario Salas, "Algumas experiencias vividas na Supervisao de Educacao basica," in *A alfabetizacao funcional no Chile*. Report to UNESCO, November, 1968. Introduction: Paulo Freire.

26. Dario Salas refers here to one of the best adult education programs organized by the Agrarian Reform Corporation in Chile, in strict collaboration with the Ministry of Education and ICIRA. Fifty peasants receive boarding and instruction scholarships for a month. The courses center on discussions of the local, regional, and national situations.

27. An analysis of the objectives and methodology of the investigation of generative themes lies outside the scope of this essay, but is dealt with in the author's work, *Pedagogy of the Oppressed*.

28. The members of the Uruguayan team were Raquel Carreira, Raquel Barreito, Enrique Mendez, Julio de Santa Ana, and Julio Barreiro.

12

OUTWITTING THE "DEVELOPED" COUNTRIES

Ivan Illich

IT IS NOW COMMON TO DEMAND that the rich nations convert their war machine into a program for the development of the Third World. The poorer four fifths of humanity multiply unchecked while their per capita consumption actually declines. This population expansion and decrease of consumption threaten the industrialized nations, who may still, as a result, convert their defense budgets to the economic pacification of poor nations. And this in turn could produce irreversible despair, because the plows of the rich can do as much harm as their swords. US trucks can do more lasting damage than US tanks. It is easier to create mass demand for the former than for the latter. Only a minority needs heavy weapons, while a majority can become dependent on unrealistic levels of supply for such productive machines as modern trucks. Once the Third World has become a mass market for the goods, products, and processes which are designed by the rich for themselves,

Ivan Illich is co-founder and Director of CIDOC, Centro Intercultural de Documentación, Cuernavaca, Mexico.

the discrepancy between demand for these Western artifacts and the supply will increase indefinitely. The family car cannot drive the poor into the jet age, nor can a
school system provide the poor with education, nor can
the family icebox insure healthy food for them.

It is evident that only one man in a thousand in Latin
American can afford a Cadillac, a heart operation, or a
Ph.D. This restriction on the goals of development does
not make us despair of the fate of the Third World, and
the reason is simple. We have not yet come to conceive
of a Cadillac as necessary for good transportation, or of
a heart operation as normal healthy care, or of a Ph.D.
as the prerequisite of an acceptable education. In fact,
we recognize at once that the importation of Cadillacs
should be heavily taxed in Peru, that an organ trans-
plant clinic is a scandalous plaything to justify the concentration of more doctors in Bogotá, and that a
Betatron is beyond the teaching facilities of the University of São Paolo.

Unfortunately, it is not held to be universally evident
that the majority of Latin Americans—not only of our
generation, but also of the next and the next again—
cannot afford any kind of automobile, or any kind of
hospitalization, or for that matter an elementary school
education. We suppress our consciousness of this obvious reality because we hate to recognize the corner into
which our imagination has been pushed. So persuasive
is the power of the institutions we have created that
they shape not only our preferences, but actually our
sense of possibilities. We have forgotten how to speak
about modern transportation that does not rely on
automobiles and airplanes. Our conceptions of modern
health care emphasize our ability to prolong the lives of
the desperately ill. We have become unable to think of

better education except in terms of more complex schools and of teachers trained for ever longer periods. Huge institutions producing costly services dominate the horizons of our inventiveness.

We have embodied our world view into our institutions and are now their prisoners. Factories, news media, hospitals, governments, and schools produce goods and services packaged to contain our view of the world. We—the rich—conceive of progress as the expansion of these establishments. We conceive of heightened mobility as luxury and safety packaged by General Motors or Boeing. We conceive of improving the general well-being as increasing the supply of doctors and hospitals, which package health along with protracted suffering. We have come to identify our need for further learning with the demand for ever longer confinement to classrooms. In other words, we have packaged education with custodial care, certification for jobs, and the right to vote, and wrapped them all together with indoctrination in the Christian, liberal, or communist virtues.

In less than a hundred years industrial society has molded patent solutions to basic human needs and converted us to the belief that man's needs were shaped by the Creator as demands for the products we have invented. This is as true for Russia and Japan as for the North Atlantic community. The consumer is trained for obsolescence, which means continuing loyalty toward the same producers who will give him the same basic packages in different quality or new wrappings.

Industrialized societies can provide such packages for personal consumption for most of their citizens, but this is no proof that these societies are sane, or economical, or that they promote life. The contrary is true. The more the citizen is trained in the consumption of packaged goods and services, the less effective he seems to become in shaping his environment. His energies and finances are consumed in procuring ever new models of his staples, and the environment becomes a by-product of his own consumption habits.

The design of the "package deals" of which I speak is the main cause of the high cost of satisfying basic needs. So long as every man "needs" his car, our cities must endure longer traffic jams and absurdly expensive remedies to relieve them. So long as health means maximum length of survival, our sick will get ever more extraordinary surgical interventions and the drugs required to deaden their consequent pain. So long as we want to use school to get children out of their parents' hair or to keep them off the street and out of the labor force, our young will be retained in endless schooling and will need ever-increasing incentives to endure the ordeal.

Rich nations now benevolently impose a straight-jacket of traffic jams, hospital confinements, and classrooms on the poor nations, and by international agreement call this "development." The rich and schooled and old of the world try to share their dubious blessings by foisting their pre-packaged solution on to the Third World. Traffic jams develop in São Paolo, while almost a million northeastern Brazilians flee the drought by walking 500 miles. Latin American doctors get training at the New York Hospital for Special Surgery, which they apply to only a few, while amoebic dysentery remains endemic in slums where 90 percent of the population live. A tiny minority gets advanced education in basic science in North America—not infrequently paid for by their own governments. If they return at all to Bolivia, they become second-rate teachers of pretentious subjects at La Paz or Cochibamba. The rich export outdated versions of their standard models.

The Alliance for Progress is a good example of benevolent production for underdevelopment. Contrary to its slogans, it did succeed—as an alliance for the progress of the consuming classes, and for the domestication of the Latin American masses. The Alliance has been a major step in modernizing the consumption patterns of the middle classes in South America by integrating them with the dominant culture of the North American metropolis. At the same time, the Alliance has modernized the aspirations of the majority of citizens and fixed their demands on unavailable products.

Each car which Brazil puts on the road denies fifty people good transportation by bus. Each merchandised refrigerator reduces the chance of building a community freezer. Every dollar spent in Latin America on doctors and hospitals costs a hundred lives, to adopt a phrase of Jorge de Ahumada, the brilliant Chilean economist. Had each dollar been spent on providing safe drinking water, a hundred lives could have been saved. Each dollar spent on schooling means more privileges for the few at the cost of the many; at best it increases the number of those who, before dropping out, have been taught that those who stay longer have earned the right to more power, wealth, and prestige. What such schooling does is to teach the schooled the superiority of the better schooled.

All Latin American countries are frantically intent on expanding their school systems. No country now spends less than the equivalent of 18 percent of tax-derived public income on education—which means schooling and many countries spend almost double that. But even with these huge investments, no country yet succeeds in giving five full years of education to more than one third of its population; supply and demand for schooling grow geometrically apart. And what is true about schooling is equally true about the products of most institutions in the process of modernization in the Third World.

Continued technological refinements of products which are already established on the market frequently benefit the producer far more than the consumer. The more complex production processes tend to enable only the largest producer to continually replace outmoded models, and to focus the demand of the consumer on the marginal improvement of what he buys, no matter what the concomitant side effects: higher prices, diminished life span, less general usefulness, higher cost of repairs. Think of the multiple uses for a simple can opener, whereas an electric one, if it works at all, opens only some kinds of cans, and costs one hundred times as much.

This is equally true for a piece of agricultural machinery and for an academic degree. The midwestern farmer can become convinced of his need for a four-axle vehicle which can go 70 m.p.h. on the highways, has an electric windshield wiper and upholstered seats, and can be turned in for a new one within a year or two. Most of the world's farmers don't need such speed, nor have they ever met with such comfort, nor are they interested in obsolescence. They need low-priced transport, in a world where time is not money, where manual wipers suffice, and where a piece of heavy equipment should outlast a generation. Such a mechanical donkey requires entirely different engineering and design than one produced for the US market. This vehicle is not in production.

Most of South America needs paramedical workers who can function for indefinite periods without the supervision of an MD. Instead of establishing a process to train midwives and visiting healers who know how to use a very limited arsenal of medicines while working independently, Latin American universities establish every year a new school of specialized nursing or nursing administration to prepare professionals who can function only in a hospital, and pharmacists who know how to sell increasingly more dangerous drugs.

The world is reaching an impasse where two processes converge: ever more men have fewer basic choices. The increase in population is widely publicized and creates panic. The decrease in fundamental choice causes anguish and is consistently overlooked. The population explosion overwhelms the imagination, but the progressive atrophy of social imagination is rationalized as an increase of choice between brands. The two processes converge in a dead end: the population explosion provides more consumers for everything from food to contraceptives, while our shrinking imagination can conceive of no other ways of satisfying their demands except through the packages now on sale in the admired societies.

I will focus successively on these two factors, since, in my opinion, they form the two coordinates which together permit us to define underdevelopment.

In most Third World countries, the population grows, and so does the middle class. Income, consumption, and the well-being of the middle class are all growing while the gap between this class and the mass of people widens. Even where per capita consumption is rising, the majority of men have less food now than in 1945, less actual care in sickness, less meaningful work, less protection. This is partly a consequence of polarized consumption and partly caused by the breakdown of traditional family and culture. More people suffer from hunger, pain, and exposure in 1969 than they did at the end of World War II, not only numerically, but also as a percentage of the world population.

These concrete consequences of underdevelopment are rampant; but underdevelopment is also a state of mind, and understanding it as a state of mind, or as a form of consciousness, is the critical problem. Underdevelopment as a state of mind occurs when mass needs are converted to the demand for new brands of packaged solutions which are forever beyond the reach of the majority. Underdevelopment in this sense is rising rapidly even in countries where the supply of classrooms, calories, cars, and clinics is also rising. The ruling groups in these countries build up services which have been designed for an affluent culture; once they have monopolized demand in this way, they can never satisfy majority needs.

Underdevelopment as a form of consciousness is an extreme result of what we can call in the language of both Marx and Freud *"Verdinglichung"* or reification. By reification I mean the hardening of the perception of real needs into the demand for mass manufactured products. I mean the translation of thirst into the need for a Coke. This kind of reification occurs in the manipulation of primary human needs by vast bureaucratic organizations which have succeeded in dominating the imagination of potential consumers.

Let me return to my example taken from the field of education. The intense promotion of schooling leads to so close an identification of school attendance and education that in everyday language the two terms are interchangeable. Once the imagination of an entire population has been "schooled," or indoctrinated to believe that school has a monopoly on formal education, then the illiterate can be taxed to provide free high school and university education for the children of the rich.

Underdevelopment is the result of rising levels of aspiration achieved through the intensive marketing of "patent" products. In this sense, the dynamic underdevelopment that is now taking place is the exact opposite of what I believe education to be: namely, the awakening awareness of new levels of human potential and the use of one's creative powers to foster human life. Underdevelopment, however, implies the surrender of social consciousness to pre-packaged solutions.

The process by which the marketing of "foreign" products increases underdevelopment is frequently understood in the most superficial ways. The same man who feels indignation at the sight of a Coca-Cola plant in a Latin American slum often feels pride at the sight of a new normal school growing up alongsde. He resents the evidence of a foreign "license" attached to a soft drink which he would like to see replaced by "Cola-Mex." But the same man is willing to impose schooling —at all costs—on his fellow citizens, and is unaware of the invisible license by which this institution is deeply enmeshed in the world market.

Some years ago I watched workmen putting up a sixty-foot Coca-Cola sign on a desert plain in the Mexquital. A serious drought and famine had just swept over the Mexican highland. My host, a poor Indian in Ixmiquilpan, had just offered his visitors a tiny tequila glass of the costly black sugar-water. When I recall this scene I still feel anger; but I feel much more incensed when I remember UNESCO meetings at which well-meaning and well-paid bureaucrats seriously discussed

Latin American school curricula, and when I think of the speeches of enthusiastic liberals advocating the need for more schools.

The fraud perpetrated by the salesmen of schools is less obvious but much more fundamental than the self-satisfied salesmanship of the Coca-Cola or Ford representative, because the schoolman hooks his people on a much more demanding drug. Elementary school attendance is not a harmless luxury, but more like the coca chewing of the Andean Indian, which harnesses the worker to the boss.

The higher the dose of schooling an individual has received, the more depressing his experience of withdrawal. The seventh-grade dropout feels his inferiority much more acutely than the dropout from the third grade. The schools of the Third World administer their opium with much more effect than the churches of other epochs. As the mind of a society is progressively schooled, step by step its individuals lose their sense that it might be possible to live, without being inferior to others. As the majority shifts from the land into the city, the hereditary inferiority of the peon is replaced by the inferiority of the school dropout who is held personally responsible for his failure. Schools rationalize the divine origin of social stratification with much more rigor than churches have ever done.

Until this day no Latin American country has declared youthful underconsumers of Coca-Cola or cars as lawbreakers, while all Latin American countries have passed laws which define the early dropout as a citizen who has not fulfilled his legal obligations. The Brazilian government recently almost doubled the number of years during which schooling is legally compulsory and free. From now on any Brazilian dropout under the age of sixteen will be faced during his lifetime with the reproach that he did not take advantage of a legally obligatory privilege. This law was passed in a country where not even the most optimistic could foresee the day when such levels of schooling would be provided for only 25 percent of the young. The adoption of international standards of schooling forever condemns most Latin Americans to marginality or exclusion from social life—in a word, underdevelopment.

The translation of social goals into levels of consumption is not limited to only a few countries. Across all frontiers of culture, ideology, and geography today, nations are moving toward the establishment of their own car factories, their own medical and normal schools— and most of these are, at best, poor imitations of foreign and largely North American models.

The Third World is in need of a profound revolution of its institutions. The revolutions of the last generation were overwhelmingly political. A new group of men with a new set of ideological justifications assumed power to administer fundamentally the same scholastic, medical, and market institutions in the interest of a new group of clients. Since the institutions have not radically changed, the new group of clients remains approximately the same size as that previously served. This appears clearly in the case of education. Per pupil costs of schooling are today comparable everywhere since the standards used to evaluate the quality of schooling tend to be internationally shared. Access to publicly financed education, considered as access to school, everywhere depends on per capita income. (Places like China and North Vietnam might be meaningful exceptions.)

Everywhere in the Third World modern institutions are grossly unproductive, with respect to the egalitarian purposes for which they are being reproduced. But so long as the social imagination of the majority has not been destroyed by its fixation on these institutions, there is more hope of planning an institutional revolution in the Third World than among the rich. Hence the urgency of the task of developing workable alternatives to "modern" solutions.

Underdevelopment is at the point of becoming chronic in many countries. The revolution of which I speak must begin to take place before this happens. Education again offers a good example: chronic educational underdevelopment occurs when the demand for schooling becomes so widespread that the total concentration of educational resources on the school system becomes a unanimous political demand. At this point the separation of education from schooling becomes impossible.

The only feasible answer to ever-increasing underdevelopment is a response to basic needs that is planned as a long-range goal for areas which will always have a different capital structure. It is easier to speak about alternatives to existing institutions, services, and products than to define them with precision. It is not my purpose either to paint a Utopia or to engage in scripting scenarios for an alternate future. We must be satisfied with examples indicating simple directions that research should take.

Some such examples have already been given. Buses are alternatives to a multitude of private cars. Vehicles designed for slow transportation on rough terrain are alternatives to standard trucks. Safe water is an alternative to high-priced surgery. Medical workers are an alternative to doctors and nurses. Community food storage is an alternative to expensive kitchen equipment. Other alternatives could be discussed by the dozen. Why not, for example, consider walking as a long-range alternative for locomotion by machine, and explore the demands which this would impose on the city planner? And why can't the building of shelters be standardized, elements be pre-cast, and each citizen be obliged to learn in a year of public service how to construct his own sanitary housing?

It is harder to speak about alternatives in education, partly because schools have recently so completely preempted the available educational resources of good will, imagination, and money. But even here we can indicate the direction in which research must be conducted.

At present, schooling is conceived as graded, curricular, class attendance by children, for about 1,000 hours yearly during an uninterrupted succession of years. On the average, Latin American countries can provide each citizen with between eight and thirty months of this service. Why not, instead, make one or two months a year obligatory for all citizens below the age of thirty?

Money is now spent largely on children, but an adult can be taught to read in one tenth the time and for one tenth the cost it takes to teach a child. In the case of the adult there is an immediate return on the investment, whether the main importance of his learning is seen in his new insight, political awareness, and willingness to assume responsibility for his family's size and future, or whether the emphasis is placed on increased productivity. There is a double return in the case of the adult, because not only can he contribute to the education of his children, but to that of other adults as well. In spite of these davantages, basic literacy programs have little or no support in Latin America, where schools have a first call on all public resources. Worse, these programs are actually ruthlessly suppressed in Brazil and else-

where, where military support of the feudal or industrial
oligarchy has thrown off its former benevolent disguise.

Another possibility is harder to define, because there
is as yet no example to point to. We must therefore
imagine the use of public resources for education distributed in such a way as to give every citizen a minimum chance. Education will become a political concern
of the majority of voters only when each individual has
a precise sense of the educational resources that are
owing to him—and some idea of how to sue for them.
Something like a universal G.I. Bill of Rights could be
imagined, dividing the public resources assigned to education by the number of children who are legally of
school age, and making sure that a child who did not
take advantage of his credit at the age of seven, eight, or
nine would have the accumulated benefits at his disposal
at age ten.

What could the pitiful education credit which a Latin
American Republic could offer to its children provide?
Almost all of the basic supply of books, pictures,
blocks, games, and toys that are totally absent from the
homes of the really poor, but enable a middle-class child
to learn the alphabet, the colors, shapes, and other
classes of objects and experiences which insure his educational progress. The choice between these things and
schools is obvious. Unfortunately, the poor, for whom
alone the choice is real, never get to exercise this
choice.

Defining alternatives to the products and institutions
which now pre-empt the field is difficult, not only, as I
have been trying to show, because these products and
institutions shape our conception of reality itself, but
also because the construction of new possibilities requires a concentration of will and intelligence in a

higher degree than ordinarily occurs by chance. This concentration of will and intelligence on the solution of particular problems regardless of their nature we have become accustomed over the last century to call research.

I must make clear, however, what kind of research I am talking about. I am not talking about basic research either in physics, engineering, genetics, medicine, or learning. The work of such men as Crick, Piaget, and Gell-Mann must continue to enlarge our horizons in other fields of science. The labs and libraries and specially trained collaborators these men need cause them to congregate in the few research capitals of the world. Their research can provide the basis for new work on practically any product.

I am not speaking here of the billions of dollars annually spent on applied research, for this money is largely spent on existing institutions on the perfection and marketing of their own products. Applied research is money spent on making planes faster and airports safer; on making medicines more specific and powerful and doctors capable of handling their deadly side-effects; on packaging more learning into classrooms; on methods to administer large bureaucracies. This is the kind of research for which some kind of counterfoil must somehow be developed if we are to have any chance to come up with basic alternatives to the automobile, the hospital, and the school, and any of the many other so-called "evidently necessary implements for modern life."

I have in mind a different, and peculiarly difficult, kind of research, which has been largely neglected up to now, for obvious reasons. I am calling for research on alternatives to the products which now dominate the market; to hospitals and the profession dedicated to keeping the sick alive; to schools and the packaging process which refuses education to those who are not of the right age, who have not gone through the right curriculum, who have not sat in a classroom a sufficient number of successive hours, who will not pay for their learning with submission to custodial care, screening, and certification or with indoctrination in the values of the dominant elite.

This counter-research on fundamental alternatives to current pre-packaged solutions is the element most critically needed if the poor nations are to have a livable future. Such counter-research is distinct from most of the work done in the name of the "year 2000," because most of that work seeks radical changes in social patterns through adjustments in the organization of an already advanced technology. The counter-research of which I speak must take as one of its assumptions the continued lack of capital in the Third World.

The difficulties of such research are obvious. The researcher must first of all doubt what is obvious to every eye. Second, he must persuade those who have the power of decision to act against their own short-run interests or bring pressure on them to do so. And, finally, he must survive as an individual in a world he is attempting to change fundamentally so that his fellows among the privileged minority see him as a destroyer of the very ground on which all of us stand. He knows that if he should succeed in the interest of the poor, technologically advanced societies still might envy the "poor" who adopt this vision.

There is a normal course for those who make development policies, whether they live in North or South America, in Russia or Israel. It is to define development and to set its goals in ways with which they are familiar, which they are accustomed to use in order to satisfy their own needs, and which permit them to work through the institutions over which they have power or control. This formula has failed, and must fail. There is not enough money in the world for development to succeed along these lines, not even in the combined arms and space budgets of the super-powers.

An analogous course is followed by those who are trying to make political revolutions, especially in the Third World. Usually they promise to make the familiar privileges of the present elites, such as schooling, hospital care, etc., accessible to all citizens; and they base this vain promise on the belief that a change in political regime will permit them to sufficiently enlarge the institutions which produce these privileges. The promise and appeal of the revolutionary are therefore just as threatened by the counter-research I propose as is the market of the now dominant producers.

In Vietnam a people on bicycles and armed with sharpened bamboo sticks have brought to a standstill the most advanced machinery for research and production ever devised. We must seek survival in a Third World in which human ingenuity can peacefully outwit machined might. The only way to reverse the disastrous trend to increasing underdevelopment, hard as it is, is to learn to laugh at accepted solutions in order to change the demands which make them necessary. Only free men can change their minds and be surprised; and while no men are completely free, some are freer than others.